From There to Here

My Life's Journey

Jerry C. Davis

From There to Here

My Life's Journey

Copyright © 2015 by
Jerry C. Davis

Southern Oaks Publishing

ISBN-13: 978-1516891740
ISBN: 1516891740

Dedication

I dedicate this book to my wife Linda, our children Jodi and Brad, our grandchildren Jack and Maddie, my family, and those I have met and the friends I have enjoyed over the years.

"Every man's life ends the same way. It is only the details of how he lived and how he died that distinguish one man from another"

—Ernest Hemmingway

"When I was younger I could remember anything, whether it happened or not; but my faculties are decaying now and soon I shall be so I cannot remember any but the things that never happened".

—Mark Twain

Foreword

Have you ever wondered what molded your character and developed you to become the person you are today? Over the last several decades it's certainly crossed my mind many times. I concluded much of my inspiration was derived from reading adventure books like Mark Twain's "Tom Sawyer and Huckleberry Finn," and taking time listening to old people telling me their own personal stories. These experiences inspired me to look forward to making the most of my life and, at the same time, enjoying the places I visit and those I meet along the way. I give credit to my parents who instilled in me during my early years: do the best job you can do, work hard, be intellectually curious, respect others and always be willing to extend a helping hand. These later became the organizing principles of my life.

My parents have both passed away and are buried at Oak Grove Cemetery just east of LeRoy, Illinois. Oak Grove is a beautiful old cemetery with rows of stately headstones, each etched with the names and the dates of the people who are buried below them. When I visit my parents' graves, I enjoy taking extra time to wander among the graves, always amazed that I personally knew so many of those buried there. Each of these people had a life and a story, but many of their stories are now forgotten and will never be told. Not wanting mine to be lost, I decided to sit down, reflect back and share my life story with my children, grandchildren, family members or anyone else who may be interested.

Chapter 1

I was born in 1942, the son of Faye Edward and Zella Mae Davis. My story would be incomplete without first relating their lives. My parents were raised during the Great Depression. My Grandfather Davis worked as a farm tenant in west central Illinois and between seasons worked odd jobs to support his family. My Grandfather Sisson worked on a large dairy farm, but later took a job at a steel foundry in Cadillac, Michigan. Like so many people during that time, with few jobs available and very little money, they were forced to live on the absolute bare essentials.

Living conditions were difficult for everyone, but farm families fared much better than those in the city. Farmers and families with yards were able to grow their own food, raise livestock and store food for the winter. However, farming in those days was labor intensive and most farmers could not afford to hire anyone. Consequently, it became commonplace for farm children old enough to work to drop out of school to help on the farm. The family's children were in effect the farm labor force. It was either work on the farm or leave in search of work.

Teenagers in town were also forced to find jobs to help their families get by. Many young people who could not find jobs near home felt they were a burden to their parents and ventured to other cities to find work. Personally, I believe today's youth should read and be taught about the Depression and the effect it had on both our nation and members of their own families just over 80 years ago.

Joan, Judy and me, 1945

As a child I remember hearing my parents' and grandparents' occasional comments referencing the hard times of the Depression, the largest peacetime economic catastrophe in US history. From their experiences we were constantly reminded of the value of money and the need to work hard for whatever you wanted. Like so many children of my generation, we were seldom given spending money. When we received money, it was usually given as a reward for completing a required chore or helping around the house. As time passed, each generation earned more money than the generation before and now children are seldom required to work for an allowance or spending money.

In schools today most secondary students receive a general overview of the Depression. In most classes, the focus is on the cultural aspects and viewing those astonishing pictures taken during that time. Without actually studying the subject or hearing stories passed down from family members, it's hard for anyone to grasp or imagine our country, the United States of America, in such peril. There was no Social Security or Medicare for the elderly. No food stamps, Medicaid or public housing for those in poverty. Families were forced to live in tents, and hundreds of people stood in long lines for bread and soup. Just imagine parents being forced to take their children to an orphanage or giving their children away to friends or family members in order to survive. Historically, the Depression in the United States was the most severe depression ever experienced by the Western world and the harshest adversity faced by Americans since the Civil War. Yet today, few people can relate to the hardships and struggles of their own families during the period. Recently, there has been some renewed interest in studying the history of the Depression and the "New Deal" programs created by President Roosevelt. By studying the Depression, those interested feel with our country's current ongoing economic crisis and pending recessions, looking back at the Depression could prove beneficial in preparing the public for what potentially could take place in the future.

My father attended a small school in Liberty, Illinois. Liberty High School had only a three year program. Students wanting to complete high school went to Quincy, Illinois 25 miles away. My grandparents, with two younger daughters, could not afford for my father to continue his education. Being young and out of school, he did not want to stay at home or work on a farm. Farming was seasonal, low pay and hard work. Much of the work was still being done with horses, tending livestock was difficult and he received little or no pay for his work. Like many other young adults, my father decided to leave home in search of a job and an opportunity to become self-sufficient.

For a seventeen year old boy with no experience, finding a decent job was extremely difficult. To remedy his situation he joined one of President Roosevelt's New Deal programs, the Civil Conservation Corp (CCC). This government program was created to provide jobs to unmarried, unemployed men between the ages of 18 and 25. A key component was a requirement for all recruits to send $22.00 of their $30.00 monthly pay back home to assist their families. The organization worked on projects related to natural resources, conservation and preservation. Recruits received free travel, free uniforms, room and board, and after hour's entertainment. One of the most noticeable benefits to the recruits was the immediate improvement to their health. During the first two months of camp life, the average young worker gained 10 to 15 pounds. A testament to the widespread malnutrition and hunger Americans faced during the Depression. My father worked for the U.S. Forestry Department, spending three years in Washington State, Oregon and two years near Cadillac, Michigan.

My mother was born and raised in Cadillac and attended high school until she completed her sophomore year. During summer vacation she babysat a boy named Jerry Cook, for whom I was later named. She liked young Jerry, and the Cook family offered her a full-time job to watch over him. My mother decided to drop out of school and accepted the position of caring for Jerry the next two years.

It was not long after coming to Cadillac that my father

fulfilled his CCC obligation. He decided to stay in Cadillac, but soon found there were few jobs available. He finally took a job as a cook at a local diner. At the time few young people had extra money for entertainment. They spent much of their spare time at local dance halls listening and dancing to the popular music of the "Big Bands". My parents met at one of these dances, started dating and later became engaged. After a short engagement in 1938, they married and the following year on December 6, 1939, my mother gave birth to their firstborn, a baby girl named Joan Carole Davis.

A year and a half later in June of 1941, my sister Judy Corrine Davis was born and finally I arrived in June of 1942. I've purposely left off the exact birth dates for both Judy and I because years later we found out our actual birth dates were incorrect. When we requested copies of our birth certificates. Judy's stated she was born on June 3, 1941, not the celebrated date of June 4. Mine was also one day off, not June 10 but June 11, 1942. Our mother dismissed the certified documents as simply clerical errors. Bottom line, it in no way prevented us from celebrating our birthdays. To satisfy both our mother's alleged dates and the state's official dates, Judy and I have suggested we celebrate our birthdays as two-day events with presents on both days, but so far this idea has been met with resistance by both family and friends!

Coming out of the Great Depression with few jobs and low wages in the late 30s and early 40s, it's hard for me to imagine how difficult it must have been for a young couple just married, with little education, trying to provide for three small children. In 1942, World War II broke out and my father was classified as "exempt from service" due to having three children at home. Being exempt was certainly to his benefit, because countless jobs were being vacated by the tidal wave of soldiers going off to war. Companies across America quickly converted their assembly lines from civilian goods to the production of war materials. Two of Central Illinois' largest employers, Caterpillar Tractor Company in Peoria and Williams Oil-O-Matic in Bloomington (later to become The Eureka Company) provided job opportunities for residents still at home and my father spent time working for both companies.

After the war, as soldiers returned home jobs once again became scarce. Companies were rehiring their former veteran employees and many of the people who had temporarily filled those positions were being laid off. In support for those who served their country, many businesses started filling newly created jobs with veterans.

Although wartime production had propelled the economy into recovery, many Americans had anticipated a post-war collapse. But the economy remained strong after the war ended. Manufacturing refocused on civilian markets as the servicemen returned back home to their families.

A postwar population boom accompanied the economic boom and generated a housing shortage which had persisted from the depression up to the start of the war. To meet this crisis, the federal government and housing industry allocated undeveloped land to be used for housing construction. Technological advances created during the war allowed the building industry to start mass production of new efficient low cost housing. The Federal Housing Administration and Servicemen's Readjustment Act, backed builders and enabled Americans to purchase single family homes. Because owning a home was becoming cheaper than renting a house, home were being built in newly created suburban communities across America.

My father was always reluctant to buy a home and found it much easier to rent. He felt by renting a home with no contract or contractual lease arrangement, you could rent a house, not be burdened by costly repairs and when a bigger or better house became available, simply move out one and into the other. Moving became a way of life for my family. From information I've gathered from family members, it's believed we lived in 17 different homes from the time I was born to the day I graduated from high school. When I look at a U.S. map or a map of the towns we lived in, while moving my finger from one location to another, I find myself repeating the words "from there to here" as if I was playing a board game and preparing to make my next move. Moves became easy, especially when moving from one house to another in the same town. Dad became a well- trained expert in the art of moving. He would borrow a truck, we'd each gather up our belongings and the move was completed over the weekend. Moving out of state was another story and was much more involved. My mother quickly developed an efficient routine for long distance moving. She'd place a small ad in the local paper advertising a moving sale to sell our furniture and large items. The next step was Joan, Judy and I helping her pack as much as we could in smaller boxes, take them to the post office or railroad depot and ship them ahead of the move. When moving day arrived, we'd load the car with the remaining belongings leaving just enough room for Mom, Dad, Joan, Judy myself and our dog Buddy. Then Dad would start-up the old car and down the road we'd go.

We thank God both Mom and Dad were gifted with good personalities as well as the skills to find work. Dad however, never seemed able to find a job he really enjoyed or wanted to keep. Over the years it became apparent regardless wherever he worked, he had little interest in advancement and if emotional stress was involved, he would inform his employer he was leaving and go find another job. His countless number of job changes is what instigated the moving of our family between Illinois, Michigan, New Jersey, Florida and back to Illinois.

One of their moves however, did not result from his changing jobs. It was not until I was 62 years old that I learned the real story behind the move from Illinois to Michigan in 1945 or early 1946. One day my mother and I began talking about living at Grandmother Sissons's home in Michigan. As we talked she suddenly started telling me about the family living in Bloomington and she and Dad were having difficulties with their marriage. She contributed much of the problems to my Grandmother Davis' constant meddling in their family affairs. Finally it got to the point where Mom became so upset, she called Grandpa Sisson who sent her enough money for four train tickets to move her and us kids back to Michigan to live with them.

Even as young children, we found living with our grandparents to be definitely out of the ordinary. Our grandparents' small rural home sat several miles out in the country with no indoor bathroom, no running water or electricity. The only heat in the house was a large brown enamel kerosene stove standing in the front room. When the winter temperatures fell below zero, the large cast iron cook stove in the kitchen was kept burning to keep the rest of the house warm. During those extreme cold nights the three of us would jump in bed together in the small bedroom next to the kitchen and Grandma would pile her old handmade quilts on us until we were warm. The only lights during the evening were a couple kerosene lamps in each room. I can still remember watching Grandma sitting in her chair with one of the girls on her lap and taking the curling iron from the chimney of the lamp and carefully start curling her hair. Baths were usually taken only once a week. The water was heated on the cook stove, poured into the metal tub and the first one to get in was rewarded with being able to take their bath in clean water. As soon as they finished they jumped out and dried off, another pail of hot water was added and the next person got in. Going to the outhouse in the winter was like being in a race. You ran out the door in the snow, got inside and shut the door. As fast as possible you'd go, grab some of the pages from the stack of old Sears & Roebuck catalogs, wipe and run back into the house to get warm again.

Our mother's parents were both well up in years, and several months after our stay Grandpa suddenly died from a brain aneurysm. After his death, our father moved up to Michigan and our family reunited. Looking back, my sisters and I never realized a problem existed between our parents or knew how long their separation lasted. We only remember Dad being absent for a period of time.

Me at my grandmother's, in Cadillac, Michigan

After Dad returned, we moved from our grandparents' house into Cadillac. It was a two-story house on Linden Street across from the Ash Grade School. It was there where I began clearly remembering everything about my life. The war was now over and many returning veterans left their hometowns and started relocating to larger cities and the West Coast in search of better and higher paying jobs. Their sacrifices helped create an enormously wealthy nation, a country where anything was now possible. It was a generation who had fought to save the world and earned the right to prosper.

With all the moving and home construction taking place, Dad felt Cadillac needed another small local moving business. He bought a used 1938 flatbed Chevrolet truck, painted "City Delivery" on the doors and began moving freight, furniture, lumber and household items in Cadillac and the surrounding area. When deliveries were large or heavy and required extra help, my teenage cousin Ivan would help him out. Dad had high hopes for his delivery business, but after a year or two, the business still was unable to bring in enough money to support the family. Mom decided to get us a sitter and started working at Vogel's Dry Cleaners in downtown Cadillac. What she didn't realize at the time was working in the dry cleaning business would be her primary career throughout most of her life.

It was in this house where I was first introduced to crime. Fortunately, it was short-lived, and resulted in me receiving the spanking of all spankings. The day started off with no thoughts of crime. Mom and I walked down the street to shop at a small general store or grocery. While she shopped, I stood in front of a large glass case displaying a fantastic selection of shiny new pocket knives. The owner, noticing my interest, looked over the showcase case and asked me which one I liked, and said the knives only cost one dollar each. I became completely mesmerized by their beauty and continued thinking about how wonderful it would be to have one of those knives for my very own. After arriving home, with little consideration to the consequences, I reach into my mother's purse and pulled out a dollar bill. Later that day I returned to the store and proudly pointed to the knife I wanted to purchase. Being only five, I had little knowledge of paper money. I handed the owner the bill and was totally shocked when the owner gave me not only the knife but several more dollar bills. Immediately I sensed something was wrong. I ran home, went up to my room and put the money and the knife in a small box and hid it under my bed. A short while later the store owner, suspicious of the transaction, called my mother. When the call ended, she hung up the phone and quickly escorted me to my bedroom. After being questioned for what seemed to be a long period of time, I finally fessed up to the crime and was well aware there would be consequences for my actions. After a thorough whipping to my backside, we returned to the store where I tearfully apologized and handed that magnificent pocket knife back to the store owner. I can still visualize the stern look on his face, void of even a slight smile, as he stood there looking down at me. After accepting my apology, he gave my mother back a dollar bill, she thanked him for his call and we quietly walked home. After my short unsuccessful life of crime, I quickly realized the true meaning of the cliché "Crime Does Not Pay!"

During those early years I enjoyed living in Cadillac. It was the first time I could remember having someone to play with other than my sisters. Several boys lived in our neighborhood and we spent much of our time outside playing cowboys and Indians or drawing with chalk on the sidewalk. This was a time when Roy Rogers was very popular and known as "The King of the Cowboys". I however, liked Gene Autry and I loved singing along with him when he sang my favorite cowboy song, "I'm Back in the Saddle Again."

Dad seemed to enjoy living up in Michigan and spending time with the family, my uncles and cousins. Their favorite pastime sport during the summer was shooting targets out at Grandpa's farm. Dad wasn't a hunter but he seemed to enjoy target shooting. He finally decided to buy a gun of his own, a Mossberg, semi-automatic .22 long rifle, with a military-style stock which he kept "unloaded" in its original box under their bed. One afternoon while Dad was working someone stopped by our house and borrowed his rifle. It was returned later that day and Mom placed it back in the box under the bed. Several days later, Dad decided to go target shooting and pulled the gun out of the box and attempted to pull back the bolt to open the chamber. It would not open. Not realizing the gun was returned loaded, he pulled the trigger and a shot was fired.

Exactly at that moment, Joan and I were walking across the room side by side directly in front of Dad. Without warning, the spent bullet grazed my leg and hit Joan's leg just below her knee. The bullet hit the bone and then turned traveling down and out her heel. Everyone became frantic as Joan was lying on the floor bleeding. Mom called the police and they wrapped my wound with one of my sister's white cotton socks. Joan was rushed to the hospital. My injury was nothing more than a slight flesh wound on the back of my left thigh. As word of the shooting traveled, our preacher came by to offer help and console my parents. At that point, Dad was so upset he gave the preacher his rifle. To my knowledge, with the exception of his time in the military, it was the last time my father ever shot a gun.

Dad and me with rifle

This was not the first of Joan's childhood mishaps. When she was four or five, we went to visit our Grandma and Grandpa Davis. Joan was playing in the kitchen while Grandma stood by the gas stove peeling potatoes and putting them in a pan of water. Suddenly, Joan reached for the pan on the stove trying to get a potato. As she reached, the flames from the burner below the pan caught the sleeve of her sweater on fire. Standing nearby was Aunt Gin who grabbed Joan and put the flames from her burning clothing out with either a towel or a baby blanket. Joan was rushed to the hospital suffering from severe burns on her arms and stomach. After recovering from the accident, Joan was always self-conscious about wearing anything showing her scars. To my knowledge, she still carries them. Another incident happened when Joan was opening a door and the wind slammed the door shut pushing her arm through the window pane as the jagged broken glass cut deeply into her arm. After having survived these serious accidents, she has since fortunately lived a happy life void of tragic accidents.

Upper Michigan is notorious for its cold winters. The several months of heavy snows, icy roads and frigid temperatures pose quite a challenge for not only local and rural residents but also for local hunters and vacationers coming to Michigan to enjoy the many winter sports. Traveling down the snow covered roads in the family car was a wonderful winter experience. The view from a car's window after a heavy snow in the country changed the bare fields and leafless clumps of trees into a magical winter wonderland. The snowfalls brought out the massive snowplows to clear miles and miles of snow covered roads. As they pushed the snow aside walls of snow grew higher and higher along the roadways. Like all cars back then, Dad's car had only one small heater under the dash which provided little heat in the back seat and the defrosters only cleared two small frost free openings on the windshield. This was long before insulated clothing was available and it was always difficult to stay warm. Children wore snowsuits or layers of old clothes to keep warm. We didn't seem to mind, we were happy just to ride along, brushing the frost away from the windows with our cotton gloves to catch a view or the beautiful wonderland outside. For miles we would ride between the two walls of snow in places reaching almost to the top of telephone poles. Occasionally we would meet cars carrying Christmas trees tied to their top or a hunter returning home with a large deer lying over the front fender with its antlers securely tied to the front bumper. These large northern white tail deer provided enough meat to feed a family for the rest of the winter.

Mom's best friend from high school, Helen Kidder and her husband Merle, their children Dickey and Linda, were occasional visitors when we lived in Michigan. After arriving Merle would visit awhile then pile all the children in the back seat of his car for a wild ride down the snow-packed roads. He delighted in having his car slide from side to side and speeding up as we approached the large hump in the road at the railroad crossing. Our eyes would stay glued on the approaching hump and when the car reached the top, we were tossed off the seat, almost to the roof of the car. I vaguely recall another wonderful winter ride when grandmother's neighbor took everyone for a ride in their large horse drawn sleigh. Regardless of the weather, Mom's family seemed to not mind the extremely cold temperatures and loved being outside enjoying the winter activities in Michigan.

Me on porch in Cadillac, MI, 1946

Chapter 2

Dad's delivery business continued to struggle and it subsequently became obvious it would not produce enough income to support the family. Frustrated with his failing business, one afternoon without consulting our mother, he returned home and announced, "I sold the business and joined the Army!"

Needless to say, the unexpected news was not well received and soon afterwards he left for Fort Knox in Kentucky and started basic training.

Upon completion he was then sent to Fort Monmouth, New Jersey and assigned to the Army Signal Corp as a teletype operator and later became an instructor. Once he knew Fort Monmouth would be his permanent assignment, he rented a three bedroom apartment, Mom packed our belongings and we boarded a train to Long Branch, New Jersey.

Over the years Mom often talked about our train ride and how the fellow passengers commented on how well we behaved during the trip. I'm sure the main reason for our good behavior was because so much of our time was spent looking out the large passenger car windows as the train traveled the countryside and through the many towns scattered along the way. Finally we arrived in New Jersey, and it was great to know the family was together again. After loading our baggage in the trunk, Dad drove us to what would be our new home for the next several month. The stately old home with its huge front lawn sat back from the main roadway. It originally was built as a single family home, but later converted into several apartments. Near the east side of the property was a small pond and to the south was a water treatment plant with several individual cement separating ponds. My sisters and I spent hours playing near the small pond and enjoyed watching the baby ducks as they traveled from the small pond over to the treatment plant to swim in the separation ponds. While living there, Dad befriended a young fellow soldier named Glen Keller, from Sheldon, Illinois. Glen became a regular visitor in our home and a lifelong friend to our family. He was much younger than Dad and continually stuttered. He had a tremendous sense of humor and everyone in the family enjoyed having Glen around.

Joan, Judy and me, 1947

One sunny day my sisters and I were outside playing and found a newborn kitten covered with blood and entangled in something (possibly afterbirth or weeds) near the house. Apparently in desperation to free the kitten from the entanglement, the mother accidentally chewed off one of the kitten's front legs. Feeling sorry for the newborn and its condition, we took it to our mother who patiently helped us care for it. Pets were not allowed in the apartments so the kitten's new home was living under the back porch steps of the house. We enjoyed watching the kitten run, pounce and play in the yard appearing as though it never realized it was missing a leg. When we moved we left the little critter behind in hopes the next family to move in would enjoy it as much as we did.

The next place we moved to was an upstairs apartment in downtown Long Branch closer to our school and the Army base. The apartment house was owned by an older Italian lady named Mary Polio (or at least we thought she was old). Mary owned a small corner grocery store about a block from our apartment and owned several other residential rental properties in Long Branch. It was always a treat to go into Mary's store. The store was small but filled with countless displays of grocery goods, Italian foods, fresh baked breads and dried cod fish displayed in large wooden barrels completely covered with salt. Looking at those flat hard fish made you wonder how anyone could make a decent meal with the fish from those barrels! Mother later proved to us those once hard salty slabs of fish could actually be transformed into a delicious meal. As they say on the cooking shows, "It's all in the preparation," which required a lengthy process of soaking the fish in water for hours before cooking. My favorite item in her store was the fresh baked loaves of bread. They were absolutely delicious and fun to eat. The 18 to 24 inches-long loaves were dark brown and the crust was as hard as wood and the insides soft and delicious. When served at home I would race to the table in order to get one of the two crusty ends of the loaf. Holding the end like a cup I carefully poured milk inside and slowly started eating the soft mixture of milk and bread with my spoon. When the inside was clean of bread I finished off the delicious snack by eating the milk soaked crust. What a wonderful treat.

In the first floor apartment below us lived Bell and Junior Griffith. Mother enjoyed listening to Bell tell stories about living in Italy during the early part of the war where she and her family would hide in their basement or in barns while American planes dropped bombs nearby in an attempt to drive out German invaders. Bell was very thankful when the American forces drove the Germans out of Italy and grateful to be one of the many Italians able to come to America and start a new life in the United States.

In the basement apartment lived another young soldier and his wife. I can no longer remember their names but I vividly remember visiting them. It was where I first was introduced to the world's latest and greatest invention – one which forever changed the world as we knew it - the television. One day while playing outside they invited my sisters and me to come down to their apartment. We gathered on the floor and sat wide-eyed in amazement in front of a very small 9-inch round screen and watched the *Howdy Doody Show* with Buffalo Bob and other newly created TV shows like *Kukla, Fran and Ollie*. Televisions were extremely rare in 1948 and 1949, and even in a city the size of New York, there were only two or three channels available. I was amazed as I sat watching pictures come alive on that very small blurry black and white screen. We later found out living near New York had its advantages with the newfound invention. Most kids our age across America had to wait several more years before they would see their first TV show at home.

The apartment house had a large yard with lots of places for the three of us to play. Behind the house was a large old carriage barn that constantly beckoned us to go inside and explore. To open one of the heavy large wooden barn doors took all our power. Once inside, we'd gaze around looking at all the old items stored away and old rusty tools lying scattered about. Looking straight up, an old horse drawn sleigh appeared suspended in space above our heads. Someone years before had carefully hoisted it up to the top of the roof almost touching the rafters.

I was always a very curious child and enjoyed spending my time outside investigating everything in sight. One day while playing in the yard I found a baby bat lying among the leaves in the back yard, apparently hurt or sick. Without knowing anything about bats, my first reaction was to try it help it survive. I went in the house and found a large cardboard match box. After emptying the matches, I quickly went back outside, gathered some grass and gently placed the ailing bat inside. I was sure my assistance would help it survive, but within a few hours it died. After telling my sad story to my parents they quickly explained it was dangerous to pick up any sick birds or injured animals, especially bats. My parents, knowing I was upset and grieving my loss, assisted me in providing the little bat a proper burial in our back yard.

When summer came to an end my sisters and I were enrolled in the Long Branch Elementary School. The school was close enough for us to safely walk both to and from school each day. I was in the first grade, Judy in second and Joan in third grade. I enjoyed my new class and I still smile each time I look at the old photo taken outside the large brick school building. There I was in the front row, a freckle-faced boy, with a fair complexion, clearly standing out among all my dark-eyed, dark- haired Italian classmates.

My teacher that year was the first person to introduce me to art. She taught us some basic steps to draw faces, bodies and objects. I enjoyed her class but when the year came to a close, my overall performance did not allow me to move on to second grade, I was held back and enrolled again in first grade. I only mention this because some kids at five or six are just not mature as others, and being held back should never be considered a failure in life. Personally, I'm happy I ended up with the people I had as classmates during my school years, especially in LeRoy. If President Eisenhower was able to overcome his being held back in third grade, I certainly have no problems having been held back in first.

We lived in New Jersey about a year when my Grandmother Sisson suddenly passed away and Mom flew back to Michigan to attend the funeral. I can remember the sadness my mother felt about not being with her mother during her final days. After her funeral, Grandmother's possessions were distributed to various family members. Because we lived so far away my mother was unable to take anything. Consequently, Joan, Judy and I have almost nothing from my mother's parents to enjoy or pass on to our children.

From my early viewpoint, living in New Jersey gave our family the opportunity to spend more time together doing things. Maybe it was simply because we were getting older and paying more attention to the world around us. I can remember the day when Dad came home driving a brand new car. It was a robin's egg blue British Austin 4 door sedan with leather interior and turn signals that jumped out from the sides of the car's center- post when Dad prepared to turn at an approaching intersection. We really enjoyed that car and the family started going on weekend outings. During the summer we drove to the beach in Asbury Park to play in the sand and wade in the Atlantic Ocean. After playing on the beach we would climb the wooden stairways to the boardwalk above. The stately turn of the century boardwalk was lined with large buildings housing wonderful carnival rides, games, food and was well known for its fabulous saltwater taffy. Asbury Park was a sensational place to spend time as a child; and a great place for the entire family to spend time together.

Just a few miles from the boardwalk stood the remains of several abandoned WWII bunkers. These large gun emplacements had been placed there by the military to protect the New Jersey coastline. It was fun for kids to climb up on the top and look down inside the fortified cement structures. We also took several short trips visiting other nearby cities. Dad and Mom, like most families in the late 40's and 50's enjoyed taking us to the drive-in theater where we'd play on the swings and slides located directly below the gigantic outdoor screen. One night we had a special treat when Gene Autry's sidekick, Smiley Burnett, came out onstage in person, telling stories about being in Western movies and having fun riding the trail with his faithful friend Gene. What great memories I have of his gigantic smile as he told those wonderful tales.

Christmas that year in Long Branch was extra special. The Army base held a Christmas party for the soldiers' families and before leaving, Santa suddenly arrived to make sure every child went home with a sack of candy and a Christmas gift. My gift was a shiny red truck.

Once Dad became familiar with the area he decided the time had come to expand our weekend family trips. One weekend we loaded up the car and ventured over to New York City. We drove up the coast toward Newark and Dad drove our car up the ramp onto the Staten Island Ferry. Once the car was boarded and the ferry left the dock, we quickly got out and stood along the railings. It was fun to see all the cargo ships, ferries and small boats passing by, and suddenly we could see the Statue of Liberty, what a beautiful sight. When we finally reached the landing area in New York Harbor, Dad drove off the ferry and we were totally overwhelmed by the gigantic skyscrapers soaring into the sky. Once in the city the traffic was crowded, horns were honking and thousands of people were walking up and down the sidewalks. By luck, Dad's little Austin came equipped with a sun roof which simply required cranking a small handle to open the roof. Once Mom had it opened, what a sight to behold. Everyone's head (except Dad's) was looking straight up to the top of the buildings which appeared to us to be almost touching the clouds. One of the highlights of our trip was being able to have lunch at New York's famous Horn and Hardart's Auto-mat. There you could simply place coins in a machine, select what you wanted, pull a lever, and within seconds a carefully wrapped sandwich would fall into the tray below, napkins and all. It was unbelievable to watch this innovative contraption work with absolutely no human assistance. Our first reaction, "Gee, what they will think of next!"

After eating our food, it was time to head back home. Rather than taking the ferry, Dad decided to drive back through the Holland Tunnel which went completely under the Hudson River. It was the first time I experienced the cool sound of horns honking when the cars reached the very center of tunnel under the river. To this day, I still enjoy and cannot resist honking the horn when going through tunnels. I hope all my tunnel-honking has inspired my children and grandchildren to honk their horns in tunnels and carry on this fun loving family tradition.

One of our family's most memorable trips was going to see "Molly Pitcher's well," a famous landmark from the American Revolution and the Battle of Monmouth. Dad had read an article about Molly's heroic mission of providing water from the well to give to the army troops. After sharing the tale with the family, he decided to visit the historic site. Leaving the house, Dad carefully followed the directions from his trusty road map. However, what was supposed to be a short trip seemed to have taken hours. After getting lost a number of times we eventually came upon a sign pointing toward the site, but we could see nothing resembling a well. Finally we noticed a small historic marker on a pole indicating this was the spot we were looking for. To our amazement the site was between the railroad tracks and a busy highway and hardly anywhere to park. After walking up to the site, we realized the original site was nothing more than a large square concrete slab covering what must have once been the actual well! Disappointed, we headed back home, and for many years that uneventful family trip to Molly Pitcher's well, became a favorite family story. To my surprise, a couple years ago I read an article about Molly's well, and found out we were not the only ones who could not find the well's location. To this day, historians are still not sure of the well's exact location and over the years the sign has been moved to several different sites along the road. There's also discussions as to Molly's real name. Molly was a common name for Mary and Pitcher was a term used for "Barmaids". It's believed her name could have simply been a nickname – like Johnny Appleseed." There is however historically documented evidence showing women did indeed carry water to soldiers during the battle.

On weekends, Dad and Glen Keller enjoyed spending time listening to wrestling matches on the radio. Finally they decided to go see one and to my surprise, they took me along. The well-advertised professional wrestling match featured the famous Argentina Rocco, a legendary wrestler who was said to have killed his opponent in the ring when he first entered the sport. As for myself, I was more excited about seeing the match. It was between a man and a giant brown bear fighting inside a large steel cage positioned on the stage. I can't remember who won, but I do remember the bear was large and should have won easily. After the bear fight, to the applause of the entire crowd, Argentina Rocco climbed into the ring and within three rounds, defeated his opponent. As soon as the fight ended, a fight broke out between fans and Dad lifted me up to the top of some stored bleachers to keep me safe during the ruckus. Within seconds security officers broke up the fight and it was time to leave. What a night to remember, entertainment for all and plenty of excitement!

As I mentioned before, living in New Jersey seemed to be going well for our family but not perfect. While we enjoyed our family activities, it was still difficult to live on Dad's military salary. He finally found some part time work at a gas station and working at a large sheep farm on the outer edge of town. I thoroughly enjoyed riding with Mom to pick up Dad and seeing all the baby lambs playing in the pens positioned around the barns.

Mom took a part time job at a dry cleaners across the street from Mary Polio's store. My parents enjoyed going to her store and visiting with Mary. During one of those visits, she mentioned owning an empty house just one block away from where we were living. It was a single family residence and Mary offered to sell it to Dad on contract. This was my parents' first opportunity to purchase their very own home. The house was located on a corner next to a small white church. I liked the house and was impressed when coming down the stairway and being able to see either the living room or the dining room by looking through the wooded rails on each side. We lived there about a year before Dad completed his three year enlistment commitment. He often mentioned he enjoyed being in the service and considered staying in until he was told what was about to happen.

The Korean War was just starting and if he remained in the Army he most likely would be shipped over to South Korea. With the thought of an approaching war and leaving his family for a full year, he decided to take his discharge. Once again we reached our father's parents' home on Mill Street in Bloomington, Illinois.

Chapter 3

The ride back to Bloomington from New Jersey became another family adventure Grandpa Davis had offered. After loading up the Austin we drove onto the newly constructed Pennsylvania Turnpike. This road was unlike any other US Highway. President Eisenhower had a vision to establish an interstate highway system across the United States to provide people with faster and safer travel, plus having major roadways available for transportation of military or emergency vehicles in case of a disaster or enemy attack. This was the very first interstate highway system completed under this program. Not only was it a faster way to travel, it had restaurants built directly over the road giving travelers the ability to stop for gas and eat while watching the cars pass-by directly below them. What a sight to behold and quite a change from the two-lane highways we'd been accustomed to. We quickly realized we were no longer being slowed down by hundreds of stop lights or the congestion of city traffic while traveling long distances. After driving only a couple days, we reached our father's parents' home on Mill Street in Bloomington.

Upon our arrival, my parents had neither jobs nor a house to live in. Grandpa Davis had offered to temporarily let us move into the upstairs apartment over their house until Dad found somewhere to rent. I thoroughly enjoyed staying at my grandparents' house. It was the first time I really got to know them and I had the opportunity to spend time just hanging around with my grandfather. I loved following him around as he always had projects he was working on and he found plenty of things to keep me busy. Grandpa was a hard worker who spent most of his life working on farms, hauling grain, and delivering milk and cheese from the many farms scattered throughout central Illinois and Iowa.

I enjoyed talking and listening to my grandfather describing growing up before the invention of the car, truck and tractor. The only thing with horsepower back then was a horse, and they were used daily to ride, pull machines and pull wagons. He told me about the difficulties of traveling down dirt roads in buggies and describing all the amazing changes he had seen during his lifetime.

One story was about delivering seed and hay to a horse farm near Hudson, Illinois. At the time he was unaware of rumors that the farm was supposedly owned by the notorious Chicago gangster Al Capone. It was a beautiful farm on Route 51 with white fences and a large horse barn, much like those found in Kentucky. The one thing unusual was the location of the barn. Instead of it sitting behind the house, it sat directly in front. When entering the driveway, anyone wanting to go up to the house had to go through the barn. On the day in question, Grandpa pulled his truck into the driveway and approached the barn. The doors were closed so he honked the horn hoping someone would know he was there. Suddenly two guys came out of the barn and asked him what he wanted. Grandpa told them he was delivering an order of feed. The two men returned to the barn and again came back telling him to pull inside the barn. Once the truck was inside they shut the doors behind him. When my grandpa got out the men started helping him unload the truck. Once the truck was unloaded, the doors were again opened and he backed out of the barn and continued with his deliveries. Later Grandpa told the feed store owner about the strange event and the owner replied, "If they looked like gangsters, maybe it was Al Capone!" The owner went on to say it was the first time anyone mentioned anything out of the ordinary while making a delivery to that farm. It was however, a well know rumor that Al Capone did make several visits to the central Illinois area. During Al's heyday, Havana, Illinois, was commonly called "Little Reno." It was there where the Chicago mob established several gambling boats along the Illinois River. Al was also an avid horse race fan and owned several race horses. Grandpa felt if Al was indeed at the farm the day he delivered the feed, he may have been there looking at the horses being boarded. Grandpa saw no one other than the two men and nothing on the other side of the barn. The one thing he was positive of, the guys helping him unload the truck were not farmers, not locals and not interested in conversation. To him, they looked exactly like two Chicago gangsters.

Years later while working at Webb's, I found out one of our regular customers lived on that farm and I mentioned my grandfather's story. He told me he too had heard many stories over the years about Al, "Scarface" Capone's visits to the farm and also rumors of tunnels being on the property. He said he'd searched old county records and they showed during that time- frame Capone was operating, the farm was owned by some investors who raised and boarded horses, including race horses. Having lived there for years, he looked through the barns and house and never found any relics, tunnels or indications the property was anything other than a farm with a horse barn sitting in the front of the house.

After many years of farming, odd jobs and delivering farm goods, milk and cream, my grandparents moved to Bloomington and Grandpa took a job at the Norge Washing Machine Company. Around 1949, he retired but never stopped working. He stayed busy with his various hobbies and doing odd jobs as a handyman. One of those hobbies was raising rabbits. He kept them in an old garage next to their house and sold them to local hospitals for experimental and testing purposes. By today's standards, this would be a controversial sideline, but back then it was a necessity. In additions to supplying hospitals, he sold them to people to eat. When someone would call or see his sign on the front of his garage "Rabbits for Sale" they'd ring the doorbell, ask about the rabbits and I'd follow him out to the rabbit shed. There he would patiently stand by letting the customer pick out the rabbit of their choice. Once selected, he removed the rabbit from the cage, killed it, cleaned it, and carefully wrapped it in butcher paper and handed it to the buyer. One thing for sure, there was always plenty of rabbit feet around for anyone wanting them for good luck.

Along with selling rabbits Grandpa also sold dew worms. In the evenings he would go out with his flashlight and pick up the large long earth worms and take them down to the basement and release them in the large wooden box next to the wall. Feeding the worms became my job. Each morning after breakfast he would give me the used coffee grounds and I would carefully carry them downstairs and spread them over the dirt for food. This became a great business after the summer's heat made gathering worms difficult and fishermen could no longer find them in their yard. They quickly learned by just ringing Grandpa's doorbell, he could promptly provide them a paper cup full of large healthy slimy night crawlers.

One of Dad's old friends in Bloomington, Ollie Olson, spent most of his spare time after work in his garage working on radios and repairing electrical appliances. Dad enjoyed visiting Ollie as he worked and I found Ollie to be quite the artist. The walls of his shop were covered with his drawings and upon my request; he would quickly sketch me a cartoon character with his pencil. After letting me look at his drawing he would give me a sheet of paper to show me how he drew it, how to place the pencil correctly to make different shades, and with my being left handed, how to keep my hand above the paper to avoid smearing my sketch. I was immediately hooked on drawing. From then on, I spent almost all of my spare time drawing pictures of cars, horses or anything else that sprung up into my youthful mind. Over the years people told me I had artistic talents. However, being hyper by nature and having difficulty keeping focused on completing a tedious project, I found drawing and detailed art work to be incredibly time consuming and lacking the excitement needed to keep me interested. While I still appreciate works of art, I've lost all interest in drawing.

When fall came I started second grade at Emerson School on Bloomington's east side. It was fun walking along Oakland Avenue to school each day and making new friends throughout the neighborhood. I attended Emerson School for only one year but for some reason I kept in touch with a couple of my classmates for many years. Janice Olson was the cutest girl in our class. We stayed in contact and remained friends from those early years even past high school. We were just good friends and in all of our years of friendship we never once dated. Al Jones, another classmate, stayed in contact for many years and I later found out he was a brother to my sister-in law Sharon Boaz's best friend. What a small world it is indeed.

Once school started, my mother took a job at Advance Cleaners in Bloomington which was within walking distance from my grandparents' home. It was here where she met and became best friends with Betty Duvall. Betty and Mom ended up working together for three different dry cleaning companies in Bloomington. Betty's husband Howard was a Chevrolet master mechanic at Rust Chevrolet in Bloomington, a gun collector, motorcycle rider and a great story teller. He could tell some extremely interesting tales of his past adventures, mostly untrue, but never boring. Howard and Betty became lifelong friends of my parents. For many years they spent most every Thanksgiving Day at our house and we always knew a new story would soon be shared about one of Howard's great adventures. While living with my grandparents, after school I walked home with my sisters. If it was warm and the weather was nice, I would walk from our grandparents' house up Molten Street to the cleaners and wait for my mother to get off work. On my way, almost every house I passed had friendly ladies sitting on the front porches trying to get some relief from the hot weather. This was in the early fifties and air conditioning in houses was unheard of. They were always friendly, would wave and say hello as I passed on my way up the hill. When Mother got off work we casually walked back to the house talking about what had happened that day at school. Years later, I learned the path I traveled many times up and down Molton Street to meet Mom with all those friendly ladies, was in fact, the notorious red light district of Bloomington after dark. At nine I was totally unaware such unspeakable activities even occurred. It was hard to believe those always friendly ladies were actually "ladies of the night". I now realized I had missed my "golden opportunity" by not going up on those porches and asking them to share some stories about their lives and the business activities in those houses during the late evening hours.

I'm not sure how long we stayed in the upstairs apartment over our grandparents, but Dad managed to find a job working at Omar Bread Company delivering bread around the area. Omar Bread Company was very different from most other bread companies of its day. They developed area delivery routes much like the milk companies of years ago. The route salesman went door to door delivering bread and bakery products. It was a convenient well excepted concept for the fifties but within a few short years, the need for home delivery dwindled. People started buying their bakery and milk products while shopping as the new chain grocery stores springing up across the country. One day Dad took me with him on his route to deliver bread at Chanute Air Force base in Rantoul. We got up very early that morning and went to the bakery to get his truck loaded for the day's route. I watched as the workers wheeled the fresh baked bread being transferred on tall racks from one machine to another. Finally the warm loafs rolled off the noisy conveyor and they were placed into plastic covers. The smell of the hot fresh bread was fantastic. Once the truck was loaded, we climbed inside, slid the large side door closed, and Dad started his deliveries to grocery stores in the small towns scattered along our way to the air base. I must admit, I felt pretty important having the opportunity to tag along and go through the guard gates at the air base. It was great spending the entire day working side by side with my dad.

After both my parents found jobs we moved from our grandparents' house into an apartment on North Kelsey Street in Normal directly across the street from the Wesleyan University Stadium. The Denzer family lived upstairs. Mr. Denzer was a salesman for Funk's Seed Corn Company, Mrs. Denzer was a housewife and Mrs. Denzer's father, Reverend Talley, was a minister in a small church west of Bloomington. My parents enjoyed his sermons and we started attending Sunday morning services. Joan, Judy and I were enrolled in Franklin School, located about four blocks away. Several months later, Dad decided to leave Omar Bread Company and again took a job at Williams Oil-O-Matic. Soon afterward, Dad mentioned to a co- worker he was looking for a house to rent because our apartment was too small for our family. The co-worker, Roy Bleavins, lived in LeRoy, and told Dad there was a house for rent directly across the street from his house. LeRoy was a small rural farm town just 15 miles east of Bloomington. Knowing little about the town, Dad told us to get in the Austin and we drove out to look at the house and take a tour of the town. Everyone's first impression was LeRoy would be a very nice town to live in.

With school about to end for summer break, Dad quickly made a deposit for rent. A couple weeks later we loaded up our possessions and moved into the house at 101 East Elm Street in LeRoy. Dad enjoyed telling people how he'd told Roy that renting the house in LeRoy would be only be a temporary stay. However, LeRoy became my parents' home on and off for the rest of their lives.

Chapter 4

The move to LeRoy happened the first week of June, 1951. It was an unusual day for moving because an unexpected hail storm hit LeRoy. What started only as rain ended up with several inches of small ice balls covering the ground. Surprisingly, everything was moved quickly without any major problems.

Moving to this small rural town of only 1,500 people in 1951 was a wonderful experience for my sisters and me. The move again seemed to bring further stability to our family. Life was simple. No TV, no air conditioning, no swimming pool, no sports complex or organized activities, and no cell phones or computers. When I think back, I guess kids did have our own phones, but they consisted of two tin cans and a tight string held between them to talk. The only real form of entertainment was playing table games or being outside playing with our new friends in the neighborhood. As boring as that may sound today, it was absolutely delightful and everyone enjoyed being outdoors having fun. Sometimes this involved doing nothing more than laying down in the grass on a cloudy day and looking up in the sky at cloud formations and telling one another what we were looking at.

Across the street from our house lived the Bleavins family. The father Roy, who suggested Dad consider renting the house, lived with his wife Martha and their four children, Marieda 17, Karen, 13, Raymond, 10, and Diane, 9. The Bleavins family did not have a car, and was one of very few families whose home did not have indoor plumbing. The out- house (toilet) was in the backyard along with an underground food cellar and a shed or what was once the smoke house. Our families immediately became friends, I played with Raymond, Judy played with Diane, and Joan was friends with Karen. There were lots of kids in our neighborhood. The Hunley family up the street had eight children, the Fonger family had five children, two girls, Loretta and Helen and a brother Ronnie still living at home, the Anderson's had three children, Johnny, Ginger and Vickie. Then there was Herbie Robertson believed by some to be the Dennis the Menace of the neighborhood who lived a block away. Several other large families lived nearby but most of their children were older.

For Joan, Judy and I, moving to LeRoy at the start of summer vacation was perfect timing. With so many families in our neighborhood it took little time to make new friends. The playground across the street from the library was always full of kids with everyone having fun sharing turns on the tall swings, the center pole merry go round, see-saws and the tall metal slide. In front of houses city sidewalks were covered with pastel colored chalk with bold layouts of boxes for kids to play hopscotch. Girls skipped rope and boys and girls took turns putting on the one size fits-all roller skates that clamped to the bottom of your shoes and tightened securely to the soles by the turn of a large screw key. Boys spent much of their day playing baseball, riding bikes or just hanging around with one another. Within a couple weeks we had each made many new friends.

Baseball was definitely everyone's favorite sport. Neighborhood baseball games were played in the street and the players never seemed to mind the interruption from an occasional car. As it approached, the game quickly stopped, everyone grabbed the make shift bases and waited for the car to go by. Once it passed and the bases were again back in position the game resumed. The drivers never seemed to be concerned with us playing in the streets and would smile and wave as they passed by. The only thing keeping kids indoors during the summer was inclement weather, which was also an invitation for boys to go outside and play in the rain. Everyone enjoyed baseball. The older and better players took their games to the Washington grade school ball diamond.

The Washington baseball diamond had been there for many years. The school, originally, was built as the high school before the turn of the century. It was hard to believe this very ball diamond was once the same field that native LeRoyan Tim Hendryx played on. He was born in 1891; and, after being raised in LeRoy, he left and worked his way up through the minors, into the major league. Tim played outfielder for the Cleveland Naps, New York Yankees, St. Louis Browns, and the Boston Red Sox. I can only imagine how exciting it must have been to be a professional baseball player and play with those great teams, and my all time favorite and legendary slugger, Babe Ruth. Tim Hendryx died in Texas in 1957.

Tim Hendryx

Local kids would walk or ride their bikes to the ball field in hopes of being picked to play. The games started off with the selection of players. Two players, usually the oldest, took turns choosing the players they wanted for their team. Choices were made by how well you played and the best players were always picked first. Those not selected stood on the sidelines watching the game in anticipation of playing later. Few were disappointed because, as the day progressed, the players leaving were replaced by someone watching from the sidelines. In most cases, the wait was well worth it, by the end of day almost everyone from the sidelines would go home and sit at the dinner table telling their parents about the fun they had playing baseball.

Boys by nature are collectors and in every boy's pants pockets was an accumulation of valuable items needed for traveling about the neighborhood. In one pocket you'd find a small heavy sack of marbles to either play or trade. Shooting marbles was a fabulous way to spend the afternoon with friends. Everyone would gather around and pull out their small bag of colorful marbles to use in the game. The game was simple, draw a large circle in the dirt and each player places one of their game marbles inside. Then take out a large marble to use as your shooter. When your turn comes, kneel, flick your shooter with the top of your thumb from outside the ring and gather any marble you knocked out of the ring. The game continued until no more marbles were left in the ring. Everyone then counted their marbles and whoever had the most won. Last but not least, we'd either return the marbles to their owners or if you are playing "keepsies," the lucky players would keep all the marbles they won.

In the other pocket was a "boy's best friend," his trusty jack knife or pocketknife. Our pocket knives were just the thing for carving, whittling or to challenge a friend to play Mumble Peg. This game started off by holding a jack knife by the tip of the blade, flipping it and sticking it firmly into the ground. There are many variations of the game but ours was a very simple version. Two boys stood face to face taking turns throwing their knives to the outside of your opponent's feet. If it stuck, your opponent was forced to move his foot to the point where the knife stuck. This process continued until one of the player's feet was spread so far apart he lost his balance and fell to the ground. When we first started playing the game, a small stick (or peg) marked the spot where the blade entered the ground. The penalty for the loser was to then pull the winner's 2 inch peg out of the ground with their teeth. Needless to say, the dirt, grass and grit on the loser's face soon changed the rules to being satisfied with just having the loser fall. Sometimes if a younger inexperienced player wanted to play, we'd quickly revert back to pulling the peg out with your teeth. Amazingly, even though the knives were often thrown very close to an opponent's foot, I can never remember anyone ever being cut or stabbed by a wild throw. In the bottoms of both our pockets was a collection of buckeyes, pieces of string and on occasions, a rabbit's foot on a chain for good luck. It seems the only thing we seldom had tucked away in our pockets was money.

It was in 1951 when my grandparents sold their house on Mill Street in Bloomington when Grandpa decided to get out of the rabbit business. Their new home was a new small ranch style home in Normal. Shortly after their move, Grandpa pleasantly surprised us kids by bringing us a pure white male collie dog. We were elated with our new dog and we named him Buddy. I'm not sure if that was already his name but Buddy immediately became an official member of our family for many years to come. From then on, wherever we went, Buddy went too.

When I look back on those early years, I'm still amazed how all the neighborhood kids enjoyed playing with each other. Everyday someone was knocking on your door wanting you to come out to play. Those early friendships continued to grow while in school and I'm pleased to say many of those early friendships still exist today.

LeRoy was primarily a farming community and farming was and still is a very large part of LeRoy's economy. Farms come in all sizes ranging from 20, 40, 80 acres to well over 1000 acres. Farm land around LeRoy, or Empire Township, is considered to be some of the best and richest soil in the world. During the winter after the fields are bare the truckers passing by on the Interstate call it " the black desert" but when the growing season begins, all you can see for miles is corn, soybeans and golden fields of wheat waving in the breeze along each side of the roadways. Rural roads during the growing season were particularly dangerous. Tractors and slow moving equipment were constantly being moved from field to field and when the corn was high, drivers could not see the approaching cars at rural intersections. Unlike today, during the fifties most farmers still raised livestock and wire fences surrounding large pastures were full of cattle, hogs and sheep. Farmer's yards had chicken coops filled with chickens pecking away at any resemblance of food, seeds, or bugs crawling on the ground. Farm equipment was much smaller, less efficient and farming required far more people to plant, grow and harvest the crops. This provided an opportunity for farm laborers, retired seniors, and local boys to make extra money helping out on farms. Farm kids and local boys and girls walked up and down the rows of beans in the fields cutting out or pulling weeds and corn found growing among the beans. Seed corn companies hired crews to either walk through the tall corn or ride on the huge de-tasseling machines. Riding on the machines did not mean you would not end up walking. Those tall weird looking machines were prone to breaking down and after a light summer rain they seldom could maneuver through the black slippery mud. Every summer, Earl and Bertha Nichols ran de-tasseling crews and Mrs. Nichols (Bertha) ran her crews like a seasoned Marine Drill Sergeant. She expected everyone to work, and if you didn't, you wouldn't be working the next day. Baling hay was a job for the older muscular boys which required working in the open fields under the constant heat of the summer sun. The farmers drove the tractors pulling the baler and a flatbed wagons over the bumpy fields. The wagon crewmen grabbed the bales from the machine and loaded the wagon by overlapping each layer carefully to avoid having them fall to the ground. Once a load was stacked seven or eight layers high, it was off to the barn were they were dropped onto the long conveyor that carried them through the large door at the top of the barn to the awaiting loft crew. There they were carefully stacked to the top of the roof where they remained until they were later used to feed or bed down animals. After baling hay, the wheat was harvested and we again gathered to bale straw. Even through the straw bales were much lighter than hay, the late summer heat seemed to be hotter and the work was far dirtier. Farm related accidents were very common back then. Farmers lost fingers and arms in corn pickers, and with little safety protections on machinery, and equipment always breaking down or needing to be cleaned out or repaired, it was very easy to get injured. Farm families understood that possibility and when someone got injured, sick or someone died, neighbors, friends or fellow farmers gathered together to help with the crops.

The City of LeRoy was a "post card photo" of a typical small Midwestern rural town. Homes were neatly kept; large elm trees lined the streets with their outstretched branches shading the white clapboard houses providing relief from the summer's hot sun. Businesses filled every downtown building. The city park was round with well-maintained sidewalks from all four sides ending in the center where the large bronze Indian statue still stands proudly holding his bow and arrows. On the base under the statue were two drinking fountains providing fresh drinking water to park goers. Next to the fountain is a huge Civil War cannon mounted on a concrete base serving as a memorial for past wars. Children were always climbing up and sitting on top of the cannon. On the east side of the statue stands the park bandstand, a round white Victorian building with eighteen columns supporting the roof and large stone steps constructed in the front. In the fifties the city park's sidewalks were lined with wooden and iron benches for park goers to sit and visit. During the summer each Saturday evening local citizens gathered in front of the band stand for the evening's entertainment. With no air conditioning or TV at home, an evening in the park provided both an entertaining evening and the opportunity to visit with friends under the shade of the park's large elm trees. For many years Midge Bock directed the band made up mostly of school band members and a few adults from the community. In addition to the band, occasionally local singers provided entertainment for those in attendance. When Monday came, those same park benches became a favorite spot for the local "old-timers" to sit, smoke, visit and tell tall tales and lies to one another.

Old City Park

In 1951 LeRoy had two streets covered with hand laid paved bricks reaching to each side of the city limits. Center Street ran east to west and Chestnut Street north to south. Park Avenue, the city's only boulevard, was only two blocks long and both lanes from Center Street to Illinois Route 150 were also brick. LeRoy's main business street was Center Street, and Main Street was a residential street. Driving from the park circle east on East Center Street took you past two blocks of businesses, down a hill past the large stately J.T. & E.J. Crumbaugh Library and Spiritualist Church, the city playground, and up the hill past the high school. Once past the high school you entered what was then known as "Silk Stocking Row," where the wealthier residents of LeRoy's past had built some of the finer homes in the town. Reaching the end of Center Street, you turned south on to Park Avenue and continued past highway Route 150 one block to the LeRoy High School track and football field. It was hard to get lost in LeRoy, and no one in town used streets or house numbers to find someone's home. You simply gave any resident a name and they would give you the directions. For Joan, Judy and I it was a perfect place to live. Of course, when looking back, there were also things that were less than perfect. Behind almost every home or in the alley was a burning barrel. Food scraps and tin cans were routinely put into garbage cans to be picked up by Mr. Lewis, our local garbage man. Everything else was set ablaze in the burning barrel. Most all barrels used were discarded commercial 50 gallon drums with the tops cut out. In most cases, within a year the barrels would finally fill with ashes, the sides eventually burnt out and the barrels were discarded and the ashes scattered in the alley. During the summer months and without air conditioning, windows were left wide open to catch some fresh air or a summer breeze. This presented a problem when the offensive smoke and smell of the barrels or the odor from Staley's hog house on the northwest edge of LeRoy suddenly found its way into your house. Another practice no longer used was caring for driveways. Most driveways were gravel or dirt, not concrete. A common procedure to rid driveways and alleys of grass and controlling dust during the summer was spreading used motor oil and cinders from the furnaces over the dirt and grass. It seemed to eliminate grass and dust but riding a bicycle or walking through an alley not long after a freshly coated application of oil had its consequences. Your bike got completely spattered with oil and walking into your parents' house with the soles of your shoes coated with oil was not well received.

Central Illinois weather was very typical to other four season Midwestern states. Springtime was wet, summer hot and humid, fall had its ups and downs and winter temperatures would occasionally fall below zero. The seasons brought about changes not only in the weather but it affected what we did. In the winter we played in the snow, built snowmen, threw snowballs and rode the snow covered streets on sleds. Older boys would grab shovels and make extra money scooping sidewalks and driveways. Spring seemed to draw everyone back outside to plant flowers, plow gardens and children were again back on the streets riding bicycles and playing baseball. High school kids started thinking about the prom, graduation, getting a job or getting ready for college. Summer was the most popular season with everyone outside, finding summer jobs, enjoying the warm weather spending time visiting relatives, and for very few local families, taking a family vacation. Fall welcomed cooler weather and everyone in town became excited about spending Friday nights attending the local football games. Early winter brought back the basketball season, followed by Christmas and everyone bundled up trying to keep warm waiting for the first signs of spring when the trees started blooming and flowers began poking their heads out of the ground telling us warmer weather would follow.

LeRoy's school system consisted of a grade school and a high school. However, to keep up with the community's growth and increasing student population, the old Eugene Field Elementary School was still being used to house grades one through four. When I moved to LeRoy I started school at Washington Grade school. Our house was only four blocks away, an easy walk and even a faster ride on a bike. When the neighborhood boys walked together to school, we'd pass Etherton's old home on the corner of Washington and Chestnut Streets. Surrounding the property was a large thick well-groomed privet hedge running along the sidewalk. Inevitably, almost daily, someone was pushed into that hedge. While the thrashing victim tried to free himself from the hedge's mighty grip, the others would laugh and shout. Finally, someone would give the poor victim a hand and pull him out. After exchanging harsh words and threats to get even (which eventually did happened), we'd continued our journey laughing and tormenting one other.

As I've mentioned before, LeRoy was a friendly, neat and quiet community but by the late fifties was noticeably in a transition mode from living in the years gone by to a more modern day community with new ideas and conveniences. Very few houses without indoor plumbing quickly were disappearing, and new subdivisions were being laid out. More cars were parked in driveways and everyone started staying home watching TV and spend less time visiting with neighbors and friends. It took a number of years before I realized how thankful I was to grow up in LeRoy. It was not unlike any other small rural town during those times, but I felt the people of LeRoy were what made the community special. Like every small town, everyone knew everything about everyone else, or at least they thought they did. Seldom could you go anywhere in town that people didn't know who you were. This presented a distinct disadvantage for kids, especially boys. Wherever you went, or whoever you were with, if you got into trouble, the news traveled home faster than you could. Adding salt to the wounds, if you got into trouble at a friend's house, their parents were not reluctant to punish you as well as their own child, and your parents had absolutely no problem with them doing so. Many of my classmates' parents worked or owned businesses and were a vital part of LeRoy's economy. Kay Belmar's parents ran Land's Cafe, Betsy Bane's father was an attorney, Carole Brown's father managed Alexander Lumber Company, Sonny Davis' father worked at Schlossler's Implements, Paul Folke's parents owned Folke's Jewelry Store, Toddy Henson's father was the Mayor and owned Henson Oil, Nancy Luce's father was the Christian Church Preacher, George Mayer's father was a local carpenter, Janice McDowell's parents ran the Gravel & Ready Mix company, Hugh Niestrath's father worked at Perma-Built Homes, Jim O'Hare's father was the local Meadow Gold dairy deliveryman, Elmer Sawyer's parents ran the Brilliant Bronze Gas Station, Bill Scott's parents both worked at the school and drove the school buses, Nancy Spratt's father worked at the How and later ran the Texaco gas station, Delmar Vance's father worked at Van Deventer Ford, Katy Wilson's father was a high school teacher, and my mother worked and later owned LeRoy Dry Cleaners. Several other classmates' parents farmed and I'm sure I missed others whose parents worked in town, or had businesses in LeRoy.

Local gossip traveled like wildfire in LeRoy. The focal point usually centered on local deaths, auto and farming accidents, fires, the weather, local events or politics. Then there was the juicy discussions about births, engagements, marriages, and of course, why they got married. Avoiding gossip was difficult particularly if you discussed personal matters when talking on the telephone. The local phone service was mostly party lines, with several different families (usually 3 to 6) sharing the same phone line. Each family was given a different number of rings and when anyone wanted to make a call, they would first pick up the phone to see if anyone else was using it. If not, you rang for the operator and asked her to place your call. Once you started talking, anyone wanting to check for an open line or just wanting to eavesdrop could simply pick up their phone, place their hand over the voice transmitter and listen to your conversation. Eavesdropping was considered improper but should you accidently overhear a conversation about someone else's personal matters, it was only a matter of time before the story was being told around town. It seemed the more it was shared with others, the less accurate and more interesting it became. Juicy gossip was always a treat for nosy people, unless of course, the news was about them or someone in their family.

When I started school in LeRoy the Washington Grade School was located where the new swimming complex now stands. I was in third grade and due to the large amount of children that year my age; Washington school added a combined class of 3rd and 4th graders in one class called an overflow class. Our teacher was Mrs. Daisy Moss and I also had her as my 4th grade teacher. Mrs. Moss was a lovely lady who was always well dressed without one single silver hair out of place. She loved her students and geography; and, after lunch, she would carefully place her trusty world globe on her desk and inadvertently point to and start discussing a new part of the world daily. She also appreciated art and enjoyed having students draw or color pictures. Occasionally, she would ask students to select a fellow classmate, have them sit face-to-face and draw pictures of each others. Mrs. Moss was very thoughtful and treated everyone with a great deal of kindness and respect. I enjoyed having her as my teacher and kept in contact with her until she passed away in the early 1960s.

I was now finally reaching the age where I started branching out wandering around town and visiting friends. My forays started by walking uptown and visiting the city park. Vernelle Stencil, owner of the funeral home across the street from the park, was raising several baby raccoons in the backroom he had found while hunting on his farm east of town. The plan was to keep them until they could be later be released back into the wild. The raccoons became so tame Vernelle decided to let them loose in the City Park rather than taking them back to the woods. The animals became an instant hit and amused everyone including the old men sitting on the park benches. They climbed the tall trees and stretched out on the branches keeping a close eye on those passers-by below. If someone below acted like they had something to feed them, down they came and quickly sat up and stretched their paws out begging for a treat. As soon as the treat was consumed they'd scramble back up the tree waiting for the next person to come by with an offer. From the park the next regular stop was the firehouse. The doors were usually open displaying the shiny red fire trucks inside. When we entered a couple of volunteer firemen could be found cleaning the equipment and always seemed eager to show us around.

From the firehouse we'd cross the street to take a look inside LeRoy's old city jail. It was a small old rundown brick building with an outside door made of heavy wood and an inside door made of welded steel bars. The outside wood door was always open allowing people to view inside. By pressing your face close to the bars you could see the two small heavy barred cells, each with a small cots attached to the wall by chains and a small porcelain toilet mounted in the cell floors.

The only light during the day appeared to be from two small iron covered windows at the back. The jail always appeared poorly kept and I never remember seeing anyone locked up inside. There was a story told around town about Frankie Lane, a local mentally challenged fellow, who became intoxicated one night and was put in the jail to sleep it off. The next morning a police officer went to check on Frankie and found him yelling for someone to let him out. The officer then told him to come on out because the door of the jail hadn't been locked. Frankie simply smiled and came out and wandered on home.

Next to the jail stood the city's original tall silver water tower or standpipe. It stood at least sixty feet in the air with "LeRoy" painted proudly on both sides. The steel walls near the bottom of the tank directly above the foundation provided a perfect place for boys to paint or scratch names on its sides. In the winter when temperatures dropped below zero, the water in the tank would become so cold the frozen water would expand and start flowing over the top and run down the outside walls. Local people would drive by with their family to see the colossal wall of ice, which looked like a beautiful giant stalactite reaching from the tank's top to the ground below.

After leaving the standpipe we walked back up to Center Street and stopped into Still's Pool Hall. Even though we were young and knew our parents would object, the owners Whitey and Tuffy Stills, never seemed concerned about us being there. The pool hall was definitely the local gathering place for boys, men, local farmers and old timers to play pool, gossip and spin tall tales as well as play an occasional high stake poker game in the basement. The pool hall was always full and over the next several years it became the hangout for many of the guys I ran around with. On weekends, Still's also ran an old bowling alley attached to the east side of the Pool Hall. It originally started as a Duck Pin alley and later was changed to a Ten-Pin Alley. The lanes were small and the most unusual thing was looking down the end of each lane, and watching the hired "pin setter" replacing the fallen pins after each throw. In the mid-1950s Still's bowling alley was closed and in 1960 a new bowling alley, "LeRoy Lanes", was built on the east edge of LeRoy. The new bowling alley became a popular place for adult bowling teams, families and kids of all ages. After visiting the Pool Hall, we'd head up Center Street wandering through the various downtown stores to check out all their new items. Our main focus was looking at all the latest fishing rods and tackle at Schlosser's Hardware and bicycle parts and model plane and car kits at Gambles Hardware. There were another couple places off the beaten track we enjoyed visiting, Bishops' Hatchery on the 150 curve behind Sawyer's Brilliant Bronze Station where we looked at the hundreds of baby chicks in the heated cages. The other stop was Bebo's Shoe Shop. Bebo was a crippled gentleman whose store had a 10 foot long shoemaker's machine powered by one huge electric motor. When Bebo would turn on the motor, the complete line of various tools would come alive as he moved from one tool to another sewing, sanding, dying the new leather soles and heels and then polish the once worn shoe back to an almost like-new condition. LeRoy's merchants were always pleasant and seemed to have little concern that children were in their stores unattended. During our travels around town there was never a worry about being unwelcome or missing lunch. Promptly at noon each day the noon whistle mounted on the roof of the City Hall alerted everyone in town it was time for lunch. Other times of the day if the whistle went off repeatedly, that indicated there was a fire and alerted all the volunteer firemen within the whistle's range to get to the firehouse and man the trucks.

To promote their businesses, merchants in LeRoy periodically held drawings for their customers. Everyone enjoyed signing up in hopes of winning a prize. The first time I entered a drawing I won a bright red American Flyer wagon with wood side rails with a full case of Coca-Cola setting inside at The How Store. It was a beautiful wagon and what great memories I have of the neighborhood gang pulling each other around in it. On more than one occasion, I would tie Buddy to the wagon and try to get him to pull me. Buddy was much too smart for that. He would just stand there showing no intent in moving or just sit down waiting to be untied.

Before long everyone in the neighborhood was using my wagon for pulling, riding and hauling things between our homes. One day when there was little to do, Raymond and I decided it was a good time to pay back Mrs. Barley for all the trouble she gave us kids while playing street baseball. She lived just north of my parents and was very particular about the appearance of her yard. When playing baseball in the street near her house, if a ball landed in her yard, out the door she would come and run us off her property. Raymond and I decided we'd had enough of her scolding and the time had come for retribution. Off we went pulling the wagon west down Elm Street and across Route 150 to an empty lot jam-packed full of ragweed. We sat among the weeds for more than an hour grabbing and pulling the seed tops off the stems and tossing them in the wagon. After collecting a good size load of seed we hauled it back to our house. There we carefully calculated our plan of attack, I sat on top of the weed seed and Raymond took off pulling the wagon as fast as he could go up the sidewalk along Mrs. Barley's yard. Using our precise prearranged calculations, Raymond suddenly made a 90 degree turn while I leaned outward toward her yard allowing the wagon to throw both me and the seed into her yard. With great speed, we used both our hands and feet to scatter the ragweed seed in her lawn as far as possible. Our mission accomplished, we grabbed the wagon and ran back down the sidewalk toward home before she could get out her door. To our surprise, she never came out and we could never understand why her yard never showed evidence of ragweed cropping up. How could a yard covered with ragweed continue to be one of the nicest and most well-groomed yards in our neighborhood?

Me, Raymond and Buddy

Our house was just one block north of the railroad tracks, and a couple times a week the Pumpkin Vine, a train primarily used to haul grain cars to and from grain elevators scattered along its route between Rantoul and LeRoy, came into town. When playing outside neighborhood boys could hear the engine's whistle as it approached each street crossing. This was not only a warning for motorists to beware, but also alerted boys to quickly jump on their bikes and head to the railroad's engine turntable. The turntable was a large round pit located across the street just east of where the LeRoy

Fertilizer plant is now located. On the floor of the large wood sided pit was a single rail which supported each end of a massive rotating bridge. Once the railroad cars were parked on the side rails, the engine was uncoupled from the cars and driven onto the bridge. Then a crew member would pull the lever on a large motor and the bridge slowly started rotating around the circle. Neighborhood boys were well aware the crewmen would let us sit on the bridge behind the engine and enjoy the ride. As soon as it completed the circle, the crewman would tell us to clear the track and the engine would pull off the bridge, go past the cars and again be at the front of the train. The turntable was originally constructed for steam engines, but after the modern diesel engines replaced the smoke bellowing steam engines, turntables were no longer needed and were later dismantled and the pits filled in.

After spending all day outside playing with friends, I would come in, eat supper, and, before long, head up to my room and start reading comic books. For just ten cents you got 52 pages of reading, and when finished, you could easily trade it for other comics with your friends. Not only were the stories interesting, the ads in the back provided young boys with vital information on the latest body building programs, books on how to pick up girls, glasses that see through clothing, zit removal gadgets, cream for girls to make their breasts larger and ads requesting you to send in your drawings to see if you were good enough to take art classes at home. Guess what, everyone who sent in a drawing was eligible to take the course for a minimal charge simply by returning your weekly instruction packet. I seldom ever ordered anything but if those items are still being advertised; warning, the glasses don't work! After reading the instructions numerous times, and placing them on my head every way possible, I could not see through clothing and can only imagine how silly I looked in those large black rim glasses while staring at every girl I met coming down the street.

On the other hand, there were numerous ads about how to make money. Those were very enticing and instantly I knew I could soon become rich and win fabulous prizes. It may be hard to believe, but this was the start of my career as a salesman. My first venture was selling garden seed for 5 and 10 cents a package from American Seed Company. I sent for my sample kit, put on my best shirt, clean pants, combed my hair and started walking all over town, knocking on doors, asking people (mostly ladies) to look through my samples of the various garden and flower seeds, with the prices clearly displayed on the front. Almost everyone in town had gardens, and people started their gardens by planting seeds rather than buying plants. American Seed Company was well known for its quality and I found it rather easy to "get the sale". Customers simply wrote their name on the order form, checked off what they wanted, I thanked them for their purchase and headed to the next house. After a couple days of selling, I hurried home and my mother helped me fill out the order form. When my order finally arrived, I carefully separated the package for each customer, tied my delivery box on the rear carrier of my bike and delivered the seeds to my customers. It was always fun looking through the rewards catalog to see what prizes I could get for all my hard work. After making a careful selection, I enclosed the money I owed along with my reward request and then anxiously waited for the day my prizes would arrive in the mail. In addition to prizes I also made a little money (very little). I soon discovered my prizes never looked as good as the photos or worked quite like the ad descriptions stated.

I really enjoyed selling things and walking around town

visiting people. One of my very favorite stops was visiting our neighbor Mrs. Maggie Boyer, who lived a half block west from us on Elm Street.

Maggie was a 90-plus-year-old Irish lady who lived by herself and when I would stop by, she'd usually ask me if I could help carrying cobs and coal from the shed next to the ally into the house. She was a very proud lady and would never let me carry those buckets unless she paid me for my service. It was never very much, but the real reward was just sitting with her and listening to the stories about her life. She was a master storyteller and her stories seemed to come to life as she spoke. One story in particular I found absolutely amazing. It was about our 16th President, Abraham Lincoln. Maggie was a very young girl when Lincoln was shot. After he died, a funeral train carried his body from Washington D.C, to Springfield, Illinois where he was to be buried. Her family heard about the train's schedule, and in respect to the "Great Emancipator," her father loaded the family onto a horse drawn wagon and traveled the unpaved dirt roads to a nearby town to see Lincoln's funeral train pass. She remembered the long ride on the muddy roads and the sadness her family felt when they found out they had arrived too late to see the train. She said in order for them to get home while it was still daylight; they immediately turned the wagon around and headed back home. Years later at a LeRoy Historical Society meeting I was surprised to learn John C. Schuler, the engineer driving Lincoln's funeral train, was a LeRoy resident and is buried in Oak Grove Cemetery. The railroad gave the funeral train open track without any city stops all the way from Washington, D.C. to Springfield, Illinois. I still find it incredible to have had the opportunity to actually talk to someone who was alive when Lincoln was President and still be able to share those wonderful stories of her early life in the mid-1800s. Mrs. Boyer lived until she was around 100 years old. The last few years she was a resident in the LeRoy nursing home on the corner of Lynn and Pine Streets where she remained until she died. The nursing home was later torn down for a residential building site.

In my earlier years I firmly believed Mrs. Barley was a woman who hated kids, especially after frequently being run out of her yard during baseball games. That changed when I started stopping by to visit with her husband. During the spring and summer months Mr. Barley enjoyed sitting on the front porch and was always glad to have someone stop and visit. He was well up in years, totally blind but always had a smile on his face and he thoroughly enjoyed being outside. His spent most of his time just listening to the sounds of the outdoors, hearing the birds sing and listening to the neighborhood kids play. After a couple visits he knew who I was as soon as I would start up the porch steps. He always asked me to come over and sit down and talk, wanting to know what I had been doing and what was happening in the neighborhood. Spending time visiting Mr. Barley obviously met Mrs. Barley's approval. Before long she would come out and ask if we wanted a glass of water or ice tea. After several visits, I occasionally would even stop by when she was sitting alone outside on her porch swing. I had always thought she was a very private person but found she was a pleasant lady and enjoyed sharing her memories about her family and her early life. Her maiden name was Strayer and her family had lived and farmed in the LeRoy area for many years. During one visit shortly after our family returned from visiting my grandparents in Florida, she asked about our trip. I told her all about Florida and all the fun we had during our visit. She then began telling me about one of the first trips her family took in an automobile. Families back then seldom traveled far from home and when long distance was involved trains were used by most travelers. Before the automobile, there were very few paved or well- maintained roads in rural McLean and De Witt Counties. At the time, the automobile was wonderful for city and highway driving, but it was difficult for cars to travel the rural dirt roads previously traveled by buggies and horse drawn wagons. Her father finally bought his first car and was eager to take the family on a short trip across the county to visit relatives. I don't remember where she said they were going or the distance, but her description of the roads they traveled sounded like most of the roads were either dirt trails, gravel roads, or stretches of one lane paved cement highways. Shortly after the trip started, her father found the roads were not suitable for his new automobile. The dirt roads were slick with mud and the tracks from the wheels would hit potholes filled with water. This did not discourage her father, still determined to continue; but before long he met another car coming up the narrow road. In an effort to make room for the approaching car the right side wheels went off the road and suddenly sank into the soft mud. Fortunately, with the help of her brothers and the gentleman in the other car they were able to push the car back on the road. Finally, her father came up to an intersection where he turned the car around and returned home. Mrs. Barley also enjoyed talking about her many years of marriage to Mr. Barley. Mr. Barley (Cambie), had worked with his brother Frank for many years at the Barley Land Company in the old Brick Barley Building on the corner of Center and Chestnut Street uptown. They had one son who was in the Air Force and he and his family lived in Texas. Hearing her talk about their early life and living in LeRoy, I thought they most likely were childhood sweethearts. However, a couple years after Mr. Barley passed away, Mrs. Barley suddenly remarried, and to my surprise, her new husband, a nice gentleman from Minnesota was in fact her former high school sweetheart.

In the fall of 1951 my grandparents surprised everyone when they announced they were moving again. This time, they decided to move to Florida to spend their remaining years in warmer weather in Ocala. A short time later, both of my dad's sisters, Aunt Sis and Aunt Gin along with their families, also moved to Ocala to be near my grandparents. My dad was both surprised and disappointed to be miles apart from his family.

Dad continued working at Williams Automatic but always felt there was a better job out there doing something different, he just hadn't found it. One of his ideas was to switch careers towards electronics. Using his past military experience and taking some additional electronic courses could be the key to open the door for a new career. He researched the various companies advertising their electronic courses taught at home. After selecting the one he felt best suited his interest, he enrolled and the books soon arrived for his first course for radio repair. He seemed to be excited and knew the course would consume a lot of his extra time. He built a long work bench in the basement and spent hours after work studying the manuals and assembling the transmitter and receiver components he received through the mail. While he was working at one end of the room, I stayed busy at the other side of the room playing with my electric train sets. I spent countless hours laying out track and switches. I constructed a paper Mache' tunnel out of newspapers and glue made from flour. At the other end of the table I created a small city with buildings and plastic trees, and a small depot with people and cars and trucks parked along the tracks.

I have always loved cars and could play with them for hours

at a time. When outside, I'd lay on the ground beneath the large maple tree in our yard and make roads in the dirt around the roots at its base. At night I'd gather them up and after dinner go to my room and play with them again. While lying on the floor and giving them a firm push, the cars would speed across the hardwood floor just like a real race car. From those tiny toy cars I developed a fascination and love for automobiles. Like many people in the fifties, I waited in anticipation for the automaker's next year models to come out. To show off the new models, dealers held special events in their showrooms handing out free candy, sodas and adults could sign up for door prizes. To assure no one could see the cars until the nationally announced preview date, the cars were delivered on trucks to the dealers totally covered up. When the official day finally arrived, people would fill the showrooms and go from car to car looking at the new styles, model changes and all the latest options being offered on the cars. The most popular model was always the family sedan with four doors and a standard transmission. For the younger sportier crowd, the sleek two-door hardtops and convertibles were more popular. Automatic transmissions and power steering were just becoming popular but they too were optional and raised the price of the car. Other "extra options," for buyers was an extra right side rear view mirror, dash clock, fender skirts, full size chrome hub caps, chrome bumper guards, and even a matching colored sun-visor over the top of the windshield. Car radios were another option but they only carried AM channels and one speaker was offered in the center of the dashboard. For the young man wanting to impress the ladies, a continental spare tire kit could be added to the rear bumper. Air conditioners, power windows and electric windshield washers and seat belts were not yet available on cars and trucks. At the time, a completely loaded brand new Ford Customline two-door hardtop sold for less than $1,500.00 at Van Ford Motor Sales in LeRoy. For the wealthier folks, and there were a few in our town, a new Cadillac luxury sedan sold for $3,200.00.

I also liked motorcycles, and one day I wandered into Govia's Grocery store on the north side of the park and walked to the back where George Govia was working behind the meat counter. Taped to the top of the glass case was a cut-out of Kilroy, a bald headed cartoon guy peeking over a wall. George explained the World War II and Korean War cartoon was a favorite cartoon drawn on walls by troops stationed all over the world. I always got a smile seeing Kilroy's huge eyes looking over his big nose down on me from the counter. George liked motorcycles and out behind his store sat his prize possession, a Harley Davidson Motorcycle with an attached sidecar. I asked him about the motorcycle and in turn he asked me if I had ever ridden in one. I responded with a "No" and George asked me if I would like to take a ride. Needless to say, I quickly replied, "Yes."

George said, "Follow me," and he put a sign on the front door reading "Be Right Back," and we went around to the backyard.

George started off by showing me where to step to climb into the sidecar. Then he climbed on and cranked up his mighty machine. Suddenly the engine came to life and we started out of the lot and headed north on Main Street. With a large smile George came to an intersection and quickly turned right. Within seconds the wheel of the sidecar went airborne and once the turn was completed the sidecar bounced back down to the street's surface. I was excited beyond belief with the ride and enjoyed it as much as any amusement ride I had ever been on. I could tell George was also delighted in just seeing me hanging on for dear life laughing and enjoying my very first motorcycle ride in the sidecar of his mighty Harley.

It seemed as each day passed LeRoy became more of a permanent home for our family. Everyone enjoyed living there. Mom found a job working uptown at Holderly's Dry Cleaners. The owner, Dewey Holderly, was in his sixties and had been in the cleaning business for over forty years. He and his wife ran the business but she passed away with cancer shortly before we moved to LeRoy. After she died Dewey was having a difficult time running the business without his wife. He finally decided to advertise for help, and was absolutely thrilled to have someone with Mom's experience apply for the job. This was a good opportunity for Mom, she was working only minutes away from home, she and Dewey enjoyed working together and he didn't mind my stopping by to visit Mom at work. I soon found my visits to the cleaners to be profitable. Dewey would take me back to the small cleaning room where a huge dry cleaning machine sat bolted firmly to the concrete floor. Dewey never took the time to check the pockets of the clothes before putting them in the cleaning machine. Consequently, coins from pockets fell out and would drop to the bottom of the machine. With me standing at his side he opened the door and showed me the large rotary drum with wooden slats inside which allowed cleaning fluid to tumble wash the clothes. He told me he had a difficult time trying to reach the change on the bottom because of the small space between the tumbler and the machine's outside liner. He was convinced my small arms were just the right size to reach between the outer wall and the slats and touch the very bottom of the tank. He was right, just by slightly bending my fingers, I could scoop up coins lying on the bottom. After a couple handfuls, Dewey would smile and say, "That's enough for today," and all the coins I gathered were mine to keep. The retrieved coins always came out bright and shiny from being submerged in the cleaning fluid. After placing them in my pocket and thoroughly washing my hands and arms, my next stop after leaving the cleaners was just around the corner to Land's Cafe for an ice cream float.

On weekends, Dad started working at the Brilliant Bronze gas station owned by Chuck and Helen Sawyer. They were also the parents of one of my classmates, Elmer Sawyer. Elmer and I started spending a lot of time together playing at each other's homes. It was always fun going over to his house to play. He was the only person I ever knew who had a pet skunk. It had been unscented, but because it was nocturnal, they kept the window in Elmer's bedroom open for it to climb in and out of during the night. It definitely preferred to be outside and when it was damp, humid or raining, the skunk would come in smelling even worse than a wet dog. I'm not sure whatever happened to that skunk, but I would guess it either died or just ran off.

Elmer's parents' house was located in the northwest part of town and included over a half block of property. His bachelor uncle lived with them and kept two ponies in the barn behind the house. Elmer and I would get a saddle from the barn, put it on a pony and away we'd go. Both of us were too young to properly tighten up the cinch, but nevertheless, we took turns riding the pony around the pasture. On more than one occasion, the saddle would begin to gradually slide down the side and off we'd fall to the ground. Once free of its riders, the pony ran as fast as he could to the other side of the pasture to avoid giving us another ride. One time we both hopped on the pony and when it got tired of carrying us around the lot, it headed back to the barn. As we approached the barn we noticed the bottom door was open but the top half of the barn door was shut. Because the pony was short, it knew he could simply duck under the top door and go back inside the barn. Seeing what was about to happen, we hurriedly leaped to the ground. It took only a few rides to determine a career as cowboys or rodeo riders was not in our future.

I was under the impression Elmer never cared much for his name, especially when his mother would step out on the back door stoop and yell, "Elmer Arthur," which could be heard almost a block away. Since we felt that he didn't favor his name, Elmer, the guys decided to help him find a new name. He soon became known as "Buzz" named after the comic book character and WWII Ace Navy pilot John "Buzz" Sawyer. Elmer liked his new name and to this day is still known as "Buzz Sawyer". During those early school years Elmer was fun to be around and enjoyed going the extra mile entertaining his fellow classmates. His ability to be funny sometimes ended up with several other students, including myself, joining in with disruptive laughter. The teachers however, were less than amused and our report cards reflected their sentiments. In the "Needs Improvement Section", their comments repeatedly included remarks about work being incomplete, being disruptive and not paying attention in class. Knowing my parents would be unhappy with my report card, I carefully prepared myself with every excuse possible to explain my grades and those awful comments and recommendations. The easiest excuse was to blame Elmer for the disruptions. I had no problem doing that because I knew he was at his house trying to blame his performance and poor conduct on me. My parents however, were less than amused and I soon learned trying to blame Elmer no longer worked.

In fifth grade my teacher was Miss Hazel Thom. Her

classroom was located upstairs and provided everyone a great view of the east side of the playground. Miss Thom was a very quiet lady, never married, and lived with her old maid sister. In my opinion there's not much I can say about her as a teacher. She was nice but distant, never allowing herself to become close to her students. With her quiet voice she would carefully go over each subject, line by line, chapter by chapter directly from each textbook.

The only eventful thing I remember that year was deciding to sign up for band. Band seemed to be of great interest to the girls and if all the cute girls wanted to be in band, so did I. When I told my parents, I sensed they felt I finally found my niche, and I just might have a hidden talent for music. A few days later they took me to Miller's Music Store in Bloomington and rented me a trombone. I soon found out the slide was too long for my short arms, so back we went and I came home with a coronet. I enjoyed playing the coronet and really enjoyed practicing, especially when my sisters were trying to hear the radio or watching TV. I continued in band until I graduated from high school.

Many years later, Linda and I became neighbors to the Thom sisters. When I would see them outdoors working in their yard I'd stop and visit them and found them to be very nice and good neighbors. They kept their small house and yard absolutely spotless. Because of their age it became difficult for them to trim the large hedge behind their house. I ultimately convinced them I had the time and the trimmers needed to maintain their hedge and they finally accepted my offer. I continued trimming that hedge until they both passed away and their property was sold.

Chapter 4

Christmas while I was in fifth grade was very special. After opening my presents from under the tree, Mom and Dad told me to look out on the side porch. I quickly ran to the window and there on the porch sat a red and white JC Higgins 26-inch boy's bicycle. It had a battery operated headlight, a gas tank with a button for the horn, passenger carrier over the rear fender and chrome plated shock absorber springs on the front. What a beauty! It was snowing, but I managed to walk it down to the sidewalk, get up on it and take a ride a couple hundred feet and back. Dad has purchased the bike from Gamble's hardware store downtown. I spent many hours and many years riding that bike all over LeRoy and out into the rural country side. It was always a thrill to pedal it as fast as I could get it to go, the bike swaying from side to side as I pushed each foot down on the pedals, and looking down watching the asphalt rapidly passing beneath me. I was reminded years later by my sisters that the bike was a present to all three of us. Evidently in all the excitement of seeing that bike I didn't read the tag tied to the handlebars, and why would a girl want to ride a boy's bike anyway?

As summer vacation came around, life appeared to be going

well until one night after our evening meal. When our number of rings sounded out mother answered the phone. Immediately she told Dad the call was for him. As he started talking it was clear something very serious was being discussed. Everyone became quiet and tried to pick up bits and pieces of the conversation. It became apparent the call involved me. After Dad put the phone down, Mom and I were called into the kitchen where I was told the caller was our local police officer. The officer told Dad he was on the way to our house to discuss a recent crime involving a nearby home invasion. It was plain to see my parents were very upset and wanted to know if I'd been involved or knew anything about the crime. I immediately told them I was in no way involved and knew nothing about it. When the officer arrived he told us a house one block away had been burglarized and several items had been stolen. The house was located on the corner of North Street, just south of the Log Cabin and directly across from a vacant lot where the neighborhood kids played baseball. The police officer had already questioned the neighboring residents to determine if anyone could provide information about the incident. During his investigation, an elderly lady who lived just north of the lot told the officer she saw me and a couple other boys climb into the house and carry out items. In total shock, way beyond being scared, I told him we did not break into the house and had never even been on the property. I wasn't even sure we had played baseball on the day in question. The officer appeared to be unconvinced and told my parents he would need to question each of us further. In leaving, he told Dad, tomorrow morning he would be taking all the boys to the McLean County Sheriff's Department in Bloomington for further interrogation and fingerprinting. After he left my parents continued to discuss the seriousness of this situation and warned me I'd better be telling the truth. I went to my room and worried the whole night about what may happen the next day. When morning finally arrived, I was beyond worried. Finally lunch time arrived with still no call from the officer. Finally he called and told Mom to disregard his visit as the case had been solved. The officer said after leaving our house he received a call about someone messing around south of town in Gilmore Cemetery. When he reached the cemetery he caught a local high school boy attempting to dig up a grave. While checking out his car, the officer opened the trunk and found several items taken from the home of the neighborhood burglary. While being questioned at the county jail, he confessed to the burglary and told the officer he had acted alone. His confession proved us to be completely innocent. The officer felt the older lady had no bad intentions, and due to her failing health and memory issues, she most likely just imagined the whole thing when asked about the incident. You cannot imagine the relief I had after that call!

I must admit, we did on occasion go into a local house without permission, along with many other local kids. There was a large old house that stood on the corner of Buck and Pine Street called "the Buck house". It had been abandoned for many years, unpainted and unkempt with windows broken out and the front door always partially open. Over the years the abandoned home had fallen victim to looters, kids and local curiosity seekers. Being young adventurous boys, it was exactly what we envisioned as a real haunted house. When riding in that neighborhood, we'd hide our bikes in the weeds of the yard and enter through the front door. As you opened the door wider to enter, you were welcomed by the creaky sounds of the door's rusty hinges. Once inside you were standing in the living room, the only light inside was from the sunlight shining through the windows not covered with boards. Looking around, the walls had lost most of its wallpaper and the cracked ceiling had holes showing exposed lathe, and what plaster was left was dark and water stained. Several pieces of junk furniture remained in the mostly empty rooms. There was a very old mid 1800's huge piano with most of its parts gone. The kitchen was littered with old silverware, kitchen utensils and rusted pots and pans. It definitely was a scary place to be but interesting and exciting to explore. Lots of old junk was thrown about the floor and water- stained papers scattered everywhere. This indicated to us someone a long time ago, for reasons unknown, the occupants simply walked out the door and left. Our imaginations ran wild. We imagined the sudden exodus may have been caused by a tragic accident, a brutal crime or possibly even a supernatural experience. With every step we carefully kept our eyes moving from wall to wall hoping to find what others visitors had missed, the find of all finds, a hidden treasure. After wandering through the house and finding nothing, we ended our exploration and exited out onto the dilapidated porch, still feeling a weird sensation that a ghost may be lurking behind us. Quickly we jumped on our bikes and rode off in search of our next exciting adventure.

Summer was now in full swing, it was again time for me to put on my selling cap and hit the streets. This time I expanded my product line by selling two exciting well known products, Cloverleaf Salve and Dr. Hess Bag Balm & Udder Ointment. These products were commonly used in farming communities and very easy to sell. My sales results prompted me to continue searching through the reward catalogs for more and better great prizes. Now that I was taller and stronger, I was also able to start my next new job, mowing yards.

Across the street from our house lived Mr. and Mrs. Strayer, a brother to Mrs. Barley. They had not lived there long and Mr. Strayer came over and asked me if I would be interested in mowing his yard. I definitely was interested but mowing yards back then was not an easy job. We, like most every other family at that time, had only an old iron push mower, and the only motor it had was the person pushing it. Gas powered mowers were becoming popular but they were also expensive. After telling Dad about the offer, he quickly realized if we had a gas powered mower, I could mow our yard and find other yards to mow. He shopped around and finally came home with a used gas mower. This was great news, I was now ready to start making money in my new-found career. The mower was small and designed unlike any other mowers I've ever seen. The handle was in the center of the cover and when you wanted to turn around, you just pulled the handle over and it was now ready to go in the opposite direction. I started off charging $1.00 to a $1.50 a yard and easily could mow two or three yards a day using around one and a half gallons of gas, which was less than 25 cents per gallon. For someone not being old enough to have an hourly job, this was a great deal. Over the next couple years I ended up having around 10 yards I mowed until we later moved to Florida.

In the fifties, residents in rural towns appreciated fresh food, and many people had their own gardens. Residents also preferred fresh meat, and many bought their meat directly from farmers or uptown at Bock's locker plant. Chickens were very popular and many local people preferred buying them live and killing and cleaning them themselves. It was not unusual to drive around town and see someone step outside their kitchen door, take a chicken from a cage, place the neck on a stump, then chop off its head. Once the head was detached, the chicken would flop around on the ground until it became lifeless and died. The chicken was then dipped into a large pot of boiling water, and then the feathers were plucked from the skin. With a couple skillful cuts to the stomach, the insides and feet were removed, the chicken dipped in clean water and now it was ready to fry for the evening meal.

Mrs. Barley was one of few people who had a freezer in her basement. When her supply of chickens ran low, she'd drive out to Satchwell's poultry farm and buy a dozen chickens. Mrs. Barley was a small and very neat lady and did not like getting dirty. One afternoon, she asked me to go with her to Satchwells' to help her buy chickens. She carefully backed her spotless 1937 Ford two-door sedan out of the garage. I got the large wooden chicken crate from her garage and placed it in the trunk. We got in the car and she slowly drove out to Satchwell's poultry farm on highway 136. I was looking out the window and felt I could have walked faster than she was driving. We finally arrived, and she started selecting the chickens she wanted from the hundreds trying to stay away from Mr. Satchwell's long chicken hook. One by one she pointed them out and Mr. Satchwell carefully hooked them around the leg and placed them in the cage. It appeared the chickens figured out what was about to happen to them because they were making every effort not to be put in the crate. Finally the dozen chickens were captured, she paid Mr. Satchwell and back home we drove. I soon found out Mrs. Barley's ideas on dressing chickens was much different than most people. She didn't want her chickens flopping around on the ground because she said it would bruise the meat. Her preference was tying the chickens' legs to the clothes line and slitting their throats. This method eliminated any possibility of bruising the meat. As I previously mentioned, I had seen numerous people kill chickens, but this was my first experience in performing the actual act. I also found out the chickens were uncooperative in being tied to a clothesline by their feet. Finally, with the chickens hanging upside down securely attached to the clothes line, Mrs. Barley handed me a very sharp old kitchen knife and I started cutting their throats. Being new at this occupation, I was unaware what was about to happen. The chickens were hung just high enough that when their throats were cut, the thrashing headless chicken totally covered me with its blood. By the time I finished the job and went home, I looked like a mass murderer after a very busy night. Mrs. Barley, however, was very pleased and paid me seventy five cents for helping her.

My mowing business was now doing very well and it seemed many of the elderly people I worked for needed other small jobs done while I was there to cut their lawns. I hung window screens, cleaned basements and helped them plant flowers and trim bushes. I was now making enough money to do other things I enjoyed.

Occasionally in evenings I would go over to visit our next door neighbor, Dale Webb. I enjoyed watching him work on his project in his garage. Dale and his wife Joanne had only been married a few years. Dale owned Webb's Men's Wear, a clothing store uptown which he bought after returning home from World War II. The previous owner, Oscar Phares, had operated the local clothing store for more than 40 years. Dale and Joanne had bought Joanne's parents' house, and Dale spent much of his evening hours remodeling their house and building shelves for his store uptown. It was no secret, Dale never really cared for kids, and my mother was always worried I was getting on his nerves. For some reason, I got along very well with Dale and can't ever remember him acting as if he didn't want me around. He even surprised me one time when he offered to spray paint my bicycle during one of his projects. In addition to working on the house and store, Dale bought an all-wood Chris-Craft inboard boat which needed to be restored. Dale was a near perfectionist on every project and over the course of a year, he painstakingly restored the boat to "like new" condition. When finished, he and Joanne would go to Lake Bloomington on Sunday afternoons and cruise around the lake. One weekend they invited our family to go with them for an afternoon cruise. The boat not only looked new, it ran like new, and the entire family enjoyed spending the day riding around the lake with Dale and Joanne. This was about the same time when I developed a real interest in reading books rather than comics. I particularly enjoyed reading adventure books, like Mark Twain's "Adventures of Tom Sawyer and Huckleberry Finn" and the many tales and adventures during their youth. While moving through the pages I thought about how interesting it must be to climb into those caves, ride on a raft down the mighty Mississippi River and constantly be seeking new adventures along the way. For me, the Crumbaugh Library was the world's greatest travel agency. While there, I could visit any place in the world I wanted to go. I enjoyed looking through the books and magazines, and of course, opening a National Geographic and scanning the pictures of the topless ladies of the Congo. It was certainly one of almost every young boy's favorite "acceptable" reading materials of the time. I also enjoyed reading about Ernest Hemingway's hunting trips and looked at all the photos of him standing alongside the dangerous lions and elephants he'd killed while on safaris in Africa, and seeing the many other photos of his fishing trips off the coast of Florida and Cuba. It was hard to believe anyone could catch the gigantic marlin and sailfish he caught, some weighing more than 500 pounds. I still consider both Twain and Hemmingway to be two of our country's greatest writers and adventurists. I must confess however, as popular and interesting as Hemingway was as a person, at first I found his books hard to understand. I was around 15 when I first read *The Old Man and The Sea* and thought it was boring. Years later I read it again and thought it was brilliant. I guess he's one of those authors you just have to read at the right time in your life. With that said, he lived the life of a true adventurer. He was a "man's man" and had the rare ability to both enjoy the moment and describe in detail the lives and experiences of the people he wrote about. Wherever his journeys took him, an adventure returned with him. I was sad to hear in the summer of 1961, this extremely colorful and talented man, with so much left to give, took his own life at the age of only 62.

The Crumbaugh library was a beautiful building but I remember it could sometimes be somewhat scary. The west wing of the building was the sanctuary for the Spiritual Church. It was well known that this church held some very unusual services. There were rumors of ghosts being in the building, objects levitating during services and spirits from the past talking through a medium to those seeking to communicate with the dead. These stories all sounded very strange to my young mind. The library portion of the building was free to the public and seemed perfectly normal and free of spirits, but that changed when you needed to go to the restroom located in the basement. To get there, you first had to open a heavy steel gate, then start your descent down the stairway leading to the floor below. The steps, walls and floors were covered with solid marble. Once you reached the lower level the slightest noise from your shoes coming down on the marble floor gave out a loud all- encompassing echo. In mini-seconds it started reverberating throughout the entire basement, giving you a creepy feeling like you were traveling through a chamber of an ancient Egyptian tomb. It never took me long to relieve myself, and when finished, I wasted no time heading back up to the main floor, with a feeling someone may be following. It was a little creepy and I had no desire to have a face to face encounter with someone from the past.

When summer came to a close, I was in the sixth grade. This was when I met the teacher of all teachers, feared by all and afraid of no one, the one and only, Mrs. Mears. Most children and parents feared her. Any outburst in her class could immediately result in her dislocating your head from your shoulders or having your hands whacked by her well-worn ruler. Respect was never an option; it was required at all times. She was a large woman, very stern and in total control. One thing for sure, when she talked, you listened. And if you were stupid enough not to listen, you knew what was in store, and she always followed through. My mother was so concerned when she found out Mrs. Mears would be my teacher she went to the school and talked to our principal, Mr. Covey about putting me in another class. Her visit was in vain, and to my mother's surprise, I really liked Mrs. Mears.

There were only two times I almost crossed the line with her. The first time was when the boys in recess started walking up and hitting each other in their privates. After recess she had all the girls stay in the hallway and the boys were told to remain in the classroom. After the girls were gone she calmly walked over and shut the door. This was never a good sign. With a stern voice she explained that type of behavior would no longer be tolerated. That was all it took to stop the "nut cracking" taking place on the playground. The second time was when I think, Bill Dever, one of my classmates told us Mrs. Mears' first name was Margaret. The next morning when she entered the classroom, several of us welcomed her with "Good morning, Margaret." She seemed to be amused and started class with no noticeable reaction. Finally, it was time for recess and she asked each one of us to remain in the seats while the others left for the playground. Again, she slowly got up from her seat and closed the door. She then stated her name was in fact Margaret, but she never ever wanted to hear us call her anything but Mrs. Mears again. Then she looked over her desk and asked us if we understood! We quickly replied, "Yes, Mrs. Mears," and she then told us to join the others outside.

Years later, I got to know Mrs. Mears very well and found her to be a wonderful lady. When I attended summer school at Illinois State University, Mrs. Mears also was attending classes. She had taught for many years with only a teacher certificate, a common practice during the thirties and forties, and decided she wanted to get her degree. For several years, each summer she would take the required classes. I often wondered during her classes if she ever challenged those professors, knowing well that if she had, there was no doubt who would have won. After returning home from the Army I began serving as an election judge with Mrs. Mears. I was a Republican, she was a Democrat. The judges sat around the room making sure the election was legal and helping those voters who needed assistance. I was 24 years old at the time, and when I asked Mrs. Mears a question, referring to her by Mrs. Mears, she smiled and said, "You can call me Margaret." I then reminded her of the day in class when I was told to never call her anything but "Mrs. Mears" again. Both she and the rest of the judges got a big laugh from my story, and I respectfully continued to call her, "Mrs. Mears" the rest of her life.

Getting older brought about many new changes to the boys in the neighborhood. We'd grown taller, braver and were developing several new interests. We became curious about almost anything. We seemed to get into more mischief, and when together, what one boy wouldn't think of, another one would. A couple of the neighborhood girls were always following us around and they seemed to be an easy target for our childish pranks. I enjoyed shooting my BB gun and I shot it at almost everything, with the exception of cars and neighborhood windows. The rule was if you broke out a window you paid for it. There were two options, take it out of what little savings you had or you'd be doing extra work until the damages were paid in full. Either way, it was not a good deal. One afternoon I had my BB gun outside and saw a neighbor girl in shorts walking around her yard picking dandelions. Quickly I ducked behind the railing on the porch waiting for her to bend over. With no one else in sight, I rested my trusty Daisy BB gun over the railing and zeroed in on her rear end and fired. Having attained the level of supreme expert by shooting hundreds of targets, birds or wandering dogs, hitting her in the butt should have been an easy shot. However, my first shot was short of the target, so I re- cocked and aimed higher, bingo! Upon impact, she jumped up, let out a high-pitched scream, and ran into her house. I was pretty proud of my precision shooting abilities until her father came over and talked to my dad. After our discussion I decided it was definitely in my best interest to no longer use a girl's rear-end for target practice! In defense for shooting people with a BB gun; back then they were in no way near as powerful as the air-rifles of today. In fact, the speed of the shot BB was slow enough you could see it travel all the way to the target. Hitting someone's butt at forty or fifty feet would not break the skin. If anything, it would only leave a sting and a tiny red mark on the skin. There was one very well-known rule about shooting our BB guns. Be careful, you could shoot somebody's eye out!

Every kid in town loved going to the county fairs, festivals and local attractions. We really enjoyed the Dare Devil shows that traveled from county to county doing stunts in their cars. With lightning speed they roared around the track, sliding around in circles, jumping over ramps, balancing on two wheels, driving through a ring of fire and having a man stand on the roof of the car with his arms stretched outward as it sped around the track. They were great, and we would come home excited and ready to try out some of the stunts ourselves with our bikes. Within days we became self-certified Dare Devils. In an effort to match the climactic fire trick, we carried the lawnmower gas can to the gravel alley, dug a small narrow trench then poured gasoline into it. Now the time had come to take our turns performing the sensational dangerous drive through our own trench of fire. With absolutely no feeling of fear in our guts, one by one we approached the trench, and the boy holding a burning rolled up page of a newspaper would suddenly drop it into the trench. Wham, billowing smoke and orange flames suddenly erupted. The approaching rider quickly lifted his legs up in the air to avoid the flames. We found it to be a thrilling and even a greater experience in knowing we were now true Dare Devils. Standing in the yard watching this incredible feat was the same girl I previously mentioned and it appeared she wanted to give it a try. Deciding to make it a bit more entertaining, we poured the gas across the alley, and while she wasn't watching, poured some gas on her front bicycle tire. We all stood back and signaled her to start her approach. As she pedaled down the alley, we lit the fire and as she crossed the trench, all of a sudden flames were on the ground and on the tire. Immediately she leaped from her bike and onto the ground. We quickly extinguished the fire, and except for a very minor knee bruise, she ran home unharmed. Since her brother was involved, he bore the brunt of dealing with his parents' dissatisfaction over the incident and his sister lost all interest in ever wanting to become a Dare Devil driver or riding through another trench of fire.

Determined to improve our riding skills, we decided to take the show on the road and moved our Dare Devil show a block north to the Hunley's yard. There we built a ramp about a foot high and took turns riding our bikes over the ramp and flying through the air. Gaining more confidence with each jump, we continued raising the height of the ramp to see who could jump the furthest. Sitting quietly on the sidelines was one of the boy's brothers. He was several years older than the rest of us and wore large thick glasses, was somewhat clumsy, overweight and not at all athletic. It was obvious he could not ride a bike as well as the rest of us. As he continued to watch us fly from the ramp and landing several feet away, his curiosity got the best of him and he too decided to try jumping the ramp. He climbed on one of the bikes and started pedaling towards the ramp. From the very start, we knew there was going to be a problem because he lacked the speed to make the jump. It was absolutely apparent we were about to be eye witnesses to a potential death defying tragedy. He was now starting up the wooden ramp, and his front tire was about to go over the top edge of the ramp. To our amazement, the front wheel suddenly fell from the bike. The bike with no front wheel started its descent, the front forks then stuck deep in the ground and over the handle bars he flew landing several feet away. To our amazement, he slowly got up half dazed, thankfully unharmed and seemed totally unaware of what happened. He then carefully placed his glasses back on his head and walked away with no interest in ever jumping a ramp again.

There were some other non-injury related pranks we pulled on unsuspecting kids in the neighborhood. One we called "Swallow the Raw Egg" trick. This started off by getting fresh eggs from our mother's refrigerator. Next, using a sewing needle, you carefully pierced a small hole in the bottom of the egg and extracted all the yoke and egg whites without damaging the shell. The process took quite a bit of time, but when finished, the egg appears to look just like an unbroken egg. We then told some girls to come watch us take our turns eating and swallowing raw eggs. Very carefully we put the empty egg up to our mouth holding it with both hands. We then smashed the shell against our mouth and acted as if the raw yoke and egg white was in our mouth. Making a swallowing sound and acting as if we were chewing, it appeared we had actually swallowed the raw egg. With only the broken shell in our hands, we proudly proclaimed, "See, nothing to it." It was easy to tell they were impressed so we asked if one of them wanted to give it a try. Somewhat reluctant, one of them finally agreed. We gave her a fresh egg, she put it up to her mouth, broke the shell and the egg's insides didn't just go in her mouth, but ran over her chin and down onto her clothes. Feeling ashamed for being so naive to fall for our trick, and knowing her mother would be mad about her clothes being covered with raw egg, she ran home yelling at us and spitting out what remained of the egg.

With pranks, teasing and boys being boys, it was only a matter of time before someone got upset and it resulted in a fight. As I have alluded to several times before, things were different back then, very different. Violence on TV or in movies were years away from being seen. Our fights generally consisted of mostly threats, a few cuss words, pushing, and finally what we called, a real fight. Once a fist was thrown, the fighters would grab each other and end-up on the ground, rolling about while each one tried getting on top and pinning the other down. Sure, swings were made at one another and occasionally someone went home with a bloody nose or a black eye, but most of the hits were really the result of nothing more than a lucky punch. Everyone in our neighborhood were friends. We played together daily and within a day or two after an argument or a fight, the loser stopped pouting, his shame and humiliation faded away and we again were neighborhood friends.

Sixth grade brought about some unusual and biological changes to the boys in my class. We started spending less time playing baseball and developed a new found interest in our female friends. It was hard to believe that we, full-fledged members of the "he man, woman haters club" would ever find anything interesting in the girls we'd been annoyed with over the past years. However, we were now not yet teenagers and no longer little boys. Suddenly notes were being exchanged in class, looks with a half-smile, and eye rolling at one another became common practice. Boys hurried out the classroom door after school so they would be waiting on the sidewalk to offer to walk a girl home. Walking a girl home was fun, but in most cases, I'm sure the silly showing off was more of an aggravation to the girl than making a good impression. It was certainly in no way what I would call a true romantic experience.

Like most other boys in my class, I also became interested in one of my classmates, a girl with her blonde hair up in ringlets. I was now taller, skinny and always acting goofy. She was cute, studious, liked sports and was involved in many school activities. I made every effort to gain her attention, but found out later she just wanted to be friends. It's always painful when you don't get the girl and even more painful having to face your buddies. As soon as the word got out the girl wasn't interested in you, their constant humiliating laughter and gestures was almost unbearable. All I could do was try to turn it around so it appeared I really didn't care. I found this was a commonly used approach and this macho man's secret communiqué between pals seemed to be somewhat effective. When translated correctly, it meant "OK, so she really wasn't interested, just drop it and leave me alone."

I've often heard it said, "You'll always remember your very first kiss." Well I don't, and I would only guess it occurred when some of my friends were having a party, and unbeknownst to their parents, a game of "spin the bottle" was secretly being played without their knowledge. Once we started finding girlfriends, it seemed much harder keeping one. Romancing a girl in grade school was like playing musical chairs. You're constantly rushing around trying to sit next to a certain girl but someone else always got the seat before you did. Managing our love lives was much like predicting the weather. You know what the temperature is today, but you're never sure what tomorrow has in store.

Saturday nights in LeRoy were always special. It seemed as if everyone came to town to shop and visit friends. Families walked up and down the sidewalks, parents stopped into stores to shop, groups of kids gathered and they too walked up and down the sidewalks. It was always hard to get past Ralston's Five and Dime. Mr. Ralston stood on the sidewalk next to his popcorn machine selling sacks of fresh popcorn. Mrs. Ralston was positioned inside the store, standing behind the large glass showcase displaying a large selection of assorted candies. It seemed to be some kind of a trap and it was always hard to make that decision. Some of us would get the popcorn and those wanting candy went inside. After making their selection, Mrs. Ralston would carefully scoop up the candy behind the glass and put it into a small paper sack.

Before the television became so much a part of everyone's lives, the most popular pastime in America was going to the movies. LeRoy had a theater and you always knew when it was open, because the neon lights of the marquis of the Princess Theater could be seen up and down Center Street, proudly displaying the evenings featured film. The Princess Theater ran two shows on Saturday, an early show for kids beginning with cartoons and sing along musicals featuring the famous "bouncing ball" leading the audience to sing along with popular songs like "By the Light of the Silvery Moon".

The evening show was more for teenagers and adults. I think they may have also had a movie on Friday or Sunday nights. Back then there were no ratings for films and certainly no R rated movies. We had now reached the age of being "almost grownup" so we began going to the Saturday evening show. All our friends would congregate outside, boys in one group, girls in another patiently waiting for the doors to open. Once opened, Mrs. Freiberg would start selling tickets from her small ticket window and keeping a constant eye on the lobby to make sure everyone remained orderly. Mr. Freiberg always stood behind the candy counter by the popcorn machine lining up the bags to sell to the ticket holders on their way inside. Once everyone was seated, Mr. Freiburg suddenly disappeared upstairs to the small projector room where he placed the gigantic reels of film on the large projectors. Finally the lights were turned out and the screen came to life first showing still advertising slides of LeRoy's local businesses. Next, came the upcoming previews and finally it was time for the featured film to light up on the large cinema scope screen. Most movies ran trouble free, but on rare occasions, the movie would stop and everyone sat patiently in the dark waiting for Mr. Freiburg to get the projector running again. While Mr. Freiburg was busy upstairs, Mrs. Freiburg moved from the ticket window to the candy counter to continue selling popcorn and candy. After the movie started and sales ceased, she would start her nightly ritual of periodically patrolling the aisles. With her trusty Ever-Ready flashlight in hand pointed down toward the floor, she prudently looked across every row assuring there would be no distractions. This included; no talking, no feet on the back of seats, no throwing objects, and no overly affectionate behavior during the show. If the light beam from her flashlight suddenly was aimed at you, there better be an immediate response or it could result in you being thrown out of the theater.

Even under her watchful eye, we were never discouraged from enjoying ourselves at the movies. We'd follow the giggling girls inside, wait for them to take their seats, and quickly sit in the row behind them. When the movie started, we each started asking one of the girls in front of us to ask another girl if she would sit next to you. Suddenly there was a carefully choreographed exchange of seats. When everyone was finally seated, with luck, you ended up next to the girl you liked.

Saturday night movies at the Princess was not only fun, it was definitely an educational experience. When the lights were turned out, we were quickly presented with an opportunity we previously only talked about, this was the real thing, our introduction to romantic interactions. The process was not only exciting but very time consuming to say the least. The first step was getting that special girl to sit next to you. If she said yes you would take your seat and after the movie started, hope she would let you hold her hand. If that met her approval, you moved to the next step by carefully sliding your arm across the top of her seat and down on her shoulder. If there was again no resistance, you had now reached the level of true romance. Not exactly like the stories one would read in the romantic magazines at the library, but for us, close. We found our minds racing with a new found passion but with so little experience, we needed further instructions. Carefully we scanned the theater to watch the older boys sitting with their girlfriends. This gave us much needed pointers and confidence for what our next moves should be if the opportunity would arise. With everything happening so quickly we still needed to keep an eye on the aisle for Mrs. Freiburg, knowing her lack of tolerance for romantic escapades, which were not allowed in her theater.

As the years passed by, we gradually moved to the preferred seating in the back row. It was considered by young theater goers to be the official "necking row", and some very fond memories of the Princess Theater were made by sitting in those seats. It's not hard to comprehend why we never remembered what the movie was about, but one thing for sure, regardless of what movie was playing, we were always anxious for the next Saturday night movie at the Princess Theater.

In the mid-fifties LeRoy like most other cities around the country started changing. TV's in homes were becoming commonplace and families started staying home more to watch their favorite TV shows. The living room became the main gathering place to watch the local news, shows like The Mickey Mouse Club, Father Knows Best, The Adventures of Ozzie and Harriet, I Love Lucy, The Ed Sullivan Show, Gunsmoke and of course after school, American Bandstand. A trend was now starting; much of our evening activities stopped and less time was being spent outside with friends and neighbors or going downtown on Saturday nights. Spending time with others was now being replaced by hours in front of the small black and white screen with only a few channels to watch. Changing channels was somewhat complicated because the antenna outside the house had to be aimed at one of the only three available TV stations in the area. My dad quickly became a full-fledged TV junkie. He would spend his entire evening sitting in his chair in front of the TV. When winter came, he quickly realized there was a problem. Going outside in the cold to turn the 30 plus foot metal pole holding the antenna was a brutal experience. He finally had a simple remedy. He moved the antenna right next to the living room window. Now all you needed to do was put on gloves, open the window, grab the antenna and give it a turn. On a cold windy day it was amazing how fast he could turn that antenna. That worked for a while, but even a better remedy suddenly became available, the electric rotor. One of my father's happiest moments came when he finally brought home an automatic rotor for the antenna. It was now so simple, just go up to the TV, change the station, and select the direction on the plastic box and watch the little arrow on the rotor slowly move to the chosen direction. After several seconds, the antenna was now facing the station and the fuzzy picture tube suddenly again was clear. With all the manual labor now behind him, watching TV and eating popcorn became our father's favorite nightly entertainment.

Sixth grade also brought about some exciting changes at

school. Our class suddenly grew and new friendships were made with the addition of several new students. Two small rural schools, South Downs and Sabina transferred their sixth grade students into LeRoy. Those I recall were John Umstattd, Sue Burns, Tom Henderson, Betty Roberts, Nancy Roberts, Dorothy Roy, Judy Waller, Conrad Wilson and Butch Woods. We already had known most of our new classmates because they lived so close to LeRoy and attended the local churches and events. But now having them in our class not only created new friendships, it added some much needed talent to our sport teams. Everyone was surprised how well we got along and how we enjoyed interacting with one another. The country kids did have a distinct disadvantage. After school, they had to ride the school bus home instead of hanging out in town. Unlike today, parents didn't pick up their children after school. The town kids walked home and the country kids stood outside the school and waited for their bus. Everyone in town seemed to enjoy walking and even those with bikes would walk along with the others kids.

During summer vacation, country kids seldom came to town. Summers were a busy time on the farm, and farm parents needed their children's help to do chores, help with livestock or work in the fields. Farm kids couldn't just come into town whenever they wanted because most families had only one car. If your parents needed the car to drive to work, kids either walked or found a friend to come and get them.

Of all my friends, David Litherland's house was one of the more interesting and entertaining homes to visit. He and his brother Gary were always doing something strange and interesting, such as playing with guns, running trap lines along nearby creeks and skinning and cleaning animal hides. When entering their basement you had to do so with caution because you would find yourself walking under and around animal skins hanging from the rafters. One summer David went to visit his cousin in southern Illinois for a couple weeks and came back with a great prize, a real Indian skeleton they had unearthed from a field on his uncle's farm. The farm was located near an old Indian burial ground and arrowheads and Indian artifacts were always easy to find. When they came across the Indian skeleton, there was one thing missing, the skull. It wasn't a big deal to David so he carefully gathered the bones and brought them back to LeRoy where he placed the old Indian in a large cardboard box under his bed. When the guys would visit David, we'd pull the old Indian out and try to figure out what bone went where.

David enjoyed reading books about Indians, their lives and Indian lore. It was not unusual for him to make a quick decision and try something he'd recently read about. One day he decided we needed to fix lunch Indian style. I followed him out to the alley, we built a small fire, got some large baking potatoes from his house and packed them in fresh mud. When the fire was hot, we buried the potatoes in the coals of the fire. Then we went to his mother's garden and got several ears of sweet corn. Carefully we laid the corn, shucks still on, above the coals. After a long wait and adding more wood to keep the fire hot and turning the corn, David finally pulled our food out of the fire. We carefully peeled off the shucks from the corn and removed the dried mud and skins off the potatoes. Within minutes we were setting around the fire visiting and eating our Indian lunch. I will have to admit, the meal tuned out OK, but I still preferred eating lunch at home and took less time to consume and less work than cooking Indian style.

David always had an issue with his weight. With his round

face and a fair complexion, it was easy to tell when he was nervous or excited because his face would immediately turn bright red. With his red face, his strong interest in Indian lore and Indian artifacts, we decided he needed an Indian name. After gathering everyone's recommendations, it was obvious the name needed to have a connection with his red face and the headless Indian under his bed. When the vote came in, we honored David with his new nick-name "Red Bone," which stuck with him for many years.

David dated occasionally but kept a close eye on all his friends' romances. After a while, it became obvious he was watching much closer than we realized. Whenever one of us guys would break-up with our girlfriends, David was right there ready and willing to comfort the grieving girl. He'd make his move by giving her a call and asking her out. While some thought David's approach was funny, there were others who didn't. When questioned about the subject by the ex-boyfriend, David was just David, he simply smiled and responded with his soft slow draw, "Well, I thought since you weren't going with her anymore, I might as well give it shot."

During that school year my parents moved to the country and I too became one of the "bus kids." The house, a remodeled old school house, was about two miles east of LeRoy on Route 150. Dad rented it from a local dentist Dr. Amdor. He had recently remodeled it but decided to move back to Indiana. Not wanting to sell the property, he rented it to my parents.

It was fun living there because it had 15 acres of farm ground, a garage and a small shed located behind the house. Dad soon realized we needed a second car so he bought an old 1941 Chevrolet business coupe. It was perfect for the farm and it soon became his farm truck.

Dad put up fences along the side of the sheds for chickens then we drove to Bishop's Hatchery and bought two dozen baby chicks. Later he built another pen for two baby calves. Joan, Judy and I really enjoyed the calves and took turns feeding them from a bucket with a large rubber nipple sticking out from its side. After a few feedings the calves realized when it was feeding time. As soon as they saw us coming with the bucket, they would run to us ready for their meal. When there was a need to haul calves or sheep, Dad removed the back seat out of the old Chevy and loaded them behind the front seats.

Riding the school bus was fun, but unlike most rural kids, I had the choice of riding the bus home or staying in town. With Mom working at the cleaners, I could walk uptown with friends and ride home with her after work.

All types of food programs for your home started showing up on TV. One was a "frozen food service plan" from a company in Rantoul. They provided their customers with a large freezer, and for a monthly service charge, filled the freezer with frozen foods and meat as needed. Dad and Mom signed up and we were delighted in going to the freezer and seeing it totally stocked with the large variety of foods. The food was great and we never before had such a variety to choose from. When it would get low, my parents would either call to have it restocked, or we'd drive over to Rantoul and bring the frozen food back in our car. After six months or so, Mom noticed the monthly charges had increased and the program became too expensive to continue. Soon afterward the company came, loaded up the freezer and drove away. Boy did we ever miss not having the freezer full of food to go to.

My parents enjoyed having company visit our home on weekends. Two of the most frequent guests were Howard and Betty Duvall. On one of their visits Howard surprised me by giving me a .22 single shot rifle. He took me outside and gave me instructions on how to safely use a firearm. I quickly loaded it and practiced firing at empty fruit cans about 40 feet away. Having previous experience shooting my old Daisy BB gun, shooting a .22 rifle seemed easy, just more noise with a slight kick. Before long, I was taking it out into the snow-covered fields behind our house hunting for rabbits and pheasants. The fall plowed fields provided little cover so rabbits were scarce. I was able to flush out a few pheasants, but I quickly found out when you go pheasant hunting, use a shotgun.

LeRoy was a very quiet and safe town and seldom were there any crimes or spectacular events happening. When something did occur, it was considered to be "big news," and ended up in the LeRoy Journal. When it was "Really Big News" it landed in the county's daily newspaper "The Daily Pantagraph." One of the "big stories" involved the local railroad train, the "Pumpkin Vine", when it crashed into a liquor distributor's truck driving along Route 150. The railroad tracks had no crossing gates or warning lights, and the train only came into town three times a week to pick up grain from the local elevators. The truck driver must have been unaware of the approaching train or did not hear the whistle from the engine. Suddenly the train hit the truck, turning the cab over on the road and pushing the trailer into the ditch, tearing it in half and spilling its cargo of liquor and snack products in the ditch and into the field. Almost instantly, the news was all over town, and people hurried to the scene of the accident. It soon appeared everyone was more than willing to offer their assistance.

Pumpkinvine Crash

As soon as we heard the news, Raymond and I rode our bicycles to the crash site and watched as many of the local people helped with the cleanup. However, it was later learned the local helpers were not only picking up the broken liquor bottles, but picking up a few full bottles along with snacks and taking them home. At first, I'm sure the railroad and the liquor company appreciated the free help as it eliminated the need to hire a clean- up crew. When The Pantagraph reporter arrived he took a different view of their actions. They not only carried a photo of the crash, but made light of how local citizens came out in full force and assisted in cleaning up the wreckage. They went on to report that the local residents not only cleaned up the site around the truck, but helped themselves to the liquor still inside the trailer. There were threats by the county and state police to search out the now perceived "liquor thieves", but no one was ever captured, arrested or charged for participating in the cleanup. As Raymond and I started to leave, we found a half pint and two small bags of potato chips lying in the mud. We quickly took them back to Raymond's, cleaned them off, ate the chips and hid the bottle in Raymond's parents' smokehouse. For days we worried about being tracked down either by bloodhounds or the FBI for stealing. Finally after the heat was off it was time to drink our find. We uncapped the top and we each took a swig of the contents in the bottle. Quickly we spit it out and threw the bottle down the outhouse, never to be seen again.

For young boys, riding bikes was the only form of transportation around LeRoy. It would be hard to believe how many miles or how many tires we put on our bikes. There were no three, four, six or ten speed bikes back then, just our large old one-speed bike which took all your power to go up hills, but coasted down the hills with ease. In just over a couple years we became very good at riding our bikes and enjoyed showing off our riding skills. We could ride with no hands, ride sitting backwards on the handle bars, lay down on the seat while coasting and jerking the handlebar up to jump curbs. There was little we wouldn't try to do on our bikes. For an extra special bumpy ride, we'd carry our bikes to the top of the steps at the library, jump on and ride down. During our summer there were many special places to go on our bikes. One spot was the huge old mulberry tree sitting next to Jones' Gas Station on the corner of North Chestnut and Cherry Street. When the berries were ripe, we'd pull up under the tree and pick the purple mulberries from the low hanging branches. After eating all we could eat, the dark purple stains would cover our fingers, hands and mouth. Local people had little appreciation for these trees because the tree's most frequent visitors were birds, and after birds ate the berries, they appeared to enjoy dropping a purple mess on sidewalks, cars and clothes hanging on clotheslines. All of which were extremely hard to remove. We also enjoyed gathering buckeyes lying under the trees, sort out the largest, shiniest and darkest ones to take home. We were told by the old guys in the park that carrying a buckeye brought you good luck. They also believed carrying buckeyes in your pocket was a sure preventative for rheumatism, arthritis, or headaches. It must have been true because almost every one of the old timers had one in his pocket. One of the old gentlemen even told us having a buckeye in your pocket means good fortune in sexual matters because they resemble a man's testicles. I found that particularly interesting but I've never been able to find any medical or scientific documentation to support his claim. However, again, it must have been true or he wouldn't have shared such interesting information with us.

Occasionally, we loaded up our bikes and headed out on the blacktops on a road trips to visit our friends in the country. We'd make sandwiches, fill our canteens with water, and ride for miles. When we wanted to fish, we'd tie our fishing poles to the sides of our bikes and ride out to Salt Creek and spend the day fishing, throwing rocks at snakes, or walking back along the bank and climb up on the old massive wooden railroad trestle. In late summer, the thick thorny bushes scattered along the sides of the railroad tracks were loaded with wild raspberries and we'd stroll along picking them and eating them until we were full.

Just south of the trestle was a great place to skinny dip. The location was far from the road and hidden from the nearby farm houses. What started with just swimming and jumping from the banks, usually ended up in a "good old" mud fight. When it was time to leave, we'd jump back in the water, wash off, throw on our clothes and before we reached home, everything was totally dry. Other times we chose to walk out to the trestle on the railroad tracks kicking rocks or cans, throwing rocks at railroad signs and seeing who could walk the farthest on top of the narrow rails while sharing our thoughts about any subject that came to mind. Another favorite spots was the old elm tree that stood alongside the fence at the front of the football field. We'd stand our bikes against the tall chain link fence and climb up and sit on the limbs where it was cool and hidden from everyone. As we talked we'd take out our pocket knives and start carving initials on its trunk. Some were designed with a heart with our initials and the initials of the girl we liked that week.

Sitting high up in the tree totally hidden by the branches and leaves it was the ideal spot to pull out the single cigarette we sneaked from our father's cigarette pack the night before. After lighting it up, we'd pass it around trying to impress each other with our abilities to inhale without choking or attempting to blow a smoke ring. I'm sure there were times the neighbors thought with all the smoke coming out of the branches, the tree was on fire. Fortunately, there were no fires and had a fire truck come down that street with its sirens blaring, we would have been long gone before it arrived. If that tree is still sitting there, it would be interesting to see if all those old carvings are still etched on its trunk.

Halloween - Joan, Judy and me

In the fall when the leaves on the trees started falling everyone knew Halloween was approaching. Halloween was always a fun time in LeRoy. Each year the school and local merchants held a contest for students to paint Halloween paintings on the front windows of businesses uptown. I teamed up with Larry Zook and braved the cold one evening to paint a large graveyard scene which won first place in our class. All the winners received prizes, and we had our pictures taken for the LeRoy Journal. The following Saturday, contestants again gathered uptown and cleaned their paintings from the windows. The main event for Halloween was the annual Halloween parade and costume contest in the city park. There almost every kid in town would gather by various age groups to be judged. The contest drew scores of kids wearing a wide variety of mostly home-made costumes. Ghosts, hobos, angels and goblins were always the most popular. Homemade costumes were simple and easy to make. It took only a few minutes of rummaging through Mom's rag-pile in the hallway closet to find old worn-out sheets or some of Dad's old clothes. By cutting two small holes in the middle of a sheet for your eyes, you could throw it over your head and tie a strip torn from the bottom around your neck, and you were ready to go. Sheets were also popular for girls to make angel costumes. My favorite costume was putting on old worn- out clothes, multiple pairs of socks and a pair of Dad's old shoes. To finish off the costume, I'd rub candle soot on my face and I instantly was transformed into a homeless hobo looking for something to eat. Before leaving home, I'd carefully grab a bar of soap and hide it in my pocket should we be denied a Halloween treat. As we walked around town almost everyone's porch lights were lit and the person answering the door was happy to greet us in our costumes. The conversation was always the same, "What's your name?"

After telling them who I was, they would almost always reply, "Oh, you're Red Davis' boy". Then with a smile they'd hand me a homemade cookie, apple or a single piece of penny candy. After Halloween, everyone knew winter was about to begin. The winter months were cold but we still played outside except when the temperature forced us indoors. Midwestern winters seemed colder back then and created bitter cold winds that would chill you to the bone. We made every effort to stay outside as long as we could. Finally, when almost frozen, we'd run inside the house and either stand over the floor registers or in our case, close to the large old silver radiators standing next to the door. Radiators were great, you could lean against them, turn around and before long you'd be thawed out. They were also a great place to lay your wet gloves. Another way to speed up the process was going into the bathroom or kitchen and soaking your hands in water. Finally the feeling of tiny needles piercing your skin would go away and it was time to go back outside.

Everyone's favorite winter sport in LeRoy was sledding. Living in the flat farmlands of McLean County there were few places to be found to ride our sleds down hills. The most popular place was the LeRoy Country Club. It had some nice smaller hills but was always crowded with young children whose parents carefully watched making sure everyone was careful, took turns and was well-behaved. Older kids preferred going west of town where Rusty's Rainbow Garden once stood. There the hills were steeper and everything imaginable was used to ride down the snow covered hills; sleds, shovels, garbage can lids and even an occasional discarded car hood or trunk lid. Sledding was fun, but when the streets were covered with snow and ice the number one winter sport for boys was hopping cars on Center Street.

Hoping cars was a sport that didn't require using a sled. When the streets were slick, cars had great difficulties traveling up the Center Street hill. Boys stood patiently on the corner just a block east of the Princess Theater waiting for an approaching car. As it started up the hill the driver knew they couldn't stop, because if they did, they would get stuck on the ice and have to back all the way down the hill. All we had to do was run to the back of the car, grab onto the large chrome rear bumper with both hands, squat down and enjoy a thrilling ride up the hill. You quickly learned there were two spots on the bumpers to avoid, riding behind the wheels where you'd soon be covered with snow from the spinning tires, and being directly behind the exhaust pipe. The trick was to avoid dry spots or areas where the city had salted the streets. Once we reached the crest of the hill, we quickly let go and ran back or hopped another car down the hill to catch our next ride back up. Continuing to hold beyond the top of the hill was not a good idea. If a driver realized you were still hanging on to their bumper, they would pull over, jump out and give you a scolding about the dangers of hopping cars. Hopping cars were not real dangerous because the cars were never able to get up much more than ten miles per hour. For those who wanted to ice skate, kids piled in cars and drove out to Howard Virgin Park to skate on the small pond. This however, was not as popular because the surface was often rough and for most kids, owning ice skates in LeRoy was rare.

My teacher for seventh grade was Mrs. Covey. She was also the wife of our principal, Mr. E.J. Covey. Both Mr. and Mrs. Covey were well known for being strict, and both had somewhat of a serious demeanor. From stories I've heard about nuns in Catholic schools, Mrs. Covey met every requirement of a nun. As long as you did your work and paid attention in class, things went okay. If you got out of line, she would without hesitation, pull you out of class and march you down the hall to Mr. Covey's office. Between the two of them, problems with disorderly students were infrequent and always corrected immediately. I still remember her sitting at her desk and giving us work to do while she quietly reviewed our papers. Periodically, she would stop, look around, get up and walk the aisles checking on everyone's progress and making sure no one was cheating. It definitely was one of the quieter classes in school. She had a love for English and history, and admired Abraham Lincoln and the writings of Edgar Allen

Poe. I thought Poe's poem "The Raven" was totally boring and why should anyone be required to recite it. Abraham Lincoln, on the other hand, was more to my liking. One of our Lincoln assignments was to write or create a project about his early life in New Salem, Illinois. I looked through a book and found a picture of young Lincoln working in the New Salem general store. At home, mother had received a gift set of towels in a nice cardboard box. When opening the top, the bottom inside part had a lift-out cardboard frame with clear plastic to display the neatly folded towels inside. Seeing this nice unusual box, I decided to use it for my project. On the inside bottom of the box I drew the interior of the store. Then I drew and cut out my drawings of Lincoln and his customers, carefully gluing the folded bottoms of the cutouts to the box. After placing the display cover over my work, it created a 3D effect of the people and the store. I turned my project in and received an A+. Mrs. Covey was so pleased; she asked if she could keep it to show other students. More than 20 years later, she came into Webb's store and handed me my project back. To my surprise, it looked just like it did the day I turned it in. She said it was one of her favorite Lincoln student projects and I was totally shocked she had saved it all those years.

One of the most unusual days in Mrs. Covey's class started out with George Meyer sitting quietly in class. He had reached in his pants pocket and realized he had an unused 22 rifle shell left over from target practice the day before. George became bored and innocently started playing with the shell and finally poked the bottom of the shell with his pencil. Suddenly the shell went off startling the entire class. First, everyone looked at George who appeared to be in a total state of shock. There was little time for George to regain his composure because Mrs. Covey was racing straight down the aisle towards his desk. Within seconds, she yanked George out of his seat and headed out the door to Mr. Covey's office with George's feet hardly touching the floor. For many years we reminded poor George about the bullet explosion in class.

Later I learned that a shell fired outside the chamber of a gun does not send the bullet out with the power to hit or injuring anyone. Because he was holding it with his fingers, it most likely only traveled a few feet, very similar to having a small fire cracker go off. But I can assure you, it certainly made our day in Mrs. Covey's class interesting.

8th grade basketball

That same year, sports became everyone's top interest. Most of the boys in the class participated in baseball, basketball and track. Living in a small town was great because almost every boy had the opportunity to play. I was growing fast, now over 5'8" and weighing 135 pounds. Taller than many of my classmates, I started out as center on the basketball team and really enjoyed playing. I was thin, my lower leg muscles small, and my upper leg muscles more developed. Our coach, Mr. Kitchell, was amused by my odd physical condition and decided to call me "Bird Legs." After bringing the basketball down court, whenever I passed the ball or took a shot, he would yell out, "Way to go, Bird Legs." When I was on the outside looking for a shot, he would yell out "Shoot it, Bird Legs. Shoot it." I found this name very annoying and certainly did not want to be stuck with that as a nickname. I decided once I crossed the center line with the ball; my main objective was to immediately pass it to another player. If the ball was passed back to me, I quickly passed it again without attempting to look for a shot. Needless to say, I seldom scored, but I successfully avoided having to hear coach Kitchell's spontaneous outburst from the bench about my legs. Track was my real sport. I was thin, fast, had endurance and could jump. During my seventh and eighth grade years, I won several track events and was one of the better grade school broad jumpers in McLean County.

All the girls in our class idolized Coach Kitchell. He was athletic and handsome, and had recently graduated from college where he played ball. The boys also liked him, he was a good coach, and we found another good thing about him, his wife. She came to visit him at school and attended all the games, and every boys thought she was a raving beauty, which she was. To our young eyes, she looked like a movie star. LeRoy grade school was about to hold their annual grade school dance in the old high gym for seventh and eighth graders. The event was always held a couple of nights after the high school prom. The eighth grade boys would go over after the prom to help clean up for our dance, and both teachers and our parents chaperoned the event. Going to our first school dance presented some real challenges. Grade school boys knew little or nothing about getting dressed up, having manners, or dancing with a girl. To help with this problem, the school posted a bulletin, and to every boy's delight, Mrs. Kitchell offered to give lessons to anyone interested in learning how to dance. It appeared most everyone was interested, especially the boys. The dance classes were held after school in the old high school gym. Mrs. Kitchell had the girls go out on the dance floor and form an inner circle, holding hands, while the boys formed an outside circle around them. The girls moved counter-clockwise, the boys clockwise until everyone was told to stop. The person in front of you was your dance partner. Another innovative match-up was for the boys to form a line on one side of the floor and the girls on the other side. Then everyone turned around and walked backwards towards each other until you bumped into your new partner. One by one, Mrs. Kitchell walked us through the basic steps of how to do the "Box Step." When everyone had the steps down, the girls and boys went out on the floor to practice. When the lessons were finished, she told us we all did a really good job, but the boys all thought having her as our dancing instructor "was just about as good as it gets." Shortly after our lessons, it was time for my very first date. I finally mustered up enough nerve and asked a classmate, Betsy Bane to the dance. My parents took me into Bloomington, bought me a suit, dress shirt, clip on tie and a new pair of dress shoes. The night of the dance, my mother dropped me off at the high school and I walked to

Betsy's house. Unbeknown to me or Betsy, a couple of her neighborhood friends and her brother, Bob, were hiding in the bushes waiting for our departure. From her house we walked to the dance and, afterwards, I walked her home.

The next summer Dr. Amdor decided to move back to LeRoy, so we moved from there into an apartment above Bebo's shoe shop until my parents could find another house to rent. After several months we moved into a large house on the corner of School Street and the LeRoy Lexington Blacktop. It was a large house with an acre of yard plus a barn and four acres of pasture. Dad bought a two-wheel walking tractor with a plow and disc and planted a large garden between the house and the pasture. At first he seemed to enjoy the garden, but the responsibility in caring for the garden eventually fell to us kids. After a while I can only describe it as a total weed patch.

Dale Webb was the McLean County Republican Chairman, and asked me if I wanted to make some extra money. I immediately said, "Yes" and he told me I would be riding around Mc Lean County with Vernelle Stensel putting up Republican political signs. Vernelle was a close friend and supporter of the county coroner. As we rode down the county roads, Vernelle would spot a place for a sign and pull off the road. As soon as the car came to a stop, I'd grab a sign from the back seat, take the hammer and a couple roofing nails, and quickly jump out and tack the sign to the pole. From my perspective it was an easy job. Traveling around the county with Vernelle Stensel was also fun because he knew almost everyone in the county. He even bought my lunch in addition to what Dale paid me for my work. I guess that was when, where and why I became a life-long Republican.

Now that we again had a home with a barn and a few acres, it was time for me to get into farming. I heard that John Kline, a local cattle farmer, each winter bought a train car load of pregnant Western ewe sheep and put them in his barn and waited for them to lamb. As soon as the lambs were large enough to sell, he sheered the sheep and took both the lambs and ewes to the auction barn to be sold. During lambing, several of the baby lambs were rejected by their mothers, and without individual attention and care, the newborns would die. John certainly did not have the extra time to hand feed orphan lambs. Rather than letting them die, he decided to give them away to someone willing to care for them. I jumped on my bike and rode over to John's and told him I would like to have an orphan lamb. He told me he would call when one came available but I was to understand that when an orphan is born, there is only a short time without care they would survive, so whatever time of day it is, I must pick it up immediately. Finally one evening, John called and Dad took me over to pick up the newborn lamb. John gave us instructions on how to fix the milk, and what needed to be done so we wrapped it in a blanket and carried it home. We fixed an area in the basement and I officially became a sheep farmer. That winter, I picked up several lambs and was able to save six. Mom was glad when we finally moved them from the basement to the barn because the basement became infested with fleas from the straw in my make-swift sheep pen.

The first lamb we raised was called Peaches. She was everyone's favorite and instantly became a real pet to the family. Sheep, when raised from the bottle by a person seem to believe you are their parent. We would let her out of the barn, and she would follow us around the yard wanting to be fed. Everyone fed Peaches so much she became pot-bellied and developed a real need for constant attention. The others

113

lambs were raised closer together and acted more like farm animals. We found out there was truth in the saying that sheep always follow the leader, and Peaches loved both the attention and being the leader. She was always the first one standing at the stall door when we entered the barn, and by watching us lift the hook to lock and unlock the stall door, she figured out how to unlock the stall door by herself. One evening, Mom was in the kitchen fixing supper when she heard noises outside. Peaches had opened the stall door with her nose and brought the other sheep up on the back porch wanting to be fed. Soon after, the hook was replaced with a different type which helped keep her in the barn. To some city peoples' surprise, baby sheep have tails, and as they grow, farmers cut them off. Well, I had never cut any lamb's tail off, so when the day came to remove the tails, I decided to use a double edge razor blade to perform the task. It sounded like the perfect tool, it was razor sharp and should make a clean fast cut. I grabbed a lamb and without hesitation, proceeded to detach the tail. Suddenly, the lamb started kicking, and I was completely unable to accomplish the task. Immediately, blood started shooting from the incision and in a near panic, I stopped and ran across the road to the local veterinarian, Dr. Merdink and explained my dilemma. He dropped what he was doing, grabbed a bag and followed me back to the barn to evaluate the situation. He then pulled out a tool and quickly positioned it over the tail and placed a heavy rubber band above the incision. Once the rubber band was tight, the bleeding stopped and the lamb ran off. Dr. Merdink smiled and suggested I no longer try cutting off tails but find someone with a rubber band tool for the other sheep. He also discouraged me from ever attempting to perform surgery with a razor blade. Then he smiled and returned to his office and was kind enough to not send me a bill for his services.

Later in the evening I called a friend whose father had a band stretcher, and we banded the other sheep. I'm sure those sheep were much happier with the rubber bands than for me trying to remove their tails with a razor blade.

Along with raising sheep, we ended up with a milk cow, a dozen laying hens, some banty chickens and a mean giant black rooster. Howard Duvall brought us the rooster and it had spurs two inches long on its legs. Howard told us it was his mother's. It soon became apparent, wherever Howard got the rooster, they definitely wanted to get rid of it. It was unquestionably not a people friendly rooster. Walking anywhere near the barn required constant watching out for the rooster. When you were not paying attention, he would quickly come up behind you and bury his spurs in your legs. Trying to defend myself, I finally put a wooden two-by-four near the barn door. I decided if that rooster attacked me from behind again, I'd grab that board and hit him before I got spurred. Sure enough, one day I looked down and there he was about to attack. I grabbed the board, he started to run, and I threw the board at him in hopes of knocking him down. Instead, I missed the rooster and accidentally hit one of the laying hens, breaking its leg almost in half. Knowing my parents would not appreciate my actions, I grabbed the hen, took her into the barn and wrapped the injured leg with tape and a couple of sticks. The chicken fully recovered, but ended up with a huge bump over the near break and never laid an egg again.

Finally the rooster met his match. One morning I went out to the barn and sometime during the night the banty roosters had ganged up on the old rooster and killed him. He was lying on the floor below the roosting rails with holes all over him. Unfortunately for the old rooster, there were no tears or sadness and everyone felt it was again safe to go out to the barn.

During the summertime, Joan and her friends would drive over to the Farmer City Fairgrounds to roller skate. The fairgrounds had built a large wooden rink with a tent roof for skaters and it was always crowded with kids from the surrounding communities. I enjoyed tagging along trying to develop my skating skills. It was obvious the older boys were good skaters and loved to show off to impress the girls. Learning how to skate worked out perfectly because within a year someone converted the upstairs of the A&P building in LeRoy into a skating rink. This now gave the LeRoy kids a place to go. The only problem with the skating area was the several roof support pillars down the center of the floor. You constantly had to watch for them particularly when skating backward. With as much fun as we all had, the rink only stayed in operation for about a year before it was closed due to the cost to upgrade the building to meet fire and safety code requirements. It was too bad because everyone enjoyed roller skating over the A&P on weekends.

One hot summer day, David Litherland and I rode our bikes over to the City Service Gas Station and restaurant to get a Coke. Next to our table sat two older girls who had recently graduated from high school. We suddenly turned our attention to their conversation when they began talking about driving up to the frog pond north of LeRoy to skinny dip. When boys are around thirteen, and hear words like "skinny dip" we quickly developed an interest in riding our bikes the three or four miles to view this remarkable event. As soon as they piled into the old green Kaiser parked outside, we jumped on our bikes and pedaled up the LeRoy Lexington Blacktop. Finally reaching the pond, we hid our bikes in the weeds and proceeded through the tall grass until we could see both girls splashing in the water, not naked, but wearing only their panties and bras. Evidently our concentration should have been more focused on not making noise. Suddenly both girls realized they were being watched and looked in our direction and spotted us half hidden in the weeds. One of the girls was tall, lean and very muscular, and from what we had heard, she was absolutely no one to mess with. Realizing we had been spotted, we scrambled back to our bikes and headed back to town. In what seemed like only a few minutes, that green Kaiser came speeding down the hill behind us in hot pursuit. We pedaled as fast as our bikes would go and thankfully reached a small bridge over the drainage ditch just south of the King's farm. Down the ditch we rode and quickly disappeared beneath the bridge. As soon as the girls reached the bridge the car stopped and they both jumped out and leaned over the railing threatening us and yelling for us to come out. Finally, they either got tired of yelling or knew we planned on staying under that bridge, so they got back in their car and headed for town. After a few minutes we came out, got on our bikes and headed home, constantly thinking if they came back they would beat us to death. Thankfully, we got home unharmed and we made a sincere effort to keep as far away from those two as possible. Looking back on this I ask myself, *was it worth it? Absolutely!*

Kids love summer and one of the first things that comes to mind to a young person is no school and going swimming. As great as that sounds, LeRoy, like so many of the small towns in the fifties had no swimming pool and the closest places to swim was Miller Park in Bloomington or Lake of the Woods Park in Mahomet. What we did have was our local swimming holes; the frog pond, salt creek and a couple gravel pits several miles east of town. Having so few places to swim, few kids took swimming lessons and our parents were constantly warning us of the dangers of sneaking off to go swimming. After telling them we understood, we'd stop at Moss' gas station and buy a used patched car or truck inner tube. After filling it with air, we'd carefully wrap a strip of rubber or an old rag around the tube and cover the valve stem to prevent it from cutting or scratching our bodies.

Our favorite swimming hole was the gravel pits near Arrowsmith. Even though it was farther away, it was deeper and surrounded with higher banks to dive from. While it was dangerous swimming in gravel pits there were other dangers with swimming during summer. The biggest fear for children during the fifties was Polio, a highly contagious virus infection that inflamed nerves in the brain and spinal cord, causing paralysis of the muscles in the chest, and in severe cases the legs and arms. The Polio epidemic was rising faster than the population growth rate of the United States at the very height of our nation's baby boom. In almost every store a March of Dimes cardboard poster was next to the cash register showing a picture of a child in braces, on crutches or in an iron lung encouraging customers to place dimes in the small slots to raise money to help find a cure.

Polio was on everyone's mind and cities across the nation tried to halt the spread by closing public pools and parks and telling kids not to drink from public water fountains. Finally in the later fifties a vaccine was created by Dr. Jonas Salk and it was distributed throughout the world. By 1962, Dr. Salk's "miracle in medicine" ended Polio and the era of fear around the world.

With the sudden population increase of young children across the county and in McLean County, in 1956 the LeRoy school district decided the old Washington School building was no longer large enough to support the large number of students. The solution was to build a new grade school on the north east edge of town. During the construction, I was in eighth grade and our class was moved from Washington School to the basement of the high school. We really enjoyed being there and our classrooms were directly across from the cafeteria. What fun it was watching the high school students in the hallways. They were constantly flirting, holding hands and involved in deep conversations as they walked between classes. Suddenly we felt much older and worldlier than before. However, it didn't take long before the boys realized the girls in our class were much more interested in the high school boys than us. We still thought we were pretty cool and figured they would soon take interest in us. When the new school was completed that spring the entire grade school started moving into the new building. It was a beautiful building, the rooms were large and everything was new. My eighth grade teacher was Mrs. Roberts. She was an older lady and in the afternoon while we were quietly working on our assignments, she would occasionally dose off and start snoring slightly until she would suddenly wake up and try to act as if she hadn't been napping. In her earlier years she had been an art teacher and she felt I had the talent to study art. Never passing up an opportunity to not study in class, for the rest of the year I found myself being the official class artist. She had me working on art projects continually and I quickly found this to be an easy escape from having to learn much of anything. It was not uncommon for her to send me down the hallway during class to decorate the display cases or make posters for upcoming events. Mrs. Roberts was a fine person with good intentions and desperately tried to add a little culture to our lives. As for learning anything in her class, I later realized I was not learning what I needed to know before entering high school.

Bill, Jim, Donnie, Buzz

Everyone enjoyed being able to finish our last year of grade school in the new school. It was a large facility with outdoor playgrounds and a brand new ball diamond. The gymnasium was large and at noon it also served as the cafeteria. It was fun to play basketball in the gym and then go into the large locker room to shower. With wet towels scattered about, it wouldn't be long until someone would grab one and snap it on the bare rear of some unsuspecting classmate. Our principal, Mr. Covey, was constantly patrolling the locker room to make sure everything remained spotless. When he found us doing anything he disapproved of, he would line us up to hear his lecture on our wrong doings. You could tell the degree of his anger by the way he paced back and forth in front of us. Then he would suddenly stop, face us, and take up his legendary stance. Bending slightly forward with his arms straight down, he would start swinging them in opposite directions from knee to knee like two pendulums on a clock. Then he'd suddenly shout, "That's O-U-T Out". At that very second, both hands flew straight up over his shoulders in unison, fist clinched and his thumbs pointing straight back. Without hesitation, he asked us if we all understood. Naturally, we'd all respond by saying, "Yes" and nodding our heads up and down like a bunch of trained penguins. There was one particular incident where we thought Mr. Covey was about to go into cardiac arrest. One of the boys brought a dirty book to school known as an "eight page bible." He had found it hidden at home, most likely by his father and wanted to show the book to the boys. This small paperback was as evil as you could get, with extremely graphic stories and photos. This was certainly not something for our young minds but it became an instant hit. The excitement soon ended when one of the guys gave it to a girl in our class to look at. She immediately gave it to the teacher, who in turn gave it to Mr. Covey. Within minutes, every boy in the class was marched into the gym, the doors were shut and we assumed our normal position of lining up and hearing the wrongs of having this terrible evil filthy book on the school premises. With his face turning bright red, he shouted out, "This garbage is absolutely unacceptable to be on school property and whoever brought it to school and anyone who saw it should be ashamed to have looked at such filth." He repeatedly asked us who brought it to school, but no one dared to give out the name of who committed the terrible deed. I no longer remember who brought the book to school, but unlike the books we were given in school, I can say the boys studied that book one page at a time.

The last incident we had with Mr. Covey was near the end of

that year. Some of the boys decided to skip school one afternoon and go to my house and play poker. They knew my parents worked so it was a safe place to hide out for the afternoon. After we arrived at my house and hid our bikes in the barn, we were there only for about an hour before someone looked out the window and saw Mr. Covey's green Chevrolet pull into the driveway. We immediately started hiding behind furniture, in closets and away from the windows. Finally he walked up on the porch and knocked on the door. With no answer, he started walking around the house, looking in the windows trying to see if someone was inside. After circling the house several times and seeing nothing, he got back into his car and drove off. Knowing trouble was in the wind, everyone took off for home.

I quickly rode my bike up to the cleaners and told my mother I didn't feel well at school and decided to come up to the cleaners rather than go home. The next day I handed in my written excuse for not being in school. When I handed it to Mrs. Roberts, she told me Mr. Covey had called several of the boy's parents to tell them we had been absent and to confirm if they were sick. Fortunately, my written excuse said my mother knew I was ill. I'm not sure if anyone got punished for skipping school that day.

While in grade school I started what would became a lifelong friendship with Ron Bane. Ron and I both liked sports, girls and all the other things boys liked. Although he was one year behind me, we started spending a lot of time together. I also enjoyed spending time out at his parents' farm. Ron had an old Cushman motor scooter which was handed down to him from his brother, Jerry. We'd get on it and ride up and down the blacktop by their farm. Riding on the scooter was fun, especially when his neighbor, a local high school beauty, would be lying in her front yard sun bathing.

Ron Bane and myself

When Ron was younger he had taken tap dancing lessons with one of his classmates, Sharon Spratt. Occasionally Ron and Sharon performed on stage at local events. This gave Ron an edge at dancing and like me, he very much enjoyed listening and dancing to the latest Rock 'n' Roll music.

One afternoon while I was visiting his home, Ron's mother took us into the dining room, turned on their record player and gave us a lesson on how to jitter-bug. I quickly found that I really enjoyed dancing. Over the next several years we would double-date and seldom did we miss a school or local dance.

In small towns, especially back when I was growing up, children started school with little regard to the social class of other students or their parents. Most of the families in our town were working families or farm families and not considered wealthy. In other words, we never thought about it and there was really no need to. Our homes were each blessed with parents, and siblings who loved and enjoyed one another. There was always food on the table and most every child was aware there was very little money for extras or frills. And believe me, that's not all bad. Kids were kids and most

123

everyone dressed alike and everyone enjoyed playing with each other. Due to the number of students required to make up teams, and the low number of kids in our classes, it took about everyone's participation to support the various school activities. The one area I really lacked during my early childhood development was etiquette. Like all kids, at home we were told to sit up straight, chew our food, keep our elbows off the table, eat your vegetables, not to reach across the table, and clean your plate because there were thousands of children starving in China. I've always found it hard to sit still, and extremely hard when sitting in front of a freshly cooked plate of Mom's spaghetti. The heaping bowl was like a magnet forcing me to reach into the dish and grab one of those flimsy strands and place it between my lips and start sucking it down. Back then, spaghetti came packaged in much longer lengths and when sucking it, the suction created a loud slurping sound as it entered my mouth and raced toward my stomach. It always drew immediate attention and everyone would suddenly be looking at me, especially my mother. Without even looking, I knew exactly what she was about to say, "That's enough of that," whereas, I would quickly grab my fork and continue eating. As improper as it was, I found it humorous and it always brought laughter from both my sisters. Especially after inhaling the spaghetti and the entire area surrounding my mouth was covered with Mom's delicious thick red tomato sauce.

My mother did attempt to instill proper etiquette at our house but it was basically a lost cause. Why worry about such trivial matters anyway. Like most families in rural communities, our family never dined out in restaurants and seldom attended social dinner functions other than family get togethers. Our evening meal, "supper" was eaten at the dining room table and everyone enjoyed sharing in family conversation. I can't

124

blame my mother for my lack of etiquette, she tried but finally gave up out of pure frustration. Gradually I realized on my own there was definitely a difference in my manners and table etiquette from others when I started visiting the homes of my friends or later going out on dates. My mother was right, my etiquette and social manners were indeed inferior compared to many of my friends.

I always enjoyed spending time and staying nights at Ron's house. His parents were always gracious and made me feel at home. One afternoon during my senior year Ron's mother asked me to come into the kitchen to sit down and talk. She started discussing the importance of going to college. She said if I needed any help in getting admitted or seeking financial assistance, she would gladly help me any way she could. I vividly remember this because it was the first time I ever had an adult talk to me about my future or going to college. I've never forgotten that conversation or her kindness in offering me her assistance. With spring approaching there were three major events coming up before our grade school graduation. The school dance, class trip to Springfield and of course, graduation. Everyone looked forward to the coming events, but this dance, viewed as a Grade School Prom, seemed to generate the most excitement. Since Ron was in the seventh grade, this would be Ron's first real date so we decided it would be fun to double- date. I again asked Betsy and Ron asked Carole Brown. Both accepted. After hearing our parents cover all the basic rules for dating, we felt we could use some firsthand advice from someone who was actually young and currently dating. It just so happened Ron's brother Jerry and his girlfriend Shirley, both high school seniors, agreed to drive us to and from the dance. We were convinced Jerry, being well seasoned, knew everything about women and dating and would be readily available should we need his advice. As I remember, he did in fact offer us a few pointers along the way.

Once we arrived at Betsy's house, I got out and walked up to the porch, rang the doorbell and was invited inside. When I met her parents I am sure they could tell I was extremely nervous and my primary mission was focused solely on getting her out the door as quickly as possible. From there we picked up Ron's date Carol and continued to the dance.

The dance started off a little slow with everyone awkwardly trying to maneuver around the dance floor. Every boy's arm was stretched out to avoid any bodily contact and making every effort to not accidentally step on their partner's feet. After the fear gradually diminished everyone seemed more relaxed and the evening went very well. Ron and I felt lucky to have dates and noticed several girls dancing with each other and boys, without dates, awkwardly going from girl to girl asking, "Wanna dance?" When the dance finally ended, Jerry and Shirley picked us up to take the girls home. We were now reaching the final stage of our date, the one most feared by every young boy who had never been on a date before. Arriving at Betsy's house, we walked up on the porch and as planned, Jerry turned out the headlights. I don't remember if I really had intentions of trying to get a goodnight kiss, but when Jerry suddenly turned the headlights on to assess my progress, any hopes of that were immediately shattered. Already nervous and rattled by the unexpected glare of the headlights, I quickly thanked her for going to the dance and she went inside. I returned to the car to be greeted by laughter. From there we drove to Carole's house and Ron well knew what was in store. His trip to her door went much smoother than mine. As for my dancing, Betsy must have been somewhat impressed because we attended many dances together throughout high school including her being my date to the Senior Prom.

A couple weeks before graduation our class loaded on two school buses and we were off to visit the State Capital in Springfield. First we toured the State of Illinois Museum and then to the Capitol building. The museum was interesting, but I was amazed at the size of the Capital and being given the opportunity to visit both chambers of the House of Representatives and the Illinois State Senate. Looking back, my impression then is much like today's U.S. Congress. Once inside, it appeared very few of the State Senators were interested in what was going on. Most of them were reading newspapers, smoking cigars or cigarettes and visiting with each other while a speaker stood at the podium reading what I believed to be a bill and very few of his fellow senators appeared to be interested. Finally came the roll call and the large tally board behind the podium lit up displaying everyone's vote. The bill passed.

Several weeks after our trip to Springfield, graduation day arrived. The ceremony was held in the grade school auditorium and my class was the first class to graduate from the new LeRoy Grade School. We again dressed up and our parents sat proudly in folding chairs watching as fifty-three eighth grade students received our certificates for passing the state requirements.

While graduating from grade school was an exciting milestone, this graduation meant more to me than to most of my fellow classmates. In March, my parents had told us we were moving to Florida when school was out. I would be leaving all my friends in LeRoy. My uncle, who was working as a salesman in Florida, helped my dad get a job working in

Clearwater at Bankers Life & Casualty Insurance Company. My parents felt this would be a good opportunity for my dad and make it possible for us to again be near my father's family. Living in a warmer climate, void of snow and near the Gulf coast, it would be an added benefit. Before Dad accepted the position, we started getting rid of the livestock. As soon as the sheep were sheered, we sold them to a local farmer. The worst part of selling the sheep was saying goodbye to Peaches. The farmer assured us he would not butcher her and we all watched as they were loaded onto his truck and he pulled out of the driveway. The cow and the chickens were sold to another farmer.

With that out of the way, Dad quit his job in Bloomington and went down to Clearwater and stayed with my grandparents and started his new job. While finishing the school year, Dad looked for a house and wanted it ready for us to live in when we moved. This left all of the work and the preparation on Mom, my sisters and me. The girls helped Mom sort and pack boxes, I helped with selling our furniture and getting the boxes shipped to Florida. Shortly afterward Dad called saying he found a house in Dunedin, Florida, and during our last week of school, he came back to LeRoy on a bus to get the move underway.

A couple days before leaving, one of my classmates, Katy Wilson, had a party at her house and told me it would be a good time to say goodbye to all my friends. It was great that she had the party and everyone was having fun until a policeman came to the front door and asked to talk to Katy's parents. Mrs. Wilson came to the door and quietly stepped outside on the porch to discuss the problem with the officer. He told her the neighbors had complained about the loud noise, and the party had to stop. Shortly afterward, she came back in and told us, "It's okay. Continue enjoying yourselves, but just keep the noise down."

It was obvious moving away from LeRoy did not please everyone in the family. The following fall Joan would be a senior in high school. In addition, she was madly in love with her latest boyfriend Byron, who was about to join the Navy. Judy would be a sophomore and really couldn't figure out why anyone would want to move anywhere. I too hated leaving my friends but was actually excited about living near the water where I could swim in the ocean, sunbathe and look for new exciting experiences. I'm not sure if Mom was really happy about it, but as usual, she went along with it and was busy trying to get everything ready for the move.

Chapter 5

Moving day finally arrived. We loaded up the car and started our drive to Florida. It seemed like every trip we made was a beginning of another adventure. Back in those days, there were very few interstate highways, no GPSs, and the poorly lit two lane roads were void of those large green directional signs over the highway to guide you along your route. The only marked signs were the small state highway signs poorly placed along the road or on a pole when you were about to approach an intersection. Dad had his travel plans down to a science. Before leaving he bought several folded-up paper maps of all the states we would be driving through. Whenever he thought he was lost or wanted to know how much further it was to the next town, he would pull off the road, unfold the appropriate map and start reading. State maps were for sale on racks in every gas station and an essential tool when traveling unfamiliar roads. They were much larger than today's maps and almost impossible to read in the car. It was not uncommon to see a confused traveler parked along the road, standing outside his car with a map spread out over the hood.

Reading a map correctly can be a real challenge for anyone, but trying to refold it to its original neatly per-folded condition is down-right frustrating. If you've never attempted this feat, you will find it's nearly impossible and the map usually ends up poorly folded and twice the thickness.

To us, our father appeared to have the skills of a professional map reader. Finally with a look of accomplishment, and having determined our location, he would get back in the car and pull back on the highway to continued our journey. Dad's 1954 blue and white Chevy Bel Air four-door allowed us plenty of room, but over the last year the car had developed some serious transmission problems. The shifting bands in the automatic transmission would occasionally slip and the reverse gear had totally stopped working. With the moving cost and paying rent on two homes, my parents didn't have the extra money to get the transmission fixed. Since it would go forward with no problem, Dad decided there was no reason not to drive it to Florida and have it fixed later. The car was absolutely packed, Mom and Dad were in the front with one of us between them and two of us sat in the backseat with Buddy. In the trunk Mom had packed a metal cooler full of food for us to eat along the way. At the last minute, before leaving, Glen and Phyllis Keller decided they would follow us down, so we packed additional things in their car. On the drive south Dad carefully calculated how we would make every stop along the way without using the reverse gear. Most of the gas stations back then had only two gas pumps, so Dad would carefully wait for a gas station with few cars and stop there to fill up the tank.

The old highways were great for families traveling because scattered along the roadways were small pull-off areas with picnic tables to stop to rest or eat meals. This was perfect because we could pull right back on the highway without backing up. Traveling over 1500 miles required us to stay one night in a motel. Finally, we found one with a sloped parking area and a spot right in front of the room. Early the next morning we got into the car, Dad started the engine, put the car in neutral, and Glen looking both ways to make sure no cars were coming, and gave the car a push. While the car rolled backwards, Dad turned the wheel, and we coasted in a perfect position to drive forward with no problems. With Glen and Phyllis following behind, we continued our journey to Florida. Occasionally we needed to stop for gas, eat, or to use a restroom. This gave us kids an opportunity to take turn riding in Glen's and Phyllis' car. It always was fun being around Phyllis because she could find something funny about almost anything. Most highways were two lane roads and went directly through the main business district. Phyllis really enjoyed riding down the main streets, particularly the small communities. She would look at us and say, "Watch this." When the next car approached, she'd reach over, honk the horn and start waving at the approaching driver saying, "Hi, you dummy!" The people riding in the car, unable to hear what she said, appeared to think they were meeting friends and quickly smiled back and waved. We all laughed and drove on until we reached the next town where she would repeat her joke again.

In the fifties, cars didn't have air conditioning and during the summer everyone was forced to ride with the windows down. Dad had to be extra careful not to shake off his cigarette ashes or throw his cigarette butts out the side window. That could easily send ashes or the discarded cigarette back into the opened rear window and onto the passengers or burn a hole in the cushions of the back seat. Riding with the windows down also made it difficult to hear the radio. Cars didn't have rear speakers, so mom would turn the volume up to allow us in the back to hear and sing along with the music. When we entered a town and started slowing down, she would turn the music down.

Traveling through the Deep South was very different than it is today. The rural two-lane highways passed hundreds of tiny dilapidated houses with poor families setting on their front porches seeking relief from the summer heat and hoping to catch an occasional breeze. The houses sat so close to the road passersby could look through the open doors and see scarcely any furniture or anything else of value inside. Poorly dressed children ran and played in the red dirt yards with no grass, swing sets or toys.

Long distance travel for families was very uncommon for the average family. Cars were less comfortable, far less dependable, and it was not unusual to see cars stopped along the roadway with flat tires, overheated engines or an occasional busted radiator hose. We occasionally would see cars with a strange looking canvas bag, called "desert bags," tied to the car's front grill to keep the water cool for drinking. During our trips we were always able to find numerous ways to keep entertained. On both sides of the highway there were thousands of large billboards advertising everything known to man; information about an approaching tourist site, roadside food stands, souvenir shops, fruit stands and signs stating you were approaching a restaurant known for their "World's Most Famous Hot Dogs or Hamburgers". Our favorite signs were the small red and white signs on posts about a quarter mile apart reading out a variety of catchy jingles.

VIOLETS ARE BLUE ROSES ARE PINK

ON GRAVE OF THOSE WHO DRIVE AND DRINK

– BURMA SHAVE.

It was easy to get lost while traveling the rural highways because they were poorly marked with small highway signs often placed miles apart. If you missed a turn, it would be miles before you realized you were on the wrong road. Driving through the larger cities was also confusing, turn lanes were rare and as many as four or five different highway signs could be posted on one pole at an intersection.

Another uncommon sight was passing areas where prison chain gangs were working along the roadways. Signs were posted stating, "SLOW DOWN, PRISONERS AT WORK, DO NOT PICK UP HITCH HIKERS". It was a bit scary watching the guards standing motionless with their shotguns, while prisoners shackled in leg irons and wearing dirty striped prison clothing, ordered to work in the hot sun. Our eyes would focus on the faces of the prisoners, not knowing what they did, but knowing we didn't want to end up in prison or be forced to work under those harsh conditions.

Everyone in the car was excited when we finally crossed the Georgia state line entering Florida. In keeping with our family tradition, we all got out of the car to take our picture standing next to the "Entering Florida" sign. Then it was on to our next stop, the Florida Welcome Center, for a free glass of fresh 100% Pure Florida Orange Juice. Five hours later we arrived at Dunedin, Florida.

Visit to Tifton, Georgia

Our new home in Dunedin was a small cottage-style house with a large screened-in front porch. Inside was a combination living room and dining room, a kitchen, two bedrooms, and one bathroom. The house had no furnace, no air conditioner, and the only source of heat was a small fireplace located in the living room. The backyard was large and very deep and full of citrus trees. It was a real treat to step out the back door and find trees full of oranges and grapefruits just hanging there ready to be picked. At first I wasn't sure where I would be sleeping but soon found out my bedroom was the front porch. Dad had purchased several roll-up bamboo curtains to cover the screens and the landlady, Bessie Smith, who lived next store, gave us a daybed. Each night I would go out on the porch, roll down the bamboo shades, put my blankets and pillow on the bed and climb in and go to sleep. I really didn't mind sleeping on the porch except for nights when it was either raining hard or too cold to stay outside. On those nights, I carried my blankets into the living room and slept on the floor.

It was nice to again be living near my grandparents, aunts, uncles and cousins. They all lived in the area and their homes were not far from ours. Grandma was still fun to be around. She and I would entertain each other by reciting the local TV ad jingles to one another. We especially loved the one with the Southern Colonel character in his all white suit and hat, smiling and saying, "Y'all heard what the Colonel said, 'I'd even go north for Southern Bread'."

Grandma always appeared happy, but that could change in a second when her Irish temper took over. Once while I was at their house, she was standing behind the ironing board ironing and talking to my grandfather. He was telling her something and suddenly she became angry. Abruptly, with a stern look she picked up the iron and shouted, "Paul, one more word from you and this iron will be lying flat against your face!" It was obvious she had forgotten I was standing there. I'd never seen her temper flare up so severely before. Startled but amused, I laughed. She looked over at me, and she too started laughing as if it had all been a joke. It absolutely wasn't a joke, and as Grandpa and I left the house, he said to me, "That woman is crazy." In later years, Cousin Linda's husband Bob Hampton, started kidding with her and calling her "Crazy Grandma." Everyone was surprised because she thought it was funny. From that day forward the grandchildren affectionately referred to her as Crazy Grandma. Grandma was a true homebody. Grandpa did all the shopping and bought everything needed for the house. Seldom do I remember her leaving the house or even being out in the yard except for when she went to church or to a family event. She spent most of the day cleaning and cooking inside and humming or whistling old hymns. She enjoyed having the family over and occasionally she would go places with them. On one of those occasions, Dad, Mom, we kids and Grandma loaded up in Dad's 1948 four-door Studebaker, which unlike most cars, had rear doors that opened up from front to back.

While we were riding down the road, the rear door next to Grandma suddenly flew open. Cars then had no seat belts and the suction and the wind created by the open door started pulling Grandma out of the car. Fortunately, Dad was able to slow down and pull off to the side of the road without losing our dear Grandma. She later laughed about the near tragedy but after thinking back on all those temper tantrums, Grandpa may have wished she would've been pulled out of the car!

Grandpa stayed busy and just like in Bloomington, he always had some type of money-making project. He bought an old garage and had it moved to their backyard and removed the siding and replaced them with wire screens. Inside he built partitions and added several large cages on each side where he started raising parakeets. He had hundreds of parakeets in all different colors. On shipping day he would carefully box up the birds and send them to the Hart Company to sell to pet stores. Most every week a delivery driver would stop by and pick up the young birds. It was fun to go inside the shed with him to feed the birds or get them ready for shipment. He'd close the door behind us and I watched as he gathered the parakeets one at a time. Occasionally, one or two of the birds would fly out the cage door and it was my job to take the long handled pole, with the mesh net at the top and gather them from the rafters above.

Moving to a new town may sound difficult for a teenager, but I found it very easy to make friends. Our landlady had a granddaughter Judy's age and she kindly took us around and introduced us to all her friends. Her father owned a local gas station and hired me to help out on Saturdays. Dunedin had a large youth center where I started going on weekends. Families were always moving in and out of the area and the new kids were always welcomed.

While it may sound as if I liked the kids in Florida more than those in LeRoy, that wasn't the case. Dunedin was connected to Clearwater as Bloomington is to Normal. Dunedin was eight times larger than LeRoy and Clearwater was nearly twice the size of Bloomington. The simple fact was, there were just so many more things to do and a lot more kids to do things with. Living near the Gulf of Mexico, with its beautiful white beaches made it a fantastic place for any teenager to live. However, I faithfully continued to correspond and keep in touch with many of my old friends in LeRoy.

I quickly realized the most popular place for most every teenager in town to gather was the Dunedin Community Youth Center. The large building had a basketball court, a huge trampoline, and kids would bring their favorite records from home to listen to and dance. The center had very strict rules. Once you arrived for the evening, you could not leave and come back in. There was no fighting, smoking or cussing allowed inside, and if you were asked to leave, you were banned from coming back. The boys seemed to always start off playing basketball but gradually joined with the others to dance. I was amazed at the size of the trampoline and found out kids interested in diving used it to improve their body coordination. While I did not want to become a diver, I did take lessons and it was definitely a blast to use. However, most of my attention was centered around dancing and making new friends. It wasn't long before my new friends introduced me to the greatest thing about living in Florida - going to the beach. It was so cool. Thousands of people lined the beach, lots of guys and girls sunbathing, a large in ground pool where someone was always climbing up the ladder to the highest diving board to show off doing flips, twists, back jumps and jack knives executed with precision. Large groups of guys and girls wandered up and down the beach, going into junk shops, food stands, and renting chairs and umbrellas from beach side vendors. The longest road on the beach went south, and once you drove past the public beach area, the pavement ended and you would drive onto the sand along the water for at least a half mile. On weekends, teenagers spent most of their spare time at Clearwater beach. Older teens in the evening headed to the south end and built bonfires and partied for hours into the night. In those days, there were no high rise condos, only a few single or two story motels scattered along the roadway of the beach. All you needed for the day was a bathing suit, a towel, sunglasses and baby oil with iodine to protect you from getting sunburned. Every chance we'd get, we put on our flip flops (also called thong sandals), a t-shirt, swim suit and threw a towel around our neck and walked up to Bay Shore Drive to hitch a ride. With thumbs in the air, within minutes a car would pull over and tell us to get in. If the driver was not going to the beach, they'd drop us off downtown Clearwater at the foot of the causeway bridge. There standing with our thumbs up, another car would pick us up and take us out to the beach. Riding in cars along the coastline highway with the windows down was great. There was nothing better than listening to the sea-gulls, inhaling the salt in the air from the Gulf and having the wind blowing in your face. It was incredible. Beach bound hitch-hikers stood positioned along the roadway heading toward the beach everywhere. At the time there was no fear for kids to hitch a ride when going from one place to another in Florida. Local drivers seemed to always know you were either going to the beach or heading home. For those of us without a driver's license, hitchhiking was our main mode of transportation traveling around town.

After a full day at the beach we'd hitch a ride back over the causeway, get out and walk north to the local record shop or across the street to the local boxing club. From there it was just a couple more blocks north to our favorite pizza place. The small pizza shop was located in a tiny building positioned right at the edge of the sidewalk. It was only big enough to hold a large pizza oven, a drink cooler and a small counter. The proprietor stood on the sidewalk selling sections of a four by six inch piece of pizza for 10 cents or 12 pieces for a dollar to those passing by. There were no tables or chairs; we either sat on the curb or ate it while we walked. After finishing our pizza, we'd cross the street again, put out our thumbs and hitch a ride back to Dunedin.

In the late 1950s, Florida driving permits were issued to 14-year-old. Having the permit allowed you to drive a car with your parents, or a motorcycle during daylight hours only. Many of the guys my age had Cushman Eagle scooters or motorcycles and rode them everywhere. I immediately applied and received my permit. One of my friends and classmates Kenny Imes, had a large evening paper route. He'd fold up the papers, slip them in plastic sleeves and place them in the two canvas bags over the motorcycle's gas tank. He then took off down the street pitching papers in driveways along his route. His route was primarily in two large residential subdivisions. Kenny could consistently deliver over a hundred papers in less than 25 minutes. This paid for his motorcycle and gave him extra spending money. When we had plans to do something after his route, I would help him get the papers ready and ride with him. It would be hard to imagine how many miles we rode together on the shiny black and chrome Zundapp 200CC motorcycle. Florida's lifestyle was far different than living in the Mid-West. Several of my friends' parents owned boats and we'd take them out in the bay and use them to water ski. Parents enjoyed their kids having parties at home, and seldom was there a weekend when someone wasn't having a house party or a beach party. One of the girls I met was Jane Ann Puckett, who lived around the corner from our house. Living so close, I would stop by her house to watch American Bandstand. She was really more of a friend than girlfriend, and I was more interested in being with my friends, so the relationship was short lived. However, to my friend's and my surprise, the next year she was the winner of the Miss Clearwater Teen Beauty Contest. WOW!

The other distinct difference about living in the South was segregation. Dunedin, like all Southern towns, has a separate area where Afro-Americans lived, then called "colored people." They were not allowed to attend the white schools or go to the public beaches. When riding public buses they were required to sit in the back and public drinking fountains and restrooms were clearly marked "whites only" or "blacks only". Most surprising to me was when I would walk uptown, which required me to pass what was then called "colored town". When I approached a colored person on the sidewalk, they would step off the sidewalk and let me pass before continuing on their way. At the time it was a way of life in the South and later would be changed for the better of all people not only in America, but around the world.

When summer ended I entered 9th grade at the Dunedin Junior High School. It was a brand new school complex, and my class had well over a 150 students. Joan and Judy went to Clearwater High School which was a huge complex. I was grateful I had made friends over the summer and felt totally comfortable going to my new school. I'd estimate approximately 70 percent of the students were children of parents who had moved to Florida in the past few years. The students were accustomed to having new students come into the school almost daily, and everyone seemed to get along and enjoyed one another. A couple of weeks after school started, the group I ran around with decided we needed someone to run for Student Council President and I became a candidate. We made campaign signs to hang in the halls. I gave two speeches at our school assembly, but to my disappointment, I came in second. However, as runner-up, I served as our class representative on the school's Student Council. That in turn was beneficial in my being selected as Student of the Month by the Dunedin Rotary Club.

Me running for Student Council President

School started out well, but I did have a couple of problems along the way. In science class one morning, our teacher was writing on the blackboard and one of the guys in the back loudly said, "Quack!" The teacher quickly turned around, but could not see who made the noise so she continued writing. Suddenly, a couple other guys chimed in, "Quack-Quack." And as everyone quietly laughed, four boys and I were asked to step out in the hall. The teacher said she would not put-up with our foolishness and to go directly to the principal's office to discuss why we were disrupting her class. She handed us a folded piece of paper and told us to give it to the principal. Off we went to the office, still thinking the disruption was funny. The principal was a big man and a former Marine officer. Hanging on the wall behind his desk was his large college fraternity paddle with several large holes drilled through it. He told us to line up and informed us the number of "*Quacks*" written beside the names on the piece of paper, would be the number of *whacks* each of us would receive with his paddle. I had never experienced this form of punishment before. One at a time we walked up to the side of his desk. He calmly instructed us to bend over and grab the back of our knees. I could not believe the pain I felt when he whacked my rear end six times with that paddle. Once he was done administering our punishment, he sternly explained to us this was officially our first offense, after three offenses, we would be given two options; One, our parents could enroll us into a private or military school, or Two, we would be expelled and sent to a Florida juvenile facility until we were sixteen years old. He then asked if we understood the process, and without hesitation we responded, "Yes sir." We then returned to our classroom where we each gingerly sat down without saying a word. The real mystery was how that teacher knew who made the "Quacks" in her class.

I was surprised when I received my second offense later that year. On my way home from school with Kenny one afternoon, we came upon a crowd that had gathered on the sidewalk. In the middle of the crowd, two girls were having a full-fledged "cat fight". They were hitting, kicking, pulling hair and yelling names at each other. Kenny pulled his motorcycle to the curb and we joined in watching the battle. Finally some parents came along and separated the two girls, and the crowd dispersed.

The next morning, I, along with several others, was called into the principal's office. We were each asked if we had been spectators at the fight. We replied, "Yes," and were told because we made no effort to stop the fight, we each would receive a "warning." I was shocked with the news but relieved my second trip to the principal's office didn't result in his taking down the paddle. For the remainder of the year I made a sincere effort to avoid my third warning. A classmate from our neighborhood did receive three far more serious warnings and was sent to a reform school in Tampa. I'm not sure if my second warning, as minor as it was, would have resulted in reform school, and I certainly did not want to be in a position to find out!

The name Dunedin is a Scottish name, and Dunedin, Florida, up until 1960, was the home of the U.S. P.G.A. Professional Golfers of America. In tribute to the city's namesake, the school's band, "the Highlanders," over a hundred strong, wore Scottish style uniforms and was led by four students playing bagpipes. The band was well known and traveled around the state marching in numerous parades, some several miles long. I soon found marching to be a test of endurance, in addition, with the heat from Florida's hot sun scorching pavement, many of the band members had blisters on their feet. A remedy was quickly found by wearing an extra pair of socks was when marching in parades. The community strongly supported the band and the band's uniforms were paid for by the band boosters' club. Annually club and band members walked door to door throughout the community asking for donations to support the band.

Nancy Ansbaugh, one of the girls in my class, lived four blocks from my house. Her parents' house was everyone's favorite place to go. Nancy's parents loved having her friends visit and never complained when a group showed up for a get-together. We often gathered in their living room to visit and play each other's records. The guys really enjoyed visiting with Nancy's older brother, Richard. His hobby was looking for bugs and snakes, and he was always skinning or dissecting a recent find. We called him "the snake guy". He would go out into the palmetto fields and stop by construction sites where they were clearing land to build subdivisions. He became friends with several of the construction workers and when they found rattlesnakes (and there were many), they'd kill them and save the big ones for Richard. Richard used an old gunny sack to carry the dead snakes home. There he would cut off the head and rattlers, remove the skin, stretch it out and take the hide to the back porch. The next step was to tack the tail end to the ceiling, then stretch the skin flat and tack the front end as well. Once stretched and firmly tacked, he'd measure the length of the hide which was usually around five feet long. Then he'd take a couple pieces of short two by four boards and slide them between the ceiling and the skin in the middle of the hide. Within a couple days, we were amazed to see how the weight of the boards had stretched the skin. After taking it down, the skin would be almost a foot longer than before. People were really impressed when Richard would show them a six-foot-long snake hide without the head or the tail. The heads were mounted with their mouths wide open, and he'd later sell the heads, rattlers and giant skins to the local souvenir shops near the beach. Richard gave me a couple of those skins, and I later gave them to Ed Canton, our biology and science teacher in LeRoy. Dunedin Junior High sports program included basketball, track, baseball, and swimming and diving. The school sponsored dances in the gymnasium Friday evenings during the school year. With the school being so large, the dances were always packed and line type dancing was popular before I ever saw it on TV. Many times more than a hundred kids would line up in rows and start dancing to records or a local band. With only a change of a song, the line dance would suddenly become the stroll, giving couples the opportunity to show off their skills while strolling down the center to the opposite end.

Music has always been a large part of my life, and concerts for nationally known artists were always coming through the Tampa Bay area. I was very fortunate to see one of the best Rock and Roll shows of the time. Alan Friedman brought his famous Rock 'n' Roll Review to Tampa, causing great excitement to every teenager in the area. The entertainers for the show were Bill Haley and the Comets, Buddy Holly and the Crickets, the Everly Brothers, Jimmy Rogers, and the Royal Teens. For anyone my age, the Royal Teens sang the one hit wonder "We Wear Short Shorts". The band's composer/piano player, Bob Gaudio, later became one of the Four Seasons. The local radio station held a talent contest for local teens to find the best singing talent in the area. The contest winner performed on stage with the stars during the show. My sisters, without my knowledge, registered me for the contest. A few days later I received a notice in the mail with the date and the time for my audition. As tempted as I was to give it a try, I didn't go. I knew there was no way I could ever win, so I simply continued practicing my singing at home just to annoy my sisters. The greatest thrill from the show came when we found out our seats were located right below the railing in front of the dressing rooms. I had the very rare privilege to meet each one of the entertainers and get their autographs. What a wonderful memory I have of standing there visiting with Buddy Holly and the other entertainers that evening.

After attending the concert in Tampa I continued to go to Rock & Roll concerts for many years. In 1975I had the opportunity to be a guest for an evening backstage with the Rolling Stones in Chicago, courtesy of an old friend from Saybrook, Marion Shelton. Marion was the stage foreman traveling with the show. I took a Pantagraph reporter along to write an article about Marion and our evening back stage. Needless to say, having the opportunity to meet the Stones was also thrilling and quite the experience.

Going out with girls in Florida was somewhat different because the kids I knew were more into traveling in groups. Many times no one in the group actually had a date. But as the evening progressed couples would pair up, especially when at the beach. In the early evening, blankets were spread out on the sand and beach goers got ready to watch the sunset. As the evening got darker, everyone would move their blankets closer to the nearby pier to get light from the pier's tall mounted lights. Couples would stroll along the beach watching the incoming waves and catching the cool breeze as the water rushed towards shore. As the evening continued on, blankets begin to disappear and couples gradually moved under the pier to spend time together away from lights and the crowd to test each other's boundaries. At 10:00 p.m. the public beach closed and it was time for everyone under 18 to head home.

Several months after our move, Joan's boyfriend Byron Woodrum joined the Navy and after basic training was stationed at Panama City, Florida. Over the holidays he came down to visit and surprised her with an engagement ring. Joan gladly accepted and immediately started making plans for her wedding in October. After the holidays Dad told us he was not happy living in Florida. He liked selling insurance, but the weather was too hot and he soon found finding new customers was difficult and an ongoing challenge. Around April, both Mom and Dad felt it was best for us to move back to LeRoy as soon as school was out.

Chapter 6

When the school year ended, everything was packed and we were ready to make our move back to LeRoy.

Chuck and Helen Sawyer had occasionally called my folks and knew my parents had made the decision to move back. Chuck mentioned there were very few houses for rent in LeRoy and offered to let us stay at their house until we could find another place to rent. Knowing I had little time left in Florida, I took every opportunity to go to the beach and spending time with friends.

After all the furniture was sold and boxes of personal items shipped, we loaded up the car and started our journey to Illinois. It seemed the closer we got to LeRoy, the more I missed Florida. Right then I made a personal commitment to someday again move back to Florida and live near the Gulf of Mexico.

Finally after two days on the highway we arrived in LeRoy. Chuck was right, there were absolutely no houses to rent. Not wanting to overstay our welcome at the Sawyers, Dad purchased a repossessed mobile home in Bloomington and had it moved to Roark's Trailer Park in LeRoy. It was a newer model with lots of room but it was nothing like living in a house. My room was in the middle and everyone was always walking through my room to get to the back bedrooms.

Dad found a job selling cars for Galloway Buick and the best thing about the job was them allowing him to drive one of the demo cars home. We really enjoyed traveling around in a new Buick with all the latest whistles and bells. I can't, however, recall any of those cars having air-conditioning. One weekend Dad took us over to Sheldon, Illinois to visit Glen Keller's parents. Clarence and Mary Keller lived on a large farm about five miles out in the country. During our visit Dad was outside talking to Mr. Keller when he suddenly became sick and thought he may be having a heart attack. Mr. Keller said we needed to take Dad to the hospital but he could not drive because of his bad eyesight. He told me to help him load Dad into the backseat and for me to get in the driver's seat. I was just about to get my Illinois driver's license and without hesitation, I started his car and within seconds we were speeding down the blacktop toward the hospital. Suddenly Mr. Keller noticed a freight train approaching the crossing on his side of the car and yelled, "Speed it up, we need to beat the train to the crossing!" I pushed the accelerator to the floor and within seconds we drove over the crossing as the approaching train's horn blared as it came down the tracks.

After Dad's examination, the doctor told him it was just an anxiety attack and for Dad to see his local doctor when we returned home. It goes without saying that was an exciting ride, and for the remainder of Mr. Keller's life, he enjoyed talking about racing the train to the crossing.

Shortly afterwards I received my driver's license. Proud to be able to drive, I loaded up Dad's 54 Chevrolet with friends and off we went to the Bloomington and the Normal Steak & Shake. Having a license called for me to start looking for my very own car. With jobs working at the A&P grocery store on Saturdays and after school, evenings part-time at the Standard Gas Station, and working holidays at Webb' Men's Wear, I had enough saved to buy a car. It wasn't long before I found a real sharp 1951 Black Chevrolet 2 door Sedan.

As the months passed by I realized how great it was to be back with all of my old friends in LeRoy. I was now officially a high school student at LeRoy High.   I not only enjoyed being in high school, I was impressed with the size and architecture of the high school building. It was a large two story brick structure with classrooms on both floors and additional classrooms in the basement. The principal's office was on the first floor and across the hall were the rooms for typing, bookkeeping and business class. Upstairs was the English classes, study hall, library, and the music office. The biology class, chemistry/physics class, home making, shop and cafeteria were located in the basement. On the west end of the building was the auditorium, a gathering place for band, school plays and other special events. I really liked the auditorium with its rows of cushioned seats, the balcony, the tall open ceiling with ornate, giant hanging lamps suspended by gold chains and the auditorium stage with huge maroon velvet curtains that opened and closed with a pull from a hidden chain. Toward the back of the stage was the iron circular staircase used by play members to go downstairs to the dressing rooms. It was always fun to read the names, written on the plastered walls by the iron stairs, by all the kids who had been in plays many years before us.

On the east side of the stage sat a very large, stately reed pipe organ with two rows of keys and a large wooded bench. Mounted on the top were long gold metal pipes pointing up toward the ceiling. The organ, originally purchased by the Universalist Church for a reported $10,000, was moved to the high school after the American Legion purchased the building in 1927. It was used for many years but sat silent while I was in high school. The grand piano in front of the stage had replaced the organ. The auditorium was the central meeting place for school plays, band practice, band concerts, student assemblies, graduations, special functions and community activities.

On the east side of the school was the original gymnasium. In the fifties the school realized the need to build a much larger gymnasium next to the old one. The old gym then became the place for ball practice, weight lifting, school dances and the annual prom. In back of the school building was the Ag building which was used for teaching vocational agriculture. Many of the Ag students were also members of the Future Farmers of America. In 1959, construction started on a new middle school behind the new gym and included a new cafeteria for both middle and high school students.

LeRoy High School was very much like other small town schools back in the fifties. Students were very involved in activities and extremely proud of their school. Because of the school district size, few classes exceeded 30 students. Friendships were not divided by each individual class, but instead, were united as a complete student body. Everyone enjoyed participating in whatever they were interested in and the school and the teachers supported all extracurricular activities. They included sports, dances, plays, carnivals, homecoming parades, bonfires, student trips, school yearbook, honorary groups, and the student council.

Extracurricular activities required a teacher to be present, and in most cases, they received no extra pay for their involvement during or after school activities, it was simply considered to be part of their job. Like most schools, sports was the main school activity, and the students, teachers, parents, and townspeople all turned out to support their team.

LeRoy's students concerned themselves with having fun while learning and making the most of what the school and LeRoy had to offer. We were conscious of current events but national and political issues and a teacher's political opinion was considered inappropriate and seldom brought into the classroom. The country was well aware of the lingering issues between the United States and Russia and in our earlier grade school years, students practiced classroom survival techniques in the event of a nuclear attack. During my senior year in high school John F. Kennedy was sworn into office as President and tensions quickly grew into confrontations between President Kennedy and Russian President Khrushchev. To stop the flow of Soviet East Germans to Western Europe, Khrushchev ordered the construction of the Berlin Wall. Closer to home, President Kennedy authorized a covert mission (The Bay of Pigs) in an attempt to overthrow Cuban leader Fidel Castro. Tensions continued into the following year when the Cuban Missile Crisis was watched on everyone's TV fearful that Soviet missile sites would be sitting just 90 miles away from our coastline and aimed at American cities.

With the exception of the comic and sports sections, children and teenagers seldom read newspapers. Televisions changed that and suddenly families gathered together in their living rooms and watching the news became a regular evening event. The evening news made us more aware of the issues of segregation, racism, urban crime and conflicts around the world. However, while we became more aware those issues, they seldom affected anyone in central Illinois. In many ways we lived very protected lives, free from the worries of those living in troubled areas around the world or in America's largest cities.

It seems like once friends, always friends, and it was great just hanging around with the friends I had known for so many years. One of those friends was Monty Raley. Monty was definitely a fun person to be around and when our group was together, things were never boring. Monty's parents owned a very unique mobile home which at the time the manufacturer called the mobile home of the future. It was long and roomy and at the back were two bedrooms; one down and one up and a sleeping area over the stairway. Once when his parents went away for the weekend, Monty stayed home alone and while they were gone, that mobile home became party central. We considered it a safe place to be because if neighbors complained about any unusual activities during his parent's absence, upon their return, his sweet mother, a kind and religious lady, would simply reply, "You must be mistaken because my Monty's a good boy and would never do anything like that". (Boy, if she had only known what her dear innocent Monty and his friends were up to during their absence). Needless to say, we all looked forward to hear that Monty's parents were planning to leave town for the weekend.

While music was enjoyed by generations for hundreds of years, everyone now had radios, record players and TVs. With a simple turn of the dial, you could hear every type of music. The fifties brought about an increased interest in a new type of music called "Rock and Roll". Teenagers listened to records or had radios with them everywhere they went. Cars

154

only had AM radios and some of the newer radios had FM
stations, but reception was mostly limited to larger cities.
While we were 13 and 14, our group enjoyed getting together
and listening to WHOW in Clinton, Illinois. It was a local
station that played the latest and greatest "rockabilly songs".
Songs like; "A White Sport Coat and a Pink Carnation" by
Marty Robbins, "Wake Up Little Susie" by the Everly
Brothers, "Honeycomb" by Jimmy Rogers, "Party Doll" by
Buddy Knox, "Whole lot of Shaking Go 'in On" by Jerry Lee
Lewis and of course, Elvis Presley, the soon to be and well
deserved absolute King of Rock and Roll. The main reason
we listened to WHOW was the music and the DJ took
telephone request. When you called into the station, you could
dedicate a song from you to your girlfriend and the DJ would
then read the request over the air. However, sometimes the
request was factious, and the next day the named girl
mentioned was either embarrassed or extremely mad wanting
to know who called in the request. In the late fifties radio
stations started changing their formats to the new sound. In
1960, WLS radio, formerly a national country music station in
Chicago, changed their format to Rock and Roll. WLS had
the most powerful AM signal in Chicago. In a very short time,
WLS became the number one Rock and Roll station in the
entire Midwest. While in your car or at home listening to the
radio in your room, WLS was everyone's favorite. They also
had a great lineup of DJ's; Art Roberts, Mort Crowley, Jim
Dunbar and the legendary Dick Biondi, who became an
instant sensation playing hit songs and singing his signature
song "On Top of a Pizza" over the airwaves. Rock and Roll
was definitely the sound of the fifties and everybody spent
hours listening to their radio or watching every teenager's
favorite TV show, American Bandstand.

Without a doubt, as I have mentioned before, I loved music

and as Joan Jett later so perfectly sang in her 1982 recording "I love rock and roll, put another dime in the jukebox baby". There were, of course, exceptions. For example, if you were out parked with your girl after 10:00 p.m., the station to listen to was Franklin MacCormack's "All Night Showcase" on WGN in Chicago. My favorite segment of his show was "The Torch Hour". It was a great late night show. He interspersed romantic music with amazing stories, poetry reading and incredible segways into commercials. I can tell you, if you were alone with a girl and listening to Franklin's deep, soft baritone voice reading Elizabeth Barrett Browning's love poems with the soft romantic music playing in the background, the evening can be best described by singer Nat King Cole's soulful love song, "Unforgettable".

I was one of the oldest boys in my class and one of the first to have a driver's license and a car. When going on dates or riding around town with friends, I was usually the driver. On weekends, the place to take your date was Bloomington to a movie, Casella's for pizza, or burgers, fries, and an orange freeze at the Steak and Shake.

There was always someplace to go or something to do; school events, dances, going on a date, running around with your buddies or just hanging out and having fun. The most noticeable thing happening to our old group of guys, who for so many years just wanted to hang out together, suddenly started dating and wanted to spend most of their time with their girlfriends. It was apparent everyone had grown older and our high school years were passing by much faster than we realized.

My family had totally readjusted to living back in LeRoy but realized living in a mobile home was less than a pleasurable experience. It certainly lacked the room and the comforts of living in a house. The trailer park was not well kept. It was noisy and during the winter that trailer was downright cold. My bed was right next to a window and the sweat on the window would leave a layer of ice on the inside of the glass. Finally, my folks sold the trailer and we moved into a house on West North Street, in the same block we lived on when we first moved to LeRoy. We again became next door neighbors to Mrs. Barley, but now on the west side of her home. Mom really enjoyed living back in our old neighborhood and was working again at Dewey's Dry Cleaners.

Joan and Mom were busy working and planning for her upcoming wedding. Their time proved to be well spent because the ceremony at the LeRoy Christian Church was a total success. It was both beautiful and an exciting event for Joan, Byron, friends and the families. Shortly after the wedding Joan packed her things and moved to Norfolk, Virginia to be near Byron at the naval base. It wasn't long after Joan's absence from living at home made me realize the three of us, always together and so close, our lives were changing. We would now take our turns leaving the safety nest that our parents created; and, before long, Judy and I, in the next few years, would also be leaving home and going out into the world to start our own lives. Our childhood was beginning to fade, and all those wonderful experiences of our youth would be selectively cataloged into lifelong memories.

Joan and Byron had bought a 1955 Black Chevrolet Bel Air convertible but Byron was not able to take it to the base. They left it at my parents' house and I began driving it on dates and cruising around town. One thing for sure, that car was what they would now-a-days call a "Chick Magnet". Girls loved riding in it. The guys also enjoyed cruising around town with the top down with the radio on, hoping we could attract the attention of the local girls. Most people thought it was mine even though it wasn't, but I really enjoyed the times I spent in that 1955 Chevy convertible.

Family photo with 1955 Chevy

When school again started, I went out for the football team. I was a running back and not really that good. I quickly found attending games and practices did not allow me the time needed to work and make money. I soon realized I had to choose between playing football or driving my car and dating. I chose to keep working, having my car and going out on dates.

Being a sophomore at LeRoy was certainly different from when I was there as an 8th grader. Everyone had grown up and all of the crazy grade school stuff was long behind us. There were, however, some times when it appeared our brains were still far from being fully developed. It was immediately apparent there was a distinct difference in the way everyone now acted and dressed. Girls came to school with starched blouses, everything neatly ironed, and their hair perfectly done or pulled back in a ponytail. The boys too, wore ironed shirts, some with the collar up in back trying to have the look of James Dean or Elvis Presley. Their hair was always combed, filled with "Butch Wax" allowing their crew cuts to stand straight up. For those with longer hair, it held your hair perfectly to the sides of our head and ended with a perfect DA. Boys wore their shirts tucked in and belts in jeans were required to meet the school dress code.

LeRoy High School

Major changes were taking place in boy-girl relationships. When teachers were not present in the hallways, couples would hold hands, personal conversations were taking place next to lockers, everyone enjoyed flirting and several of my classmates were now going steady. On a less serious note, that didn't mean we still didn't take time for a few pranks along the way. One ingenious creation was when a group of us boys figured out a way to disrupt classes and not be detected during the disturbance. It was a very imaginative, uncomplicated trick. We would carefully take a paper clip, bend it to form a hook, scotch tape a lit cigarette upside down to the clip, tape a firecracker to the upper half of the cigarette, hang the paper clip in the locker and shut the door. This innovative time bomb in the locker gave us plenty of time to go to our classes and wait for the cigarette to burn up to the firecracker's wick. Several minutes later, the firecracker would explode, the locker door flew open and everyone sitting in class would wonder what happened in the hallway. After a couple of these explosions, someone blew the whistle on us and the hallways again were quiet. For a while the principal thought he knew who the pranksters were, but never found any incriminating evidence to actually nail us.

School was fun but certain classes were not so fun. For me, Algebra was an absolute nightmare. Mr. Wilson, we called him "Chrome Dome", was the father of my classmate, Katy Wilson. Mr. Wilson was a good teacher, but if you weren't interested in math, it could be a very difficult class. I'm sure he was aware there were a few of us students who were confused and frustrated with the symbolic set of numbers, variables, operators and delimiters, but he never made us feel clueless of what he was trying to teach us and he made a sincere effort to help us understand. His knowledge of math, algebra and chemistry was far better suited for the smarter students. When the first report card came I knew I was in trouble. I did not do well and naturally my parents were concerned and set up a conference with Mr. Wilson. He told them, "Math doesn't come naturally for Jerry, but if he pays attention and works hard I'm sure he'll finally understand it." It appeared he had the patience to persevere until a light bulb could finally be lit over my head, but it didn't. I was lost and had given up. Finally, boredom overcame me while I was sitting in the very back of the class by the blackboard. A freshman boy sitting near the front row was goofing around while Mr. Wilson was busy writing on the front blackboard. I chalked up an eraser and threw it at the freshman. Just as it

160

was about to leave the very tips of my fingers, Mr. Wilson suddenly turned around and watched as the carefully thrown projectile hit the unsuspecting freshman in the back of his head. It was a perfect throw. Mr. Wilson calmly asked me to leave the class and sent me down to the principal's office. Our principal, Mr. Lewis, felt I would be better suited to join Mr. Torry's General Business class for the rest of the semester. I have to admit, I always liked Mr. Wilson. He was a nice quiet man who loved his family and to most students, he was a good teacher, especially for those students going on to college.

After returning to LeRoy years later I enjoyed visiting with Mr. Wilson after he retired from teaching and driving the school bus. He became very involved in community organizations and a regular attendee at our Class of 61 reunions for many years.

Mr. Torry's class was totally different and one I actually enjoyed. In addition to his teaching responsibilities, he was also the Assistant Principal and coached basketball and baseball. He was very professional, somewhat stern and always in total control of his class. When talking to you, it appeared those dark piercing eyes were attempting to read your mind. He enjoyed teaching and definitely loved sports. He promoted sports participation and was always fair to everyone. I really got a lot out of his classes. To my surprise, I had an interest in business and even enjoyed bookkeeping and business applications. Reading those books and filling out those huge bookkeeping entries with the countless columns helped me to understand basic financial analysis in solving common problems in both business and personal financial matters. Today's computerized programs have greatly simplified those time consuming tedious processes. We no longer have to worry about our handwriting or calculating the totals with the old large-handle adding machines or using simple addition and subtraction. Using today's computers, calculations are calculated and processed in a matter of seconds. After teaching several years at LeRoy, Mr. Torry moved to Washington, Illinois where he became the Superintendent of Schools until his retirement. One of my most enjoyable classes in school was band. Our band director was Edward Carter. Mr. Carter was a wonderful guy and a fun person to have as a teacher. At times he should have applied a bit more discipline and the students knew he was amused when the unexpected occurred. During practice it was not uncommon for someone to stick a sock down the tuba or remove the mouthpieces from an unsuspected trumpet player's horn between songs. Even a loud wrong note during a number would bring a smile to his face. I played my coronet and one day he asked me if I could help him out and switch over to the French horn. I thought I was doing OK on the French horn until the band's annual concert rolled around. With a grin he told me, "I know you haven't been playing the French horn very long, but during the concert could you just pretend to be playing?"

I replied, "You don't want me to play it?"
"Not even a toot!"

For students who smoked, Mr. Carter's office was the best spot in the school to go and he never seemed to mind. It was located on the second floor just above the west front doors next to the auditorium. The window was open almost year round and smoke was always coming out of it. I could never understand why no one ever caught anyone smoking there because the ground below the window was covered with hundreds of cigarette butts. Overall Mr. Carter was a kind man who really cared about his students and would go out of his way to help anyone. He was proud of his band members and always proud of both the concert band and marching band when they performed, regardless of how good or bad they really were.

During my junior year Mrs. Smith was my English teacher. Mrs. Smith was one of the oldest teachers I ever had anywhere. I'm not sure how old she was but in the eyes of her students, she was older than Moses. Dressed in her old 1940's style clothing with her old lady shoes and silver rimmed granny glasses popular long before John Lennon was born, she would stand at the front of the class and slowly begin to teach. Before long everyone became mesmerized and carefully watched her talk because her dentures never seemed to move as often as her mouth. With a rapid machine gun sound she would attempt to relocate her loose dentures to their proper position in order to continue teaching. It was in many ways a mind numbing class. On warm spring days, the large windows of her second story classroom were always opened to draw a breeze into the classroom. Boys sitting by the window would keep a sharp eye out for cars driving up and down the street. On occasions, Mrs. Smith's husband, old as well, would come walking up the sidewalk on his way home. Walking at a slow pace, we could see sticking out of the pocket of his sport coat a brown paper wrapped sack. It was our summation it had to be a small bottle of booze, as he always seemed to be in a hurry to get past the high school property. I am of the opinion Mrs. Smith's ability to teach English had passed years before she taught in LeRoy. I know this sounds disrespectful, but I cannot imagine Mrs. Smith having ever been an outstanding teacher. She had little control over the class and rather than going into further details, I will only say by midterm, myself and a couple other students were re- assigned to another class.

Wrongful conduct has its consequences, and in my case, in order to graduate, I would need to take two English classes my senior year. When my senior year started both Mrs. Smith and Miss Steege had left LeRoy and their replacements were both recent college graduates.

My junior English teacher was Sarah Turner. I really can't say much about her because she did not complete the total year. What I will say is she was nice and easy on the eyes.

My senior English teacher was Karen Newell, without a doubt, one of my favorite high school teachers. I can remember sitting in the classroom the first day of school and this young teacher right out of college walked into the room to start her class. The guys in the room instantly sensed this was going to be a fun year. We immediately could tell this young teacher, with little experience, would have no idea how to control a class and she looked like a real push-over. Wrong, wrong, wrong! To our surprise, within minutes we found out she was in total control as she stood there in front of the class laying out her agenda for the year. I really never cared much for English and certainly seldom discussed literature, poetry or Shakespeare. I can say by the end of the year I actually enjoyed it. It was obvious I liked to talk and had a problem keeping my mouth shut. However, unknown to many, I had a real fear of talking in front of the class or in front of groups. Mrs. Newell's approach to teaching was to have students get up in front of class and give talks and read reports. I would cringe when she would say, "Jerry, it's your turn" and almost freeze up.

Years after graduating, I became involved in community

organizations and was often asked to speak at various group functions. I still found speaking somewhat difficult but I always remembered what Mrs. Newell told me one day in class. Speaking in front of people builds confidence. It's just like taking a test, if you've studied your material, prepared your notes and talk about what you've learned, you have nothing to worry about. You'll do just fine. She was the only teacher I can recall to mention the importance of public speaking. For anyone considering going into business, education, government service or involved in your community, public speaking is an accentual piece of participation and success. Public speaking should be taught in every school today.

Mrs. Newell was not only an exceptional teacher who continually offered everyone lots of advice and encouragement. Most everyone considered her an outstanding teacher and after all these many years, she still keeps in touch with many of her former students from our class.

I would guess most of my classmates would agree one of the most interesting classes in high school was Mr. Ed Canton's biology class. Most of us thought he was a real cool guy who continually gave everyone challenging projects to do in class. He loved science, nature, conducting experiments and was excited about teaching and believed education in the classroom should be fun. Mr. Canton challenged his students and made everyone feel special and welcomed in his classroom.

Me, Mr. Canton and Nancy Luce

It's a well-known fact that having a car, while a teenager, without restrictions can have a negative effect on your grades. I agreed; but it certainly made my school life much more enjoyable. I didn't have to ride the school bus to games after- hours games. I traveled with whomever I wanted and went anywhere I wanted after the games. Most of my friends were in sports and many did not have cars. After games we'd take our dates to school dances or go somewhere to eat. Saturday nights we'd go to Bloomington to a movie or to Casella's restaurant for pizza.

Dating in high school was fun and definitely an experience, some good and some not so good. There's no better way to explain it. It was very much like "On the job training". We were somewhere between a boy and a man and found it far more difficult to win a girl's heart than what you see in movies or read in books. Teenage boys back then were no different than teenagers today. It's just a fact, falling for a girl and believing she will in turn fall for you doesn't always work out. What starts out as a potentially perfect romance can end up with someone wanting to break up and move on. At that moment it can be devastating, and in most

166

cases it takes at least a couple of days or even as much as a week to fully recover. Based on my personal experiences at winning a girl's heart, I must admit, I certainly fell short of my goal. I never went steady or exchanged class rings with anyone while in school. In retrospect, I can only say Woody Allen's satirical definition on finding love is fitting. He cited, "Love is the answer! But while you're waiting for the answer, sex raises some pretty good questions."

During the summer months I stayed busy working for local farmers walking beans, baling hay or straw and cultivating fields. On Saturdays I carried out groceries and stocked shelves at the A&P. During my breaks I would stop in Dale Webb's store and one day he asked me if I would like to work part time there. That really interested me because in the fifties and sixties fashion had become very important to everyone. Women and teen's fashion magazines and movie magazines were very popular with the ladies, and GQ was popular for men. However, a newly created magazine called "Playboy" quickly became both men and boy's favorite publication. Playboy featured the latest fashions and some other very intriguing interests for males. Parents considered Playboy to be inappropriate for boys but it was available at stores. Of course, merchants kept them hidden under the counter away from those who could be offended. For teenage boys it was a "must read". It was not only the new found fashion guide, but it showed some cool things to buy and neat places to go and things to do for the suave and sophisticated man about town. It also included great articles, adult jokes and interesting stories. Each month, in the middle was a wonderful monthly centerfold that would look great on any man's wall or in a dorm room, but definitely not recommended to display in your parents' home. It was in your best interest to keep these wonderful magazines out of sight from your mother's watchful eye. Looking back on those articles on self-improvement and how to be desired by women, it appears we may have spent far more time looking at the pictures and not near enough time reading about how to become suave and sophisticated.

I enjoyed working part time at Webb's, waiting on customers, earning extra money and buying and wearing the latest styles at a generous discount. When we were not busy with customers, Dale would send me to the back room to sort through the return goods, writing a note on each item describing the problem and boxing them up for shipment back to the company for credit. One of those items was a pair of shoes with a defective leather sole that came unglued and separated. I described the damage, boxed them up and sent them back to the manufacturer. A couple weeks later Dale received the shoes back with a note stating the Return Goods Department could not find anything wrong with the shoes. Dale removed the shoes from the box, folded the shoe sole up, and it immediately displayed the separation. He handed the shoes back to me and told me to send them back again. I asked him, "If they couldn't find the damage, what should I write on the note?"

He pointed to the separated sole and said, "Tell the blind bastard to look here," and walked away. I went to the back room, folded a piece of white paper in the shape of a paper airplane and wrote on the top, "Look Here You Blind Bastard," inserted the pointed end into the opening of the leather and shipped the shoes back to the manufacturer. In a few days, Dale received a call from the vice president of the company who was outraged at the note I had sent to their return goods inspector. Dale calmly told him he would discuss the situation with me and assured him it would never happen again. When I got to work Saturday morning, Dale started laughing as he told me about the call. I replied, "That's what you told me to tell him."

Dale replied, "Well it worked, the inspector found the damage and gave me my credit." I was surprised at how many times Dale told that story to his friends and customers.

In the fifties and early sixties everyone who had a car spent hours upon hours cruising up and down Center Street from the city park back to the high school. Cars were loaded with boys, others full of girls and guys with their girlfriends on dates. After cruising, the streets, many of them ended up at Ramey and Helen's Log Cabin restaurant along Rte. 150. After finding a parking place, the "curbies" or "car hops" took your order, attached a tray to the driver's side window and before long returned with your food and drinks. With all the car windows down everyone visited between cars. After eating, people got out and started going from car to car. Before leaving, some of those not on dates, switched cars, paired-up and left together. The cruising continued but before long the route would change. Rather than driving the streets of LeRoy, the cars with couples managed to take a convenient detour outside of town to spend some time alone at their favorite parking spot.

Everyone, especially boys, had an interest in cars. Cars were driven with pride and given the greatest of care. Regardless of weather conditions, if your car got dirty, as soon as the sun would shine your car was washed and swept out. Teenage boys started reading Car Craft, Rod and Custom and Hot Rod magazines. Each magazine had articles showing photos of hot rods, customized cars and pages and pages of auto accessories, some for looks and some for performance.

Keeping with the trend, several local guys started a car club called, "The Dragging Drifters" and met weekly on the west edge of town at the Victory Inn. The club didn't last long but it was fun listening to everyone talk about cars, what they were doing to them and the modifications they wanted to make. They also talked about local drag races and the guys who had been to the several new drag strips around central Illinois gave reports.

Drag racing had become one of the favorite pastimes for the local guys with cars. It was not uncommon to hear someone say, "Let's go out to the blacktop and burn some rubber." We constantly made every attempt to maximize our car's performance. Blizzard's gas station sold the highest octane leaded gas in town and Charlie Bolden's welding shop was where we'd go to have Charlie weld two inch diameter by four inches long iron pipes with screw-off caps directly into the exhaust, right behind the front tires. When you wanted to race, you reached under, unscrewed the caps and suddenly straight pipes were running out the side of your car. Drag racing was usually a spur of the moment thing, and we'd pile in our cars and head either north up the LeRoy Lexington blacktop or to our most popular spot, the Sabina blacktop, flat enough to see for miles and normally free of traffic. Once leaving the city limits we'd drive about a mile or so east until we could easily see the official starting line on the road, a large area of dark black tracks covering the asphalt left from spinning tires from previous races. Once we could see no oncoming cars, we'd line two cars up side by side and a race was about to start. With the wave of a rag or a shirt, the accelerators were pushed to the floorboard and the cars suddenly took off with the roar of the engines, tires smoking and everyone in the cars cheering their drivers on to keep the pedal to the metal until they crossed the small painted mark on the road, the finish line. For as many drag races that took place, I never heard of anyone around LeRoy ever getting into a wreck by drag racing, and almost every boy raced not only their own car but many raced their parents' car as well. Some older guys around town had the money to buy those high powered cars we read about, but it still was exciting and most enjoyable when you won a race. Driving and cruising around town was the in thing to do. Everyone, both boys and girls, watched for who was driving the sharpest or fastest car and who was riding with them. Regardless of the car's age or condition, drivers took pride in their cars and everyone who rode in your car was expected to treat it with the same respect. There were exceptions, one evening after a game Ron and I took our dates to the Steak & Shake in Bloomington. It was a cold night and Ron's date Carole was sitting in the back drinking hot chocolate. Suddenly out of the blue she lifted the floating vanilla wafer from the cup with her spoon and propelled it over the seat and onto the dash board of my car. Everyone laughed but me. It was totally unlike Carole to do such a thing, and at the time, the thought did cross my mind to let her walk the fifteen miles home in the cold.

During school lunch break, students could either eat in the school cafeteria or run uptown and eat at a restaurant. After school, a large number of kids would head for Dunk and Marj's for a soda or milkshake. Within minutes the place would be packed and every booth and table was filled. The jukebox played the latest top tunes and the boys would take turns playing the two pinball machines towards the back. Girls enjoyed huddling together in the booths chatting away about what happened that day at school, who was going with whom, who just broke up with who, discussing movies and of course, talking about boys. The guys also sat in booths, some with their girlfriends or just idly stood around with their collars turned up, drinking a soda or licking on an orange pop-up. Regardless of who you were, it was important to look cool.

Dunk and Marj's Restaurant

Dunk and Marj's was also a popular place to go on weekends. If you wanted to find something to do or try to find someone, just stop by Dunk and Marj's and ask the person working behind the counter. They could quickly tell you what was going on or where you could find the person you were looking for. One Sunday morning David Litherland and I stopped in and sat down with Monty Raley and Bill Scott. We started talking about someone in town who had gone up to Chicago to visit the museums. It was early, so we decided to drive up to Chicago and see the museums ourselves. We pooled our money and off we drove in my dad's old green

172

Buick. After visiting two museums, it was time to load up the car and start home. It's a wonder we made it home because we had underestimated the cost for tickets, parking, food and gas. When we finally pulled into LeRoy, every last penny was gone and the gas tank was completely on empty. But what a blast we had taking our one- day trip to the great "Windy City" Chicago! In mid-summer, I took a job working for McLean County Asphalt and traded off my 51 Chevy for a 1954 Midnight Blue Ford V8 Customline two-door sedan. The total price was $595.00, and my trade-in was $300.00. The Ford was in excellent condition, and when waxed and detailed it shined like a million bucks. I really enjoyed that car and gradually added chrome drag pipes along the sides, lowered the front end and pin- striped the dash board. Not long after getting it I went on a date out to the country club. After the dance, a bunch of us decided to head over to Farmer City to the truck stop for a late snack. I was totally unaware one of the guys went outside during the dance and wrapped a gunny sack around the end of my car's exhaust pipe. After driving about 5 miles, the heat from the exhaust set the sack on fire pushing flames out from under my bumper. Suddenly headlights from the cars behind me started flashing in an attempt to get me to stop. When I stopped, I got out and went around to the back and saw the gunny sack in flames. I quickly put out the fire and the people behind me said it looked as if the rear of my car was engulfed in flames. Fortunately, after removing the sack there was no damage to my car and we continued on to Farmer City. This was not the only trick pulled on one another's cars, and it was always just a matter of time before "pay-back" would settle the score.

LeRoy Fair Festival

Each year when our summer vacation came to a close, the most exciting event of the year came to town; "The LeRoy Fall Festival". This was an annual event started in 1935 when LeRoy celebrated its 100th year centennial. A few weeks before it would start, posters were plastered on telephone poles and in all the merchants' windows. The first official activity to announce its coming to town started with the LeRoy Fire Department washing down Center Street. Boys and girls would ride their bikes uptown to watch the firemen spraying water on the streets with their mighty hoses and pushing the dirty water into the curbs drop boxes. It wouldn't take long before temptations could no longer keep someone from riding their bike or running out into the street. Instantly firemen, well trained from dealing with children from past years, completely covered you with the water almost knocking you down. In a short time almost all the boys were in the streets and soaked to the skin but enjoying every minute of the fun. Once the carnival trucks rolled into town, many of the local boys had an opportunity to make some extra money. We'd go uptown and keep a sharp eye out for the carnies to start unloading their trucks and looking for help. For several years I helped setting up the Ferris Wheel. The carnies, usually covered with grease from the oily equipment, were very careful to make sure we were putting the large bolts in their proper position. Once the rides were assembled, we'd stand back and the carnies would hit the switch and the rides would come alive. In appreciation, the ride owner would hand you a few crumbled up dollar bills and tell us if we brought our girlfriends up to the festival, they'd give us a couple free rides for a job well done.

Within four days of the carnival arriving in town, the Fall Festival transformed LeRoy from a small sleepy town into a massive gathering of fair goers. The park had a large stage constructed on the north end of the city park and hundreds of folding chairs in rows for the evening crowds to watch the shows. Around the park were several large thrill rides and on each side of the east west walkway, lines of tents were filled with merchandise from local businesses, food vendors selling a variety of food and local and state politicians handing out pins and brochures.

Monday through Thursday the stage shows featured local talent, beauty queen pageants and the Air Force Band from Chanute Air Force base in Rantoul. The Friday and Saturday shows absolutely packed the park to see various acts and entertainers previously featured on National TV shows. The LeRoy fall festival was the largest "free" festival in Illinois, providing professional entertainment for everyone to enjoy. The park and streets were absolutely packed and it was fun strolling down Center Street with a date, playing the games, riding the rides or just sharing a huge cotton candy swirled around a paper cone. The midway was crowded with young and old couples and both men and boys demonstrated their skills by tossing balls at bowling pins or throwing darts at balloons trying to win prizes. As expected, most of the games and machines were "rigged" and after several attempts, you were better off to take your date for a ride on the Ferris Wheel, Merry go Round or Tilt-a-Whirl. To top off the evening, dances were held under a huge big top tent set up behind the old LeRoy State Bank. Famous dance bands such as The Tommy Dorsey Orchestra, Guy Lombardo, Tiny Hill and many other well-known bands played into the night. On one occasion the tent was honored by the presence of a young country singer who played small venues while working her way to the top in Nashville. Arriving with her husband in their old car, Loretta Lynn took the stage to the delight of the audience. During the late sixties Rock and Roll fans gathered under the tent dancing and listening to the music of REO Speedwagon, The Buckinghams and the New Colony Six. For years the dances under the big top were popular for people from all over Central Illinois. Everyone enjoyed the festival, the entertainment and the dances. It was also entertaining just to stand outside the dance tent and watch the people inside. Many of them danced and drank until they could hardly stand up. This included some of our most upstanding and respectful citizens, who you would never expect to act in such an undignified manner. However, the Fall Festival was (and still is) a wonderful community event and everyone young and old enjoyed the LeRoy festivities.

When school started in the fall I joined the drama club and got a part in the school play. It wasn't the lead role, but I'm proud to say I'm probably one of the few who can still remember all my lines. From the back of the stage I walked up to the door, knocked, and when the door opened I said,

"Package for Randolph Foster, "Sign here please." Then I turned around and walked back out the door. Even with all the practice and being able to deliver my lines flawlessly, my performance was never written up by a notable critic and I was never offered a part in a Broadway play.

With fall in the air, and Halloween near, boys soon found it amusing to travel around town and out into the countryside tipping over outhouses. With each passing year the number of privies had dwindled, so we were forced to start looking for other mischievous things to do. One night we came across a wagon- load of corn sitting in the middle of a hog lot. We parked the car down the road and walked back to the lot, climbed over the fence and attempted to push over the wagon. The wagon was way too heavy and would only rock back and forth. Suddenly, we saw an outdoor light come on and that's usually followed by a farmer coming out the door with a shotgun, a harsh warning of what could follow. Farmers were well known to have their shotguns loaded with rock salt. Being blasted by rock salt was normally not severe, but certainly inflicted severe pain to deserving wrongdoers. We abruptly jumped the fence and took off running back to our car. While attempting to run through the thick sloppy mud of the hog pen, my right shoe suddenly came off. With the looming circumstance I chose not to stop or go back for the shoe. It was forever lost but we successfully made a clean get-a-way. The car on the other hand, was not clean and even after scrubbing the rubber floor mats numerous times, the interior of the car carried the strong scent of that hog lot for several days.

Another local folly was throwing hedge apples. While we enjoyed the sport, it also became a passing fad because farmers were moving away from having livestock and removing fences and cutting down fence rows to raise more crops. Once we gathered a supply of hedge apples, some the size of softballs, we'd drive down the country roads leaning out the window and took aim at the upcoming signs or mailboxes. Usually I was the driver because I was left handed and unable to throw the apples from the right side of the car. On one of our drives, Buzz decided to drive and got so close to the mailbox the person hanging outside the window had to suddenly jump back inside the car to avoid losing an arm.

Our most notable prank was the tomato war through downtown LeRoy. The event occurred one summer night when everyone's tomatoes were ripe, juicy and plentiful in local gardens. All we needed for the event was a couple of pickup trucks and lots of tomatoes. This problem was quickly solved when two boys went home and came back with their father's pickups. Once it was dark, we quietly went from garden to garden picking tomatoes and carefully piling them against the back of the beds of the trucks. The plan now was for each truck to drive to the opposite sides of LeRoy and then start back looking for one another. Within minutes our truck started around the city park when we saw the other truck coming up Center Street. By consequence, we met right uptown in LeRoy. Without hesitation, we opened fire, throwing tomatoes at each other as we passed. Tomatoes were going everywhere, on the trucks, the streets and sidewalks. After several passes at each other our supply of tomatoes ran low. In our attempt to restock, we could no longer find those large soft ripe tomatoes and out of desperation, we replaced our supply with small hard green tomatoes. The next battle became the last battle. It immediately became obvious getting hit by a green tomato had the potential of inflicting severe pain. There was also a concern about breaking a window, denting cars or knocking out the windshields of each other's trucks. The next day, this seemingly messy but somewhat mischievous escapade brought an outcry from the local merchants and an editorial in the LeRoy Journal stating the actions made by the malicious hooligans, left an unsightly mess and caused hours of extra work for city employees to clean up.

Everyone's parents constantly reminded us about the evils of smoking and drinking and the dangers of speeding and reckless driving. We heard the same story at school and if anyone participating in sports was caught smoking or drinking, they were immediately kicked off the team. Some girls even echoed the 1920s slogan from the women's temperance movement, "Lips that touch liquor shall never touch ours." Over time that notion appeared to change. But like all boys it seemed once we got together, those evil subjects would come up and the temptations to explore them aroused our curiosity. A few in my class started smoking as freshman, but our experimentation in drinking started a couple of years later when we had cars. Occasionally three or four guys would drive out into the country and share a six pack of beer.

Illinois law at the time allowed girls to drink at nineteen because they were thought to be more mature than guys who were restricted until they reached twenty-one. This unusual law kept us constantly on the lookout for older girls willing to buy our booze. By accident, one night when I was seventeen I bought my very first six pack of beer. I had stopped by Bonnie Robbin's Tavern on the west side of town to buy a friend some cigarettes. Bonnie was an older lady and her bar was pretty badly run down and during the early evening hours there was seldom any patrons in the place. That evening when I entered the bar, Bonnie started talking to me and I suddenly realized she thought I was someone else, someone much older than me. I finally built up some much needed courage and asked her for a six pack of Pabst Blue Ribbon beer. She set it up on the bar, I promptly paid her and quickly went out the door. When I proudly told the guys about my purchase everyone felt we now had a place to buy our booze. I tried it again but never asked for beer if anyone else was in the bar. A couple trips later I went in and a guy at the bar asked me what I was doing there. He then told Bonnie who I was and told her I was in high school. That ended my buying beer at Bonnie's.

Drinking wasn't really a major problem while we attended high school. Living in a small town, drinking starts rumors and rumors soon got around to other students, teachers and your parents. I however, now look back on those occasional beer runs with humor. While out with the guys in the country, it was obvious after not much more than a few gulps of beer someone in the car would suddenly show signs of being drunk. These antics, or what I will call "fake drunks", actually appeared funny and made for great stories to be told the next day. However, as we headed back into town their silly actions quickly changed into total sobriety when they realized we would soon be going home to waiting parents, or would be noticed by our town's new police officer, Bob Abner, who would quickly pull over any suspicious acting teenager.

The last two months of the school year became the busiest. The senior prom was coming up and my class, the junior class, was responsible for decorating the old gym for the prom. Decorating the gym required class members working several evenings making all the decorations by hand. Guys hung chicken wire against the walls and the girls placed different colors of tissue paper, (yes, back then they did come in white and pastel colors), individually being pushed into each hole of the wire creating their per-chosen design. The theme that year was "Sayonara" and it was my job to create a large cardboard Buddha and the servers for the evening wore oriental costumes. Everything went according to plan and the prom was a success.

When the school year ended it was again time to find a job. I went to work for Bliss Grain Company in LeRoy building grain storage bins around McLean County. Our biggest job was putting up a large storage facility on the corner of Hemlock and School Street in LeRoy. Several of my friends also worked there along with some of Bliss' full time employees. One worker was a young preacher who moved to LeRoy and a minister at a small church on the southwest side of town. I've never considered myself to be overly religious but I certainly do believe in God. Our family was lax about attending church and I am not proud of the fact that trend has continued on as one of my personal faults today. On the morning in question, the preacher and I were alone inside a bin putting nuts on the bolts and tightening them as they were being placed in the holes from the workers outside. He started telling me he was surprised by the language being used by some of the crew but he didn't want anyone to feel awkward while working with a minister. He went on to say it would not be him who judged our words or actions but God himself. He continued talking about his church, religion, his beliefs and the values of being a true Christian. I was always told there are two things you should never discuss with friends, relatives or strangers; politics and religion, especially when you know very little about either subject. I kept working and listening but most importantly concentrating on keeping up with the person on the outside of the bin. After a while the preacher suddenly asked me, "Do you believe in God and do you accept Jesus Christ as your savior?"

Startled by such a profound question, I simply replied, "Yes I do."

Suddenly he put down his tools, came over and placed his hand on my shoulder and proclaimed, "You've been saved, and you will never forget this day." I must confess, I was totally shocked by his actions or by the possibility of divine intervention. I can only say it apparently did have an impact because I continue to remember that incident to this day and I in no way make light of that event. During my journey through life, I have had occasions where I've personally sensed that someone indeed was watching over me. I'm also appreciative of the much needed assistance.

One of the highlights of every summer was the McLean County Fair. Many local boys and girls were active in 4 H Clubs and looked forward to taking their animals, sewing crafts, garden and food products to the fair to be judged in hopes of getting blue ribbons for the best entries in each class. To be a member you had to be active in agriculture so I joined and my project was growing tomatoes in our garden. I enjoyed 4 H and one evening a group from our club volunteered to provide entertainment for the members of the Farm Bureau in Bloomington. In 1958, Elvis was at the top of the charts so I decided to do an impersonation of Elvis "The Pelvis" Presley, shaking and gyrating to the record "You Ain't Nothing But a Hound Dog". All it took was a small record player, artificial sideburns, a borrowed guitar and a little practice acting like Elvis in front of the mirror at home. I can't recall how well my performance was received by the old folks, and it's probably best I don't. However, several of the girls in the club thought it went well.

The County Fair in August was definitely a great place to go. The fairgrounds were full of carnival rides, local and famous entertainers performed on the stage and a County Fair King and Queen were crowned each year. It was a great family event, an ideal place to take a date and everyone enjoyed going to the fair. Another nearby fair was the Farmer City Fair. Unlike many county fairs, the Farmer City Fair was well known for its horse races and the extraordinary activities going on in one of the large tents on the midway; the "Girly Shows". This tent appeared to be one the more popular stops for men of all ages. Right by the ticket stand a sign read: "No one under 18 Admitted". That may be what it said, but it was also well known as long as you had the money they'd let you inside. The problem for boys was trying to avoid being seen entering the tent. We would stand toward the back of the tent and wait till the line was about to end. Quickly, we bought our tickets and entered the tent. Inside, men and boys stood watching as the scantily clad ladies came out on the stage and began dancing around the small dance floor, slowly removing pieces of their clothing. As we stood there gasping in anticipation of what would come next, the music suddenly stopped and a guy appeared on stage announcing, "This show's over but if you want to see the ladies remove more, for only $2.00 you can stay for the special show". "All others please leave out the side exit." It suddenly appeared few were leaving and everybody started searching through their pockets for the two dollars. When the music started, right before my eyes with beauty, grace and untamed colorful choreography, it was an awe inspiring show. It was certainly understandable why most of the local guys never took a girlfriend on a date to the Farmer City Fair.

That summer I also worked in Bloomington for McLean County Asphalt Company. It was hard work resurfacing roads and parking lots around McLean County, but it gave me an opportunity to save extra money for school. Summer seemed to pass quickly and school was again about to start. Mom took a job in Bloomington with her old boss, Earl Wolf, who had started his own dry cleaning business. Dad was now selling insurance and because Mom and Dad's hours were different, they each had to drive a car to Bloomington. To eliminate the drive-time and save money, they decided to move back to Bloomington. The move took place four days after I started my senior year at LeRoy High. I picked up my school records and took them to Bloomington High School to set up my senior class schedule. During the meeting with an adviser, I was told that because school had already started, one of the classes I would need to graduate was full. In order for me to graduate from Bloomington High, I would need to attend summer school following my senior year. I told him I would have to discuss the situation with my parents. That afternoon, I drove back to LeRoy and talked to the principal about the possibility of finishing high school in LeRoy. Mr. Lewis was very direct. The school policy stated any student living outside the Empire Township school district was required to pay out-of-district-tuition. As I remember, the amount was around $300.00. This was financially impossible for me because I would also have to pay for my gas to drive back and forth to school. Then he said there may be another option to explore. He was willing to go to the school board and ask for their approval to let me finish my senior year in LeRoy, but there would be conditions if the board approved his request and waived the tuition. After leaving his office I was walking down the hall and met Mrs. Newell. I told her about my situation and what Mr. Lewis proposed. She asked me what I was going to do if I could not finish school in LeRoy. Being noticeably upset, I irrationally told her if the school board turned me down, I would most likely drop out and not complete my senior year. That was totally unacceptable to her, and she very sternly explained to me what would happen to my future if I didn't graduate. Two weeks later, I received a call to come back to meet with Mr. Lewis. He told me the board had agreed to allow me to finish my senior year without paying tuition since I had actually started my senior year in LeRoy. There were two conditions; First, I could not participate in any sporting events because of Illinois high school rules, and secondly, I must understand if I got into any trouble during the year, I would be expelled and would not graduate. I quickly agreed to the terms and started school the next morning. Shortly afterward, Mr. Canton, our biology teacher, asked me if I was interested in carpooling with him and Mrs. Jackson, the home economics teacher and another woman who worked at Kay's Drug Store uptown. I drove my car every three weeks, and when I had something I wanted to do after school, I would drive my own car that day. The arrangement worked out pretty well, but it was odd and somewhat awkward listening to teachers discussing their day and the issues they had with some of their students. They never mentioned names but it was never hard to figure out who they were talking about.

My senior year at LeRoy High seemed to pass quickly. I stayed involved in school events and once Christmas vacation was over, it wasn't long until spring arrived and it was now time for the Junior-Senior prom. I firmly believe every student should attend their school prom. For many students, the prom is the only opportunity they will ever have to wear a formal or a tuxedo to an event. It's an occasion where girls can wear a dress unlike anything they wore before, style their hair, and for one very special night, no longer look like just an ordinary school girl. It's like receiving a wave from a magical wand, and being suddenly transformed from just an ordinary girl into a beautiful young lady. For the boys, it's taking on the resemblance of a man and no longer a boy, dressed in a tuxedo, being a gentleman and dealing with the responsibilities of making reservations, finding out the color of your date's dress, going up to Marge Brown's Flower Shop to order flowers, and either spending hours detailing your car, driving your parents' car, or borrowing a fine set of wheels from a friend. There are also some minor issues; the horrifying experience of handing the corsage to your date and awkwardly trying to figure out where to pin it without sticking your date while under the watchful eye of a parent who was standing by observing your every move. I quickly learned to politely hand her the corsage and let her pin it on herself.

Betsy Bane and I, prom night

When it was time to leave for the prom, the prom goers' parents were almost as excited as the students. After picking up our dates it was almost a race to see who reached the school first, prom goers or the parents. As prom-goers started up the sidewalk to the door they were greeted by relatives and on-lookers lined up to watch the young couples pass by. Once inside, we danced to the music of Kenny Hess' band from Peoria. The music was great and all-in-all, the prom went well. The guys and girls all looked fantastic. After the prom ended, we went bowling until the early hours of the morning and then went home. Looking back at the photos in our yearbook, I had almost forgotten the theme of our prom. It was "Southern Plantation". The Junior and Senior prom goers were dressed in their best formal wear and the Sophomore servers portraying slaves wore tattered clothing and painted faces. By today's standards, this certainly would be considered "politically incorrect". However, as inappropriate as it may seem today, there was absolutely no racial bias inferred or intended, and portrayals of this kind back then were not considered offensive. With that said, we very much enjoyed the evening and the prom was a total success.

After the prom came the senior trip to the Lake of the Ozarks, Missouri. For some classmates the senior trip was the very first time they had been out of the state of Illinois, and when we reached the Lake of the Ozarks we were surprised to find so many things to do. We visited the dam, went to outdoor shows, swam in the lake and after reading local brochures, two girls and I decided to go over to Bagnell Dam and take a ride on a seaplane. In 1961 a ride on a seaplane was considered expensive. It cost $5.00 for a 15 to 20 minute ride. I can still remember that ride as if it were yesterday. After walking onto the pier we climbed inside the plane. I sat in the front with the pilot and the girls were seated in the small rear seats. The pilot started the plane, the attendant untied the rope from the dock and the pilot quickly instructed us to; "buckle your safety belts and hold on". Taking off and landing on the water required the plane to first idle out into open water. Once positioned into the wind and clear of boat traffic, he suddenly advanced the throttle and we were on our way. Suddenly the plane lifted out of the water and we were airborne. Looking out the side windows we could see the land and boats below us grow smaller as we continued our climb. The pilot leveled the plane and from every angle we had a spectacular view stretching for miles below us. It was absolutely an amazing ride. After viewing the lake, the dam and surrounding area, the pilot turned the plane and headed back toward the dam. We nervously watched as the skilled pilot dropped the plane to the water below. As the plane's pontoons touched the water we felt the sensation of being thrown forward. Within seconds the tail of the aircraft dropped down as the plane leveled out and glided smoothly on top of the water as we returned to the dock. When we climbed out of the plane, the pilot, with a big smile on his face asked, "Did you enjoy the ride?"

That was an easy question to answer. "That was great, I loved it." Taking my very first ride in an airplane was more than great, it was fantastic. And the memory of that airplane ride will stay with me forever.

Finally our senior trip had come to an end. Early the next morning we loaded onto the bus and headed back home. After our return, everyone's attention was now focused on class finals and graduation. After the finals, the list of graduates was posted on the hallway bulletin board. It was now official. Those listed were about to graduate from high school. On graduation day we assembled in the hallway wearing our maroon caps and gowns and walked to the entrance of the auditorium. Lined up at the doors, we waited, and when opened, we walked down the aisle past the rows of families and friends and onto the stage. After the traditional ceremony, we proudly left the stage with our diplomas. Outside we lined up again for the last time together and were greeted by family and friends. During our parting conversations, I was asked, "Now what are you going to do?"

I satirically replied, "I just want to get as far away from this place as possible." Unfortunately, there's no time machine that lets us go back in time and unsay something we wish we hadn't said. "Open mouth, insert foot" best describes my response and I could have never imagined I would end up living 25 years just across the street from the very spot where I was asked that question.

Leaving the school that evening closed a chapter of our lives as students attending schools in LeRoy. We had made thousands of memories while going to school in LeRoy and most all of them were good. We had grown up together and formed our personalities around each other. Now the time had finally come for each of us to go our separate ways.

It's only natural, after parting, for old friendships to change over time, but the special friendships we formed growing up together in LeRoy have stood the test of time and distance. After all our years apart, I'm happy to say many of us continue to keep in touch.

When fall rolled around several of my close friends left for college, while I did not. At the time I wondered if my friendship with those who went on to college would continue because I did not continue my education. That troubled me for some time but I later realized I was grateful for those past feelings. It gave me the determination to strive harder to make something of myself. The advantages of a college education is undeniable, but at that time in my life it was simply beyond my reach. I firmly believe college is not for everyone. Over the years and during my travels, I have met many successful people who never attended, much less graduated, from college. Their successes were built on an idea, hard work, determination and the ambition to turn a dream into reality.

I often think about the teachers we had while attending LeRoy High School. With total respect to all teachers, the role of a teacher has changed from teachers of the fifties. Salaries were low for a career requiring a college education. Teachers not only taught, they were like a second parent. They taught you, had the authority to discipline you, counsel you and attend to any health issues while you were at school. They attended and supervised after school activities with no extra pay, held teacher's conferences after school, and it was not uncommon for them to call your parents or even stop by your house to discuss school issues. They taught classes with 25 or 30 students without teachers' aides, graded student papers at home at night and in some cases invited students into their home to provide extra help and willingly gave advice to students with personal problems. Even their private life was taken into consideration. They were expected to be model citizens and avoid anything considered controversial. Political opinions were never expressed in class and students were taught respect for one another, their school and their country. This was all considered just part of the job and they never complained. They were amazing people, and as I look back, I can only think how proud they must have been to see so many of their former students graduate and go out into the world and become successful. Without the help of our teachers and their determination, some of us would not have done as well, but fortunately with their guidance, we were all well prepared to meet the challenges ahead.

It goes without saying that I was not one of the gifted students, or a person who seriously applied myself as I should have, while I was a student. There were things I could have done or should have done, but since you can't change the past, I can only say I certainly enjoyed most everything I did. I can say I enjoyed school and got along well with my fellow students and most of my teachers. Because the town and the school was small, it's not hard to remember my teachers' names. Some were not only teachers, they were bus drivers, neighbors and some we worked for during the summer months de-tasseling corn. Here is a list of the teachers who taught at LeRoy High School while I attended school there.

- Don Bateman: Ag, Biology
- Willard Berger: Industrial Arts, Drivers Education
- Dewey Buchanan: Girl's Physical Education, General Science, also class of 61 Class Sponsor.
- Edward Canton: Biology, Social Studies
- Edward Carter: Band
- John Durwe: Agriculture
- Robert Eudeikus: Coach, Social Science
- Joe Higgins: Coach, Physical Ed, Economics- Sociology
- Ann Heppenstall: Vocal Music
- Leonard Poole: Vocal Instructor,
- Paul Rainey: Mathematics, General Science
- Marilyn Steege: English, Librarian
- Karen Newell: English, Librarian
- Charles Sides: Boy's Physical Education, Biology. Coach
- Lois Smith: English, Latin
- Ray Torry: General Business, Bookkeeping, Baseball and Basketball coach, Assistant Principle and class of 61 Class sponsor.
- Sarah Turner, English
- Lorene: Wieting, Typing, Shorthand, Office Practice
- Lester Wilson: Math, Physics, Chemistry
- Joyce Zeiters: Home Economics
- Principal: William Lewis

Le Roy High School Class of 1961

Chapter 7

Shortly after graduation, I enrolled in summer school at Illinois State University. I continued to live at home and worked evenings at the Phillips 66 gas station next to my parents' home. On weekends I worked in the men's wear department at Livingston's Department Store. I also helped my dad out with his new cleaning business. He cleaned the offices at the Shirks Beer Nuts factory and Glass Specialty Company. Shirks was a great place to work because no one was there in the evening, and I could eat all of the beer nuts I wanted. When we cleaned Glass Specialty I met the president of the company who often was working at his desk after hours. Later that summer he asked me if I would be interested in working. He had an opening at his location in LaSalle, Illinois, 50 miles north of Bloomington, and needed someone to fill the position right away. I needed a full- time job and accepted his offer. I rented a small room in LaSalle during the week and came home over the weekends. It was a good entry level job, but I did not like the drive. It was too far away from my friends, so I started looking for something closer.

During that time I bought a 1932 Ford Model B 2 door sedan hot rod. I'd admired this car when I would see it cruising around Bloomington. It was a jewel but needed some attention. I repainted it blue and reupholstered the interior and the glass installer in LaSalle helped me replace all the old glass. It not only looked good, with its 1955 Oldsmobile Rocket 88 engine and a three-speed transmission on the floor, it ran like a dream. Regrettably, I sold it just before I returned home from service. The value of a car like that one today is astonishing.

Shortly after the summer ended I received the news that one of our classmates, Johnny Pat O Rourke had suddenly died. Johnny Pat had been accepted to the Air Force Academy but because he had not fully recovered from the flu, he temporarily enrolled at the University of Illnois. His intentions being to transfer into the academy when his health improved. His death was a total shock to everyone and a great loss to his family and his friends. When you're 18 years old, you never expect to lose a close friend so suddenly, but it can happen. As we gathered at the church in Downs, we each found solace in knowing even though this kind, friendly young man, taken so early in his life, was loved by all who knew him. There was no doubt Johnny Pat would easily be welcomed through heavens gates. A few years later we lost another classmate Kathy Rourke, and regrettably over the years to follow, several other members from the class of 1961 have also passed away but are not forgotten.

Later that fall a local railroader told my brother-in-law Byron and I that the Illinois Central railroad was hiring brakemen. We drove up to Kankakee and applied for the job. We were hired to work in the Chicago district, which served all rail traffic between Chicago, Champaign and Clinton, Illinois. We took the training, passed the test and started working in the switch yard in Kankakee. Later we were placed on the extra board. This is where a brakeman is listed "as available to work" and when crews are needed, the railroad would start calling names from the top of the list down. If that brakeman could not work, they called the next names until the number of required crewmen was completed. Working on the railroad at that time was a high-paying job. To be closer to where most crews originated from, I rented a room in a home in Homewood, Illinois. When called to work, I could easily walk to the terminal to catch my train. On the early morning of November 22, 1963, I returned to my parents' home in Bloomington after working the night in Kankakee. Tired, I went to bed and shortly before noon, Judy came running up the stairs crying to tell me President Kennedy had been shot. We both raced downstairs to the TV and watched as Walter Cronkite covered the events of that day. The country was in shock, school kids across the nation were sent home and many businesses shut down. For the next few days, families and friends gathered in front of their TVs to watch the coverage and the funeral procession as it came down Pennsylvania Avenue with the rider-less horse and the caisson carrying our fallen President. This was a sad day in the history of our country and one that people of that time will never forget.

During the winter I spent most of my time in Homewood. David Litherland had graduated from butcher's school in Ohio and took a job at Gene's IGA in Bloomington. When it snowed, rather than driving back to LeRoy, David would go to my parents' house and use my bedroom to sleep, sometimes staying for several days. It was not unusual for me to come home and go into my room and find David sleeping in my bed. Mom never knew who was sleeping there until they came down the steps in the morning for breakfast. There was one occasion when someone else being in my bed caused my sister Judy to become very upset. While I was in Chicago working, Charlene Stiles, a close friend of my parents was spending time at the hospital with her mother. Because of the cold weather, Mom told her she was welcome to stay at our house rather than drive back and forth. On the night in question, Charlene stayed at the hospital very late and decided to accept Mom's offer and went to bed in my room. The next morning, Judy, who was unaware Charlene was there, looked in my room to see if I was home. Suddenly, there in my bed she saw a woman with long black hair sleeping. Shocked and in a near fit of rage, Judy ran down the stairs to the kitchen and proceeded to tell Mother she needed to have a serious talk with her son because things had gotten totally out of control. I had brought a girl home for the night and she was still in my bed. Mother having a good sense of humor, thought Judy's outburst was rather humorous. At first she appeared OK about the girl being in my bed but then informed Judy I was in Chicago working and the woman in my bed was Charlene.

It was very easy for me to get Judy riled up and I certainly enjoyed it when I succeeded. I had a couple dates with a girl who had moved to Bloomington to work at Country Companies. She was cute but our relationship was far from being serious. However, she kept asking me to take her home to meet my parents. Not quite sure why, and not being excited about the idea, I told her I usually avoided taking anyone home because my sister lived with my parents and she had mental issues. I told her while my sister sometimes appeared normal, other times she suddenly would jump up and run over and grab people wanting to hug them. She said she was sorry to hear that and understood but still wanted to meet them.

Finally one evening I gave in and we stopped to visit my folks. Once inside, I introduced her to Mom, Dad and Judy.

As soon as she sat down, she started staring at Judy and watching her in anticipation of her jumping up for a hug. After we left she told me I had a nice family and Judy seemed perfectly normal. I told her sometimes she's ~~OK~~ and sometimes she's not. Later when I returned home, Mom and Dad said she seemed like a nice girl but Judy immediately said she seemed a little creepy. Judy went on to say she stared at her the entire time she was there. I replied it's probably because I told her you were retarded and occasionally jumped up trying to hug strangers. Needless to say, Judy did not think the joke was as funny I did.

On Valentine's Day 1964 I received a very unusual Valentine in the mailbox. It was from the United States Selective Service. It did not say, "I love you". It said I was being drafted into the United States Army for two years. It instructed me to report to the Chicago Army Induction Center in March and I should bring a change of clothing and toiletries. If I passed the induction testing, I would be drafted. When I got to the train station early that morning there were about 15 guys gathered together on their way to the recruiting center. One of them was Dick Albert from LeRoy. Once we reached the recruiting center I was amazed at the number of guys being drafted. It was definitely an interesting day. They herded us around like cattle and prodded, poked and looked at or in every orifice on our bodies. Finally, in the afternoon, they lined up those who passed and sent the others with physical disabilities or criminal backgrounds home. Once in formation we were told we were being inducted, we were sworn into the service and would be taken by train to Fort Knox, Kentucky. It was now official, like the old familiar song goes: "You're In the Army Now".

We soon found basic training was not the place to be if you're not in good physical condition; and there were some who were not. Each morning we were rousted out of bed at 5:00 a.m., dressed, made our bed and fell into formation. Then it was time to run, do pushups and fall in line at the mess hall for breakfast. Before entering, it was required we travel down a long row of monkey bars, do chin ups and then go inside to eat. The sergeant yelled at us as we entered the mess hall, "You guys take all the time you want to eat, just be back, outside, and in formation in 15 minutes." As soon as we ate, we lined up and marched over to a field to do physical fitness exercises. The instructors were brutal and if we did anything wrong they would shout, "Get down and give me 25" meaning pushups, and we'd better have the strength to do it. If we didn't, we were told to do 25 more. They were constantly yelling at us, trying to get under our skin. We marched from one field to another for more training. One thing for sure, the instructors were neither nice nor prejudiced. They couldn't have cared less about who we were or who we knew. Everyone was treated the same regardless of skin color, economic status or education. To the instructors, we were the lowest form of life on the planet, and it was their job to mold each of us into a soldier whether we liked it or not.

Various types of training continued every day with the same eating schedules. After supper we would run and then return to our barracks to get ready for the next day. Lights were turned out at 10:00 p.m. and no talking was allowed after lights out. While in basic training, we continued to be tested for our basic skill sets, aptitude, dexterity and physical abilities to determine what area of the Army we were best suited to serve. I adapted well to the training, and actually enjoyed shooting pistols, rifles, machine guns, throwing grenades, climbing ropes, and crawling over and under obstacles.

Everyone in our barracks quickly became friends. When you have no inclination of ever actually being sent to war, playing war games all day was really not all that bad. We spent a large part of the day running up and down hills screaming, "Kill, kill, kill!" stabbing dummies with our bayonets and crawling under barbed wire with real live machine gun fire above our heads. We climbed ropes and walls and learned the basic skills of self-defense. We were sent into buildings full of tear gas without our gas masks. After several minutes, we were instructed to put our mask on and find our way out in the thick clouds of gas and smoke.

After eight weeks, I graduated from basic training and received my orders to report to Fort Riley, Kansas, home of the "Big Red One" First Infantry Division. I was assigned to the 26th Infantry Battalion, Headquarters Company, First Infantry Division to start Advance Infantry training. This training was similar to basic training, but far more intensive and physical and involved tactical battlefield exercises. By then, I had gained some weight, was in great shape, and I had no trouble with the program.

After AIT training, I was able to take a short leave to go home. A few months later, my sister Judy married Chuck Cagley and it appeared I would not be able to get leave. At the last minute my four day pass was granted and I just made it home in time to attend their wedding.

My job assignment at Fort Riley was an Infantry Direct Fire Crewman for a newly developed model 28 ENTAC anti-tank wire-guided missile. It was a compact, portable weapon created by the French government with the capability of carrying a nuclear war head. It was a blast to shoot. You could hide behind a hill or in a wooded area and remove the top of the container to use it as a seat, then fire the missile and use the handle or joystick on top to guide the missile either up or down or sideways to hit a moving target within 2,500 meters. We repeatedly tested it and found it to be extremely accurate and very similar to operating a remote control airplane or playing one of today's video games.

After all my military testing was completed, my test results indicated I was eligible to consider entering a couple of officer's programs. One was OCS, Officer's Candidates School for the Infantry or Warrant Officer's School to become a helicopter pilot. Both programs required extensions of service if you agreed to enter the program. OCS, two additional years, pilot's training three additional years. I looked into both but the pilot program sounded the most interesting. I signed up to attend the helicopter pilot orientation. What was unknown by the candidates, the Army was quickly building up their fighting forces to fight a war, and infantry officers and helicopter pilots were in serious demand. This would not be a peacetime game, and a colonel at the orientation stood up and bluntly told us, "Gentlemen, a war is about to start. Look to your right. Now look to your left. One of the guys sitting next to you will not come home from this war. The life expectancy of a combat helicopter pilot under direct enemy fire is less than eight minutes." The colonel was as serious as anyone could be. This no longer sounded like just having fun flying, and his message definitely changed the mood of everyone sitting there. I went away realizing this program would not be the right decision for me, and any program requiring an extension of service should definitely be avoided. I elected to stay at Fort Riley so I could get out of the Army as soon as I fulfilled my two years. Just a few months later we found out the colonel was right, the war would soon start and the First

Infantry Division would be the first to be deployed.

In early 1965 President Johnson told voters during the election he was not prepared to send US troops thousands of miles overseas to do something the South Vietnamese Army should be doing themselves — protecting its people. He had inherited the Vietnam conflict in which the U.S. had previously agreed to provide supplies and send volunteer advisers to assist in training the South Vietnamese military. Suddenly in early March, President Johnson reversed his decision and announced US fighting forces would be sent to fight in Vietnam. He assured the public they would be in South Vietnam only as a short term measure. His orders included sending the Army's 1st Infantry Division from Fort Riley, Kansas to Vietnam. Their mission; keep the North Vietnamese government from overtaking South Vietnam. For those of us in the 1st Division, we were assembled and told we would be going to Vietnam to fight a war. There was never a mention of Vietnam being classified as a military conflict. President Johnson could never have envisioned what he had started. America had suddenly become embroiled in a war that changed the American public and its perception of war and those who serve in its military. Immediately after his speech, anti-war protesters took to the streets and on campuses across America. This conflict soon turned into a long term war so controversial and unpopular that it forced newly elected President Nixon in January of 1973, to sign a peace accord and all US troops were withdrawn after thousands of American soldiers had been injured or killed.

Once we received our official orders, the First Division went into full deployment mode. Anyone eligible for retirement or having less than six months left of active service, would not be deployed. All vacancies within the division were filled. All supplies, equipment and weapons were loaded on trains, and every soldier was given leave time to go home and say goodbye to their wives, girlfriends and families. All this was done within 45 days. Like all others being deployed, I took my 8 day leave, but found it very difficult to see all those I cared about before leaving.

After arriving back to Fort Riley, we were loaded onto a passenger train and headed to Oakland Army Terminal near San Francisco. From there, we loaded on to three ships and headed to the war in Vietnam, or what was officially classified as "A Military Conflict" in Southeast Asia.

Our battalion was boarded onto the USS *General Blatchford*. This old 1944 once retired 522 foot WWII transport ship, brought out of retirement, in no way resembled or had the amenities of ocean going ships of today. It smelled of smoke from the single large billowing stack towering above the rear section of the ship. We were told the normal number of soldiers being transported on the Blatchford was 2500, but the number of troops on this voyage would be near the maximum capacity of 3500 soldiers. Bunks were added everywhere and any chance of privacy was nowhere in sight. Once on board there was the constant smell of a combination of engine oil and grease mixed with the soot from the ship's smoke stack. Groups of soldiers were lead like sheep down to the bottom of the ship to our sleeping quarters. There were no private rooms, just large compartments full of canvas bunks held by steel racks standing four high with hardly any room for our duffel bags to be stored. The compartments were hot and traveling between compartments going to the head (bathroom), required passing through the small doorways of several other compartments. At night, the only lighting to guide you in the passage ways was the small red lights inside a glass cover over each door opening. Strange bells and whistles sounded with no one knowing what they meant. I was assigned a top bunk and found it challenging to climb in or out of my bunk without stepping on the man below. After the ship was loaded the PA announced the ship was about to leave port. We were then told to go topside for our farewell. Standing by the rails we could see two tug boats below starting to pull our ship away from the pier. Within minutes, from a distance, we could see the famous prison, Alcatraz Island. From there the ship slowly sailed toward the Golden Gate Bridge. Unknown to us land lovers; we were told of a military tradition when passing under this great bridge. All soldiers leaving by ship to war were to stand topside and throw money over the ship's side into the water below the bridge to assure their safe return. Needless to say, with the ship's horn whaling and soldiers cheering and waving to the people walking above, handfuls of coins were being thrown into the water below. The view of that bridge was just as magnificent as I remembered it from the many photos I'd seen while growing up. It was absolutely beautiful. That was the very minute I realized we were actually going off to war and many of the soldiers aboard this ship may never see the United States of America again. Our voyage across the Pacific was slow and each day was repetitive. Up in the morning, dress, go outside and stand in line to have breakfast down in the mess hall. Once we ate, we gathered again on top deck. Periodically, non-coms and officers would hold group classes on what to expect when we arrived in Vietnam; descriptions of Vietcong fighters, what uniforms or clothing they wore, fighting tactics in jungle terrain, training about the country, the extreme heat, monsoon rains, animals, snakes, proper hygiene and maintenance of our weapons and equipment. However, most of our time was spent searching for a spot to stand along the railings or find a place to sit down to read or to write letters. The only relief from the smell of the ship was an occasional gust of wind mixed with the salt spray from the ocean water below. Once the loudspeaker blared out the announcement it was again time to eat. We'd line back up to go down to the mess hall. After eating, we'd go back to the deck until they told us to line up for the supper meal. After finishing supper, because of the total darkness outside, the decks became off limits and everyone was ordered to stay below. Later on after the mess hall was cleaned we could go back down to the mess hall and spend a few hours playing bingo before bedtime. This went on for more than 20 days. The ship made two stops along the way, Hawaii for mail and later Okinawa to refuel and load supplies.

Just before reaching Okinawa the ship had entered the edge of a typhoon that caused some unwelcome excitement for everyone. Trying to eat was nearly impossible. It was difficult walking to the mess hall and once there, trays were sliding from one side of the dining hall to the other. Finally, everyone was sent back to their sleeping areas and the compartments were locked down. With the swaying motion of the ship, soldiers were becoming sick. Those sick could not get to the head and the ship continued to rock every which way. Fortunately, our compartment was located at the bottom center of the ship and we had far less motion than most. I didn't get sick, but with the sounds of sick soldiers and the smell of vomit definitely was causing problems for everyone. After what seemed to be a very long period of time, the motion gradually subsided and we were welcomed by calm weather and being able to again go topside. Later after lunch our duties were to return below and clean our compartments.

Once we arrived in Okinawa some aboard (Sergeants and

above) were allowed to leave the ship for a few hours. I managed to slip out with some others and for the next couple hours we spent our time visiting the "dives and bars" located near the main gates of the base. It was great to once again feel my feet on the ground and I will only say, "What went on in Okinawa, stayed in Okinawa."

The biggest event along the way was seeing an occasional whale, another ship and crossing the International dateline. After days at sea without knowing where we were, (somewhere between the US and Japan), surrounded by nothing but water as far as the eye could see, the ship's horn blared and the announcement was made we were crossing the dateline. A couple days later we were each given a small certificate stating the date and time of that lackluster event.

On the morning of June 23, 1965 we finally arrived at the coast of Vietnam. As we headed toward shore, our Sergeant Major, a highly decorated WWII and Korean veteran, gave us his thoughts about young soldiers about to go into battle; "Gentlemen, each of you have been given the distinct honor of defending the United States of America. For those of you who have never been in battle before, you will soon find out you came to this war as boys, but by God, by the time you depart this shit hole, you'll leave as a man."

As soon as the ship anchored, landing craft boats came aside and we were ferried to shore. We had no idea of what to expect once we landed. We were glad to find it was peaceful because we had our rifles, but no ammunition. As soon as we landed on the beach we were assembled, then loaded onto trucks and taken a short distance away to a small airstrip. There we boarded a C-130 aircraft and then flown to Bien Hoa Air Force Base. At the time that air base served as the staging area for all incoming troops. Once we arrived we ate, then were taken to the area where we would spend the night. We were ordered to dig our own foxholes and told we would be responsible for securing our immediate area against a possible enemy attack. None of us really thought we were in any danger. Considering the large amount of troops stationed at the base it appeared almost impossible the enemy would attempt to make an assault. Shortly after getting settled in, our platoon leader gathered several of us and told us to put on our gear, load up our ammo and follow him. We were one of two squads about to go outside the perimeter on an ambush patrol. For me, this would be the first of many ambush patrols to come. Within minutes we were standing in front of the outer gate listening to our instructions. The lieutenant told us for the last several nights, Viet Cong soldiers had come into the valley below and would intermittently fire up at both of the US base camps. This was a common practice for the enemy trying to start a fire fight between the two adjoined hillside encampments. He then gave us our orders. We would be going down in the valley, one squad on the far right and the other on the far left. Each squad would set up their positions and engage anyone who came down the guarded trails. This felt more like a simulated training operation than the real deal. My first thought was this possibly could be an initiation or the Army's way of messing with new troops arriving in a war zone. We soon found out this was absolutely no game, in fact, it was the real deal. Once outside, we formed a line and followed the lieutenant and a South Vietnamese scout down the hill through the tall grass and into the dense thick brush. The scout soon found a suspicious "track" or footpath, so we set up our position in the brush behind the trail.

Everyone took their assigned positions just like we had practiced so many times before back at Fort Riley. We were now hidden about 40 feet back in the brush with rifles facing the path or kill zone, and our machine gunner was positioned laying parallel to the path. Our only communication with the base camp above us was a PRC-10 backpack radio which we soon found to functioned only intermittently. Nightfall fell across the valley as we laid there hidden in the brush. The longer we waited, the longer each hour seemed to pass by. Suddenly, from on our right flank, there was a rustling sound getting louder and coming closer. Suddenly shots were fired and within seconds everyone was firing his weapon in the direction of the approaching sound. Even though the squad-members on the far left couldn't see the movement on the right, the tracer bullets from the machine gun gave everyone a location to aim at. After several seconds, the firing stopped and everything was again silent. We received no incoming fire. Our focus still remained on the far right position. Seconds later each person passed the message down from the squad-leader to stay alert. He then radioed the base camp giving them our status. The base command ordered the guards from both camps above us to hold all fire toward our position until further notice. The lieutenant then told us we would to remain in our position until daybreak. There are no words to describe the next few hours and thank God nothing else came down that path. When daylight finally came up over the valley, we searched the area and found two VC bodies about 70 feet to the right of our position. The lieutenant then told us we would be taking the bodies back with us. Everyone was caught off guard, but we gathered up our gear and dragged the bodies up the hill. Once inside the gate a jeep and a trailer was waiting and the bodies were thrown in the back of a trailer. Suddenly soldiers in the camp started running over with their cameras and taking pictures of the dead VC. I was just thankful the patrol was over and we were back safe in the camp. At the time I had no idea ambush patrols and long range reconnaissance patrols for our platoon would become an almost weekly operation for the remaining time I was in Vietnam. Many of those patrols did not involve any contact with the enemy, but others did. During those with engagement, most lasted only a few minutes and it was not unusual for the squad to expend over 1000 rounds of bullets during each encounter. If anyone ever talks about being in combat in a war zone and tells you they weren't scared, they're either lying, crazy or there's a possibility they were never in a combat situation while serving in Vietnam. War is war and war is hell. We've all talked to those who have been in wars, or read stories about previous wars, but until you have experienced war yourself, you really can't understand its true reality. You're young, scared and forced to face the uncertainty of your own existence. After returning home, the images can consume your mind but there comes a time when you realize the need to turn the key and lock those haunting memories away. Personally, I feel it's totally inappropriate to ever ask a combat veteran, "Did you kill anyone?" There's no glorification in killing, even an enemy. It's simply doing what you're ordered to do and to elaborate further on the subject, serves no purpose. Being in fire fights, on sweeping operations or on ambush patrols, once someone fires, it seems like everybody starts shooting. It's not like the movies, especially during the dark of night. In a matter of seconds it can go from absolute total silence to total chaos and the aftermath can be horrific.

Once we returned to our unit we spent the next couple hours trying to get some sleep and we packed up our gear, climbed on a deuce and a half truck and our convoy headed out the north gate. We traveled about 70 miles north on a dirt road while grabbing whatever we could find to cover our faces to avoid the clouds of red dust while the convoy continued on to what would soon become the 26th Infantry's base camp. It was located on the edge of the small jungle village, Phuoc Vinh, in an area known as the Iron Triangle or War Zone C which sat deep in the jungle along highway 13 not far from the Cambodian border.

Near the camp a makeshift runway was being constructed to support fueling aircraft and helicopters, planes transporting troops, supplies and loading Agent Orange onto aircraft for vegetation defoliation. In a U.S. Department of the Army study of herbicide (Agent Orange) spray missions in Viet Nam from 1965 to 1971, it indicates 643,769 gallons of Agent Orange were applied in the Phuoc Vinh area, the largest amount applied anywhere in Viet Nam during the war.

The small village of Phuoc Vinh years before had been a French military outpost. Once we arrived, we immediately started setting up camp, fortifying the outer perimeter and getting everything ready for military operations. Having few tents, the first several nights we slept under trucks, tarps or anything else we could find. Each day, Army personnel carriers, tank retrievers, and end loaders cleared more area while soldiers using machetes helped cut back the grass and brush to provide space for our camp. Gradually, the cleaning was large enough to start building large dirt barriers with fences holding several layers of concertina wire around our encampment. Along the fence 55- gallon drums of liquid napalm mixed with aviation fuel formed a gel-like consistency which when ignited would burn at more than 5,000 degrees and cling to whatever it touched. These well positioned drums also decreased the need for accuracy when under heavy attack. Inside the wire, over a 50 foot deep clearing laced with claymore mines surrounded our fortification and sandbag machine gun emplacements were built for our added protection and fire power. It soon appeared the first intruders to find us were rats. The smell of food from the mess tent must have covered the entire area. They came in our camp by the hundreds. It was hard to sleep with them sniffing or climbing around us looking for something to eat. Snakes were another problem. Vietnam is infested with snakes and many of them are large and poisonous. There was one incident where a soldier was bitten while standing alongside his vehicle. He was air lifted to a medical unit and survived the poisonous bite. Drinking water was another serious issue. Other than the water trucked in, purified water was not available and iodine tablets were used daily in all the water we drank. No showers were available and sponge baths were the only way to stay clean. Once our camp was in place, settled and secured, things seemed to improve somewhat daily.

Once we finally had everything in place, Lt. Liederman came into our tent and told us to listen up. He said, "Now that you have a little extra time, I want you to write a letter to your mother, wife, or girlfriend and tell them how you feel about them. When you're letters are done, give them to me; and, in the event you are killed, I will personally see that those letters are sent to the names on those envelopes. "Hopefully I will never have to send them and I hope to be able to give them back to you when you leave." I can tell you, those were the hardest letters I ever wrote.

After a couple months in camp we hired local villagers known as "hooch maids" to wash our clothes in the nearby river. After being washed in the mixture of dirty water and the bright red sand it only added more dirt to our clothes.

The Viet Cong did not want children to be near American forces or taught to be loyal to the South Vietnamese government and schools became targets for the VC. In the center of Phuoc Vinh was a combination Catholic Church and orphanage. Orphanages were everywhere filled with thousands of children whose parents and other family members were killed in the war. When entering the church, the large exterior wooden doors, and the interior walls were riddled with bullet holes left from a Viet Cong attack during a morning church service. The massacre left bodies of clergy, teachers and children lying dead on the floor. From a soldier's perspective, this was a brutal reminder of the ugliness of war and at least one reason for us being there. Now these thousands of innocent children and those who were trying to shelter them were given some hope knowing American soldiers were there to protect them.

In and around our area of operation we never ran across uniformed North Vietnamese Regular soldiers. Our primary enemy was the guerrilla fighters and local fighters, who in some cases farmed by day and fought by night. They did not wear uniforms. Their weapons varied from AK-47 rifles to old single shot rifles, Chinese grenades, mortars, crudely made land mines and lots of booby traps. In some other areas north of us guerrilla fighters resorted to fighting with crossbows, makeshift spears or nothing more than filed down sticks. It was common for them to travel in smaller groups, or in some cases just having a single sniper crawl in close enough to fire at us. At first, our objective was to secure our base camp, conduct ambush patrols, conduct local reconnaissance, and doings search and destroy missions throughout the area along the Cambodian border.

As our division expanded its operations in the outlying

regions and additional units moved into rural villages, it became commonplace for troops to find villagers beaten, shot and mutilated bodies left dead as a warning to local villagers not to cooperate with U.S. troops, and what would follow if they did. As widespread as these atrocities were, they were almost completely ignored and left unmentioned by the US press, who at the time was preoccupied with what they considered terrible atrocities being committed by our aerial bombings, ground forces and refocused their reporting efforts on supporting the anti-war movement across America. While I was in Vietnam, the 26th Infantry Battalion participated in several major operations with the First Division. One such operation was the battle of Tan Binh. Our battalion was transported south near the small village and what started out as a typical fire fight, ended up being one of the bloodiest battles to that date for the 1st Division. A full Vietcong battalion had attempted to overrun a US position and all hell broke loose. Under the light of the aerial flares being shot into the sky and slowly floating down range and the light from the napalm burning the trees and brush to our front, mortar rounds started coming in as well as small arms fire. This scene was much like a classic battleground scene out of a Hollywood war movie. Before the end of the attack, bodies of dead VC's were seen being carried away by other VC. They did this in an attempt to not have US forces determine the actual number of casualties from their assault. However, the next morning it was determined several hundred VC were killed. The First Division had successfully pushed back and defeated the North Vietnamese Regulars.

Me in a bunker with a machine gun

In thinking back on being in a war zone, there were two things that immediately come to mind. The first was the loud thunderous noise which was absolutely unbelievable. Between the whump, whump, whump of the choppers, rifle fire, the blast of artillery fire, overhead aircraft and air support bombings, it was almost deafening. When calling in air strikes the planes, especially the Navy pilots, would approach and appear to be almost tree top high as they flew over positions releasing their bombs. When the bombs exploded, the blast was ear piercing and the ground around us would shake. During that period, ground troops were not issued ear-plugs. The only ones I ever saw issued were the bulky Mickey Mouse type worn by the artillery boys firing the 12 inch cannons or to flight crew members on choppers. To this day I carry the reminder of my days in Vietnam by the constant ringing sound in my ears. The other issue was the weather. In our area of Vietnam the monsoon season started in early May and ran through August. During the monsoon the average rainfall exceeded well over 14 inches each month. In addition to being drenched to the skin, the lightning storms were absolutely the most intense lightning I have ever seen. The sky would suddenly turn from total darkness into the most amazing, brightest light show imaginable. During the torrential rain storms, even the rats and snakes were in search of a dry place. Unfortunately, that meant we would find them in our tents and bunkers looking for shelter or crawling under our tarps or climbing into our vehicles. Once the monsoon passed, the weather immediately transformed into an intense heat with daytime temperatures exceeding 115 degrees. What once was mud now had turned the bright red dirt into a fine dry power. The dust completely covered everything and the sweat from the heat formed rings of red dirt in every crevice of exposed skin. Everyone and everything was completely covered. On patrols in the jungle we waded through swamps and rivers and came out with leeches clinging to our clothes and skin. Our jungle boots would stay so wet they began rotting within weeks.

As the months pasted by we continued to make improvements to our base camp which seemed to make our living conditions better and safer. The outer perimeter was now fortified with sandbag bunkers, a mine field and a large fence row of razor sharp concertina wire. We continued to encounter sporadic mortar and small arms fire and booby traps were being planted and found around our camp and along the nearby roads and trails. Outside the confines of our base camp it was apparent the war was escalating and becoming bloodier. When out on ambush patrols engaging the enemy became more frequent and during field operations there was a steady increase in enemy activity and firefights in our area. Shortly after I returned home, a major offensive was launched by the

VC on our base camp but beaten back by our battalion and
additional division support. Our camp seemed to be a popular
spot for sniper fire. Thankfully it was more of harassment
than a threat. Most of the guerrilla fighters in our area were
untrained, unhealthy and half blind. One afternoon we were
informed of a sniper spotted nearby in the trees outside our
camp. My platoon leader decided he would leave the base
camp and try to hunt him down. He yelled for me to grab a
radio and I follow him out the outer perimeter fence. As we
were outside the wire I had trouble keeping up while trying to
position the heavy radio on my back. My platoon leader was
no more than fifty feet in front of me when he started around a
clump of trees to our right. As I was catching up he
momentarily disappeared from my sight. Suddenly I heard a
loud "Boom" and I started running toward him. When I
reached him he was on the ground yelling, "Shoot, Shoot,"
and was aiming at the area of tall grass ahead. I opened fire in
the direction and advanced forward. I saw nothing, could see
no evidence of a path, and I received no return fire. By that
time, camp guards were running out of the gate to our
position. I went back to the lieutenant and could see where he
had been hit on the side of the head and shoulder by
fragments of a wire grenade. The lieutenant told me when he
rounded the trees he saw a Viet Cong running into the grass.
He did not realize the VC either threw a grenade or just
dropped it behind him as he ran away. We helped the
lieutenant back to the base camp and he was taken to a medic
unit for treatment. The next day he returned and there was
little evidence of his wounds other than a couple of Band-
Aids. Thankfully the grenade exploded just far enough away
to hit him with only a couple pieces of very small thin wire
fragments. He was fortunate he was wearing his hard-hat,
because his helmet took the most hits and showed the marks

where pieces of wire had hit it in several places.

Vietnam Combat Operation

As I mentioned before, I always felt there was a Higher source looking out for me, especially while I was in Vietnam. My closest brush with death was late one night on an ambush patrol. It seemed the more we went out the more dangerous it got. This incident was a result of a different type of danger; "friendly fire" involving a recent troop replacement. For every soldier going home, a new recruit was brought in from the States as his replacement. This became a constant concern for everyone who had been there for a while. Many of the replacements had only been in the Army for a short time. With the accelerated troop buildup for the war, and the need to replace the wounded, dead and those soldiers being discharged, the newly drafted recruits were being sent to Vietnam as soon as they completed simple combat training. For most soldiers who had been there a while, it was apparent these young replacements were not fully prepared for what they would soon be expected to do. On the night in question, we took up our position outside a rubber plantation. The new recruit was told his job would be to cover the rear of our firing line. He was positioned directly behind me, almost foot to foot aiming his rifle in the opposite direction. No one could figure out exactly what happened, but he either became so scared or confused that he somehow managed to turn around. Unbeknownst to me, the tip of his rifle barrel was now pointed directly at me and no more than two feet away. Suddenly a shot was fired and I was immediately covered with dirt. All I could think was; there must be a VC above us in a tree. My immediate reaction was to roll over and open fire.

Suddenly the lieutenant yelled out, "Who fired that shot?"

The new recruit behind me replied, "I did, sir. Something was moving in front of me."

The lieutenant said, "Check it out."

The guy then grabbed my right boot. In a moment of total disbelief, I angrily yelled out, "You son of a bitch. You damn near killed me."

The kid was in near panic and after everyone recovered from finding out we were not under attack, I laid there listening to his agonizing whispers apologizing for what had happened. I still cannot believe how anyone aiming an M-14 rifle at something that close could possibly miss their target. That shell should have hit me directly between my legs, and if so, would have gone completely through my body. After years of thinking about this, I can only theorize he was so scared he lost all sense of what he was supposed to do. Somehow, he managed to quietly turn around and when he heard the movement of my feet, I think he just closed his eyes and fired his weapon. Thank God it was only once. I will never know what actually happened for sure, but I can only surmise the possibility that a greater power intervened and redirected that 7.65 Nato round bullet to miss me by just inches. When I think about all the young guys sent off to fight wars without being properly trained, I'm reminded of Major General William T. Sherman's description of war and those who fight them; "In our country - one class makes war and leaves another to fight it out."

In December of 1965, I was sent over to a Special Forces team near our camp for demolition training using C-4 composition explosives. Their outpost was being relocated out of our area and in the interim they provided some specialized demolition and field training to some of the guys from our unit. This did not mean I was in Special Forces, we were there only for the training. It did however, give us the opportunity to travel with them on a couple of search and destroy and surveillance missions along the Cambodian border. It was a very different type operation because this Special Forces team used Cambodian and Laotian mercenaries during these missions. Mercenaries were not considered part of the US military. The United States did however pay for their services. They had their own methods of fighting and were paid to fight and kill VC. Gruesome stories about what they did to the VC they captured were widespread. There were also stories about US soldiers committing atrocities during the war but I can only say during my time in Vietnam I saw no such actions committed by US troops. The atrocities we came across were all done by the South Vietnam police and the Viet Cong fighters

Shortly after returning to my unit I was given an unexpected surprise over the Christmas holidays. I was invited back to the Special Forces outpost to attend a special Christmas lunch with actress/comedian Martha Ray. Unknown to many people back home, she was an Army Reserve Special Forces Lieutenant Colonel and dedicated much of her time visiting only Special Forces units and outposts in combat locations throughout Vietnam. What a wonderful lady. She was very serious when discussing military operations, but once those discussions ended, she was just like we all remember her, a very, very funny lady with a very large and infectious smile. It was indeed an honor to have met her.

Christmas day in Vietnam was just another day. The only thing representing Christmas was a small scrawny Charlie Brown type tree placed outside the mess tent. It was decorated with just a few handmade ornaments and a small tin foil star on top. Charlie Brown would have been proud. Not wanting to spoil the holiday, I waited to open the two presents I received Christmas morning. The largest box was filled with homemade cookies and candy sent by the LeRoy Women's Relief Corp. When I said cookies, everyone gathered around to eat the treats as I read the very kind hand written note inside. The other present was a new watch. I had earlier written home asking my parents to take some money from my savings account and buy me a stainless steel (gold was not authorized) Timex watch. I requested an illuminated face, waterproof, rustproof, dust proof, shockproof and if possible, bulletproof. Mom and Dad decided to make the watch my Christmas present, and believe me, I spent many nights in total darkness periodically looking down at the glowing face of that watch to check the time. I can still remember Christmas night in 1965. Maybe it was because it was the first time I'd been away from home during Christmas. I was on duty that night guarding the outer perimeter bunker. In absolute total silence, I stood staring out of the long narrow gun port of the bunker walls into the darkness. There was not one star in the sky and the combination of darkness and silence made me think about all those I cared about back home and how much I wished I could be there with them.

Lt. Col. Martha Rae visiting our Recon Unit

In early 1966, the Army started providing R and R (Rest and Relaxation) to troops stationed in Vietnam. The options were either Australia or the Philippines for a period up to 10 days. With so many troops now stationed there, soldiers with less than 120 days remaining in country, were not eligible for R and R. The reason was based on the fact we would soon be going home. Unfortunately, I was one of those not eligible.

When not out on operations, everyone in camp stayed busy digging trenches, filling sandbags, building bunkers and cleaning our weapons and equipment before going back out in the field. The most exciting time in camp was when the mail was flown in. As soon as the men saw the mail clerk come out of his tent and yell "Mail Call", everyone quickly gathered around as he called out the names on each envelope. I was lucky to have several friends writing me, and received at least three or four letters a week. However, there were those who did not receive mail and it was hard to watch those walking away empty handed. You could clearly see the disappointment on their faces.

After mail call, it was back to work and waiting to get orders for that night. It made little difference if you stayed in camp or went out on a patrol because even those staying in the camp got little sleep. While in camp, no one got more than six hours of sleep each night, sleep three hours, guard three hours, and if nothing happened, hopefully three more hours of sleep. After that, it was again daylight and time to eat and be ready to move out.

Two months before I came home, our company conducted a sweep operation near a small local village. A close friend of mine and a young recruit from Colorado came upon a booby-trap of partially hidden hand grenades. Soldiers were warned to never pick up any enemy weapons until they had been properly inspected. The enemy was well aware American soldiers love souvenirs and grenades, guns and knives looked very inviting. Seasoned soldiers always looked for a mark or a small painted spot somewhere on the weapon but still would not pick them up. The VC routinely marked their booby traps so their own troops would know what not to pick up. Our instructions were to get the demo guys and have them blown up in place. On this operation, the new recruit apparently saw the grenades and wanted one as a souvenir, and attempted to pick it up. No one else saw him reach down and the booby trap suddenly went off sending him up in the air. Tom, unaware of what was happening was also hit. The kid received extensive wounds to his throat, chest and head. Tom received shrapnel wounds to the upper left chest, one piece coming out the back of his shoulder. They were quickly air evacuated to a medical unit and sent back to the states for treatment. Both eventually ended up being released from service. To my surprise I later heard the kid survived and was sent home to Colorado.

Everyone in our platoon talked among ourselves about our hometowns, our families, our friends, the war, and what we were going to do when we got home. The conversations always got around to our wives and girlfriends. In combat, it is vital that everyone be constantly focused on the mission, making sure there are no mistakes, keeping each other covered, and, most importantly, going back home alive and hopefully unharmed. Wives, girlfriends and family play a very important role in the life of a soldier. They have an impact on their mental state, their readiness and attitude. After what seemed to be a short time, everyone in the squad knew just about everything about each other's girlfriends. We either carried their pictures with us or posted them on the wall of our tents or in bunkers. One guy never left the base camp without wearing his girlfriend's scarf around his neck and another wore a handmade beaded bracelet with her name on it which he believed protected him. When anyone became aware of another squad member having troubles at home, the entire platoon was there to offer support. There was nothing worse than having a soldier receive a "Dear John letter". It not only affected the recipient, it affected the entire platoon. We were half way around the world from home with no access to a telephone and a two week turn around for letters. Receiving bad news was the last thing anyone wanted and it happened more often than one would expect. Fellow platoon members were the only support available to console and assure them that the world was not coming to an end. We used the old cliché; "There will be more fish in the sea when you get home," or whatever else we could think of. Everyone made a sincere effort to support one another and tried to keep everyone's emotions under control. In most cases talking and listening to them appeared to give some comfort, but in some cases, it didn't. One of my good friends from Ohio was completely devastated when he received a letter concerning his wife who we assumed, was having an affair. For a while we thought things were getting better but shortly after returning home he reportedly drove his car into a bridge abutment and was killed. Others received letters about losing a girlfriend but they managed to endure the pain. It's hard to explain what letters mean to a soldier far from home and from their loved ones. Regardless of letters being serious or trivial, letters were the only form of communication we had with the outside world. Each letter was read repeatedly, and every little thing written in those letters affected you. Just reading the words from a wife or a girlfriend simply saying, "I miss you and I love you" would lift the spirits of a lonely soldier.

Letters from home also provided entertainment. Off-duty time was spent sharing what was written in their letters. Before long, the topic would again move toward girls or romance, and the group suddenly became the "Dear Abby of the Jungle." We'd listen intensely, asking some very personal questions and giving out some totally "off the wall" colorful and inappropriate advice that absolutely made no sense, but brought smiles and laughter to everyone's faces. Believe me, the contents of those conversations would have even made Dr. Phil blush! One of my favorite and the most unusual letter I received was sent to me by a lady in Homewood, Illinois. The lady was the daughter of the woman I rented the room from while working on the railroad. I'd met her several times and she had a daughter about my age. She wrote in her Christmas card she had read the letter I had written to her mother. She went on to say she worried about me and all the other young men fighting in Vietnam. After hearing the many war stories her husband and his friends had told about lonely soldiers serving in Europe during WWII, she knew I too must be lonely. Inside the envelope she enclosed a check for $15.00 and she suggested I use it to buy some affection. That letter was an absolute "hit" with everyone. However, there was a problem, where in the jungle could I find a bank to cash it. Oh well, it was the thought that counts.

Speaking of letters, it was hard to believe in 1965-66 there were American soldiers who were illiterate. It was even harder to believe that some were in our company and until we were shipped overseas we were totally unaware of it. We had two guys in our unit who could hardly read or write. It soon became common-place for them to ask a friend to read their letters and help them write letters home.

Recon Squad in front of shrine

Many of the guys in our company were married, and when discharged, returned home and were happily reunited with their wives and families. For many of the single guys it was a totally different situation. Many who had girlfriends when they entered service, no longer had that same girl waiting for them when they returned. Getting drafted when you're going with someone and forced to be separated for two years can take a toll on a relationship. Young men drafted in the early

225

60s gave little thought of actually having to fight in a war. Before the Vietnam War started, most draftees ended up being stationed somewhere on a base in the US or in Europe. There was no talk of war and the average single recruit gave little thought of making definite plans with their girlfriends before entering service. During those 24 months away from home many relationships changed. Their girlfriends had lost interest or found another boyfriend, and many soldiers returning from Vietnam found it difficult stepping back into a regular civilian life. This conflict, or "war" had affected almost everyone's life, mine included. It's difficult and complicated to understand so I will sum up the topic with this quote; "There are things that you never want to let go of, people we never want to leave behind. But keep in mind that letting go isn't the end of the world, it's the beginning of a new life". - Author Unknown. I remember returning to my tent on February 1st and turning over the page of the calendar over my bunk. When I saw February had arrived, I realized I had less than six more weeks before heading home. Three weeks later I became one of what Company Commander White called; "Mama's Boys". With so much resentment against the war back in the States, the Army did not want returning soldiers to arrive home showing the stresses of war. They slowed down our field duty, gave us more food so we could gain weight and more time to sleep and rest up. Much of our off duty (which was little) was either guard duty or providing security to convoys hauling supplies. Providing convoy security had its benefits, especially when the convoy included trucks carrying beer. Truck drivers appreciated the added security and occasionally a driver would offer us a couple cases of beer when they arrived at their destination. We greatly appreciated the beer because beer was the perfect trading item in our camp. That included some unofficial dealings with our supply sergeant. For just two cases of beer, I found him extremely helpful in processing my paperwork early in camp which eliminated me from spending extra time in Saigon being processed out of Vietnam. When he told me I could possibly be back in the States several days early, I threw in my most treasured possession; my Sears electric 16 inch box fan I had bought in Kansas and packed away in our truck with our equipment. Once the camp finally got electricity out to the tents, a fan was like gold. Even the company commander expressed interest in it. To the sergeant's credit, it was a good trade. Everything went like clockwork. Six days before I was due out, my papers were in order. Before leaving camp, Captain White thanked me for serving with the 26th and among the service medals I would receive was the Combat Infantry Badge, which he stated was only awarded to a very small portion of the Armed Forces.   Holding a small card he read: "This medal is awarded for performing duties while personally present and under fire while serving in an assigned infantry, Ranger or Special Forces capacity, in a unit or brigade, regimental, or smaller size, engaged in active ground combat, to close with and destroy the enemy with direct fire." He then shook my hand and wished me the best. I in turn thanked him, saluted and I went back to my tent.

With papers in hand, I packed my duffel bag, climbed into a chopper and started my journey home. As the chopper lifted from the small round heliport pad in the center of our base camp, my feelings were very different than what I expected. While I felt fortunate to be heading home, I knew I was leaving behind some close personal friends I would never see again.

Ambush Patrol Squadron (Battle worn picture)

While I served in Vietnam with the First Division's 26th Infantry Battalion, our company lost several soldiers. I'm not sure of the exact number of those killed or wounded while I was there but most were killed or wounded during combat operations. Surprisingly, some were injured or accidentally killed by friendly fire. When the Army's 1st Division landed in Vietnam it raised the total number of troop headcount to just over 40,000 soldiers scattered throughout the entire country. The US government buildup had one major objective; vamping up the draft with the intentions of sending thousands of more troops to Vietnam. By the end of 1966, the number of troops in Vietnam surpassed 200,000 and by the end of 1969, over 500,000 troops were serving in Vietnam.

There's a common belief that the fighting in Vietnam was not as intense as it was during World War Two. I have read several military articles with statistics showing that not to be the case. The technological advancement to the Army helicopter changed everything and the military relied on the helicopter like never before. The war in Vietnam became known as "the helicopter war." The helicopter became the "work horse" for the infantry. It could rapidly transport troops and ammunition in and out of hotspots miles apart in a matter of minutes while providing firepower for ground troops. Consequently, the average infantryman in Vietnam saw far more combat during their one year tour. Medivac helicopters flew nearly 500,000 missions in Vietnam. Over 900,000 patients were air lifted. The average time lapse between being wounded and hospitalization was less than one hour. As a result, less than one percent of all Americans wounded, who survived the first twenty four hours, died. Without the helicopter, many more soldiers would have died and it would have taken three times as many troops to secure the eight hundred mile border with Cambodia and Laos.

As the number of troops continued to rise, the use of drugs by soldiers was estimated to have climbed to around 20% of the enlisted troops during their tour. Unlike the statistics, stories or movies portraying excessive drug use during the war was unlike the period of time I was there. During my tour (1965-66) there was very little evidence of drug use by soldiers in our immediate area. Our battalion was located miles from the 1st Division's headquarters. Our base camp was isolated deep within the jungle and it would have been almost suicidal to buy drugs from village locals. In addition, at that time, drug use would not have been tolerated by fellow soldiers in our platoons. We all wanted to return home safely and it was essential everyone relied on one another in order to survive. From those I have talked to who served after I returned, drug use by soldiers changed immensely. Reading some recent research it concluded the contributing factors appear to be: (1) the need of troops in stressful combat situations for self-medication, escape, and a need for pleasure indulgence; (2) the relaxation of taboos against drugs in the US; (3) the availability of illicit drugs at low cost, apparently the result of profiteering by some South Vietnamese officials; and the growing disenchantment with the war and the progressive deterioration in unit morale. Even with the passing of almost fifty years since my returning home, the effects of drug abuse and how it has affected the lives of so many Vietnam veterans and their families can unfortunately be seen with one single visit to any Veteran Administration Clinic or hospital.

It was a great feeling touching down in Saigon and even a better feeling being able to step aboard the large Pam American airplane sitting on the tarmac ready to head back to the States. Because of the runway's short length, domestic airplanes could not take off fully fueled so our plane would fly first to Japan, refuel, and then fly non-stop to California. When we landed in Japan we were told there was a change of plans. Several officers boarded and the plane was redirected to Anchorage, Alaska. When we landed in Anchorage, the officers exited the plane and within minutes we were back in the air on our way to Travis Air Force Base in California.

After getting off the plane we lined up on the tarmac, and military police conducted a random search of our duffel bags looking for weapons and war souvenirs. We then boarded buses which took us to Oakland Army Terminal. What we did not expect was the evening meal, an all-you-can-eat T-bone steak dinner, baked potatoes, fresh vegetables and a wide variety of desserts. This was the finest meal we ever had while serving in the United States Army. Early the next morning we lined up for our exit physicals, processed our final discharge papers which included the list of medals I was awarded (but never received), given a travel voucher, back pay and finally we were told we would now be on Active Reserve status for two more years but discharged from active duty in the United States Army.

Leaving the building, just outside the gate we were approached by a couple off duty soldiers standing by their cars asking if anyone needed a ride to the airport. After bargaining, five of us jumped in a car and were on our way to the San Francisco International Airport. Knowing everyone would be heading east, we started down the ticket stations looking for the quickest trip of the unfilled flights. The best fight I found to Bloomington was to first fly to Los Angeles and then on to St. Louis. I gave the ticket agent my voucher and 45 minutes later I was boarding the plane.

From the letters and magazines we'd received from home, we'd certainly heard about anti-war protesters, but it was hard to believe what we saw at that airport. They started heckling us and would get right up in our faces shouting anti-war slogans, even calling us "murderers". During our discharge processing we were told by the Army, even though we were officially no longer active military, if we got into any trouble on our way home wearing a military uniform (which was required when using travel vouchers) the Army would charge us and bring us back for disciplinary action. Many of the soldiers would have happily taken a few extra minutes to give those weirdoes an attitude adjustment, but our priority was simply to ignore them and get to our departing gates.

Looking back, one of the saddest things about serving in Vietnam was returning home and realizing the lack of respect or compassion for those returning from war, most of whom did not volunteer, but were drafted and proudly fulfilled their commitment to serve their country. We were sent to Vietnam with an objective to defeat the enemy and win the war. As soldiers we completely understood our enemies had the same objective and their job was to kill and defeat us. For that reason alone, I can understand the ill feelings from families on both sides who lost loved ones during that war. I cannot however, forgive the anti-war protesters at that time. They certainly had the right to oppose the war and the US government, but never should have brought the hundreds of thousands of servicemen who were drafted and those who enlisted into their protest. Those protesters knew nothing about war, nothing about being a soldier or the humiliating effect they had on all those who served. Bottom line, many more wealthy and more fortunate kids were able to avoid being drafted by merely enrolling in college or had the political connections to keep them out of the military. Others with little respect for their country evaded the draft and left the United States. I'll never understand why those who so cowardly left the country were offered conditional amnesty by President Ford and later a blanket pardon by President Carter, while the thousands who so valiantly served were treated with total disrespect, and over the years have been denied the support, medical care and benefits so many veterans badly needed. My personal opinion remains; those who protested the Vietnam War and left the country to avoid being drafted were simply cowards and should have never been allowed to return to the United States without prosecution. To make matters worse, many of those radical protesters and draft dodgers later became teachers, professors and elected politicians in state and national politics.

Shortly after landing in Los Angeles I boarded my next flight to St. Louis. When the plane landed in St Louis the fog was terrible. Outbound flights had been grounded and there were no more flights scheduled to Bloomington until the next day. I grabbed my duffle bag and hurried outside and caught a cab to the train station. Riding along in the thick fog, I was beginning to wonder if the driver could even find his way. Finally we arrived at the train station and luckily there was a train leaving for Bloomington in a couple hours. It was scheduled to arrive around 5:00 a.m. Once on board, I leaned back and took a nap, waking up just before the train pulled into Lincoln. The heavy fog had lifted and a soft, gentle rain had begun to fall. As soon as we arrived in Bloomington, I got off the train and started looking for a cab. To my surprise, there on the platform stood Vernelle Stensel, the funeral director from LeRoy. Vernelle was there to pick up a body from the train. With his big grin he welcomed me home and told me there was no need for me to wait for a cab. He said he would give me a ride home as soon as he loaded the body from the train. Once it was placed in the hearse, we were off to my parents' house. Because I had been discharged early, I had not called my parents or anyone else because I wasn't sure exactly when I would be discharged or when I would arrive home. Within minutes Vernelle pulled up in front of my parents' house. It was still dark but I could see the light from the window and knew they were up getting ready for work. After I thanked Vernelle for the ride, he smiled and said, "It's nice once in a while to have a live person ride in this thing." I laughed, got out and headed to the front door. Dad and Mom had just gotten up and were both sitting in the kitchen. I can still see the look on their faces when I walked in the front door. They were definitely surprised and excited I was finally home. I told them there was no need to take off work because I really needed to sleep. Dad went to work but Mom insisted on staying home. It definitely felt good to be back. I did try to sleep but there was just too much going through my mind to stay in bed. Finally, I went back downstairs and spent the morning visiting with Mom, Joan and Judy.

Chapter 8

When you've been gone for an extended period of time it's a special feeling to be home, catching up on all the news about our family and friends and having some free time to relax. Even the smell of my mother's kitchen and the smell of fresh coffee on the stove brought back old memories of years gone-by. Mom told me she received a call from Wiley Pontiac saying the car I ordered while overseas had arrived and was ready to pick up. With that news, I went upstairs, got cleaned up and before long we were off to pick up my car. When we drove into the parking lot I could see it setting right outside the show room door. It was a brand new beautiful midnight blue Pontiac Grand Prix with a factory four-speed transmission and a posi-traction rear end. What a car!

As soon as the paperwork was completed I jumped inside and headed back to the house. Later that afternoon I called a few of my friends to tell them I was home. We agreed to get together and celebrate my homecoming. The evening went extremely well and it was a great feeling being back and visiting with old friends. They started telling me what had happened while I was gone, who had gotten married and all the new places to go. One of them told me he had a great idea.

The next evening a dance was being held at the Consistory featuring Al Pizzamiglio and his band. He had bought two extra tickets for his sister-in-law and her boyfriend who were coming down from Chicago. His sister- in-law was already there but at the last minute her boyfriend called telling her he was unable to make the trip. Jack said, "Help me out, my wife feels bad about going out and leaving her sister at home. Just tag along with us, it will be fun. She's nice, attractive, likes to dance and I bet you have nothing better to do."

He was right, I didn't, and Al's band was one of my favorites. I replied, "OK, but how do you know she'll even go?"

He smiled and said, "Don't worry, I'll take care of everything."

The next evening I met them at their apartment and found his sister-in-law to be exactly as described, nice, attractive and later found out she also liked to dance. At first she seemed to be somewhat uneasy about the arrangement and within minutes after getting into the car, she told me she had a boyfriend and how her sister and brother in-law insisted that she go. I told her I completely understood and was just happy to be home and going to a dance. I'll have to admit, I enjoyed the evening and it was great dancing and listening to the music of Al's band.

For the next few days I continued going out with the guys and catching up with some other friends. I drove over to Ron and Carole's house in Roanoke and Ron and I went out for a few drinks to catch up on all the latest news. The next weekend I had a date and went over to one of my previous favorite spots, Club Peoria.

The following Monday I decided it was time to go to work. I drove out to LeRoy and visited Dale Webb at his store. Dale had written me while I was over-seas saying he would like to discuss having me consider working for him when I got home. While I was in the Army, he had added another clothing store in Farmer City and was in the process of buying two Red Wing shoe store franchises, one in Champaign and the other in Detroit. He was also considering buying out a clothing store in Gibson City or possibly opening a new store in Normal, but those stores never materialized. I definitely was interested because I really did not want to return to the railroad. Under the railroad's military leave policy I had six months to report back to work from my discharge date. I explained to Dale my time-line and told him I would give it a try for six months. If we both felt things were going well, I'd stay; if not, I'd return to the railroad. We agreed and the next day I started working at Webb's Men's Wear in LeRoy.

I enjoyed working for Dale and also enjoyed the morning drive to and from work on route 150, at speeds far over the 55 MPH speed limit. Once I arrived in LeRoy, I stopped at the Log Cabin for breakfast and then headed on to the store. The downside of the job was the hours. The store was open Monday - Thursday 8:00 a.m. to 6:00 p.m., Fridays 8:00 a.m. to 8:00 p.m., and Saturdays 8:00 a.m. to 9:00 pm. Total work hours per week, 65 hours or more.

It didn't take long before I was aware of a car meeting me each morning on my way to work, it was always full of girls. And, they'd wave as I passed by. I had absolutely no idea who they were but it was fun meeting them each morning. A week later on a Sunday afternoon I pulled into the Steak & Shake in Bloomington and noticed the driver of that car who always waved was sitting in one of the cars with another girl. The space next to their car was vacant so I backed in, rolled down the window and started talking to them. The driver was a very cute blonde, and the girl who always waved was sitting in the passenger side. In the back seat was a guy but nobody seemed to be paying any attention to him, including me. Finally I asked the blonde if she had any plans that night and would she like to go out. At first she hesitated but said, "Yes," and she gave me a time and location where I could pick her up at her house. She said, "I live with my parents in Holder on the corner across from the grain elevator. Look for a white house with some white ornamental furniture and a blue gazing ball on a pedestal in the front yard."

Having been through Holder many times over the years, I said OK and headed home. Later I took off from Bloomington and headed out on the Ireland Grove road to Holder, or at least that's where I thought I was. I drove around the small handful of houses scattered about and nowhere did I see ornamental furniture in a yard, let alone a gazing ball.

Finally it hit me; *I've been out of circulation way too long. How could I have fallen for a line like that?* I bet those girls are still laughing, having sent me miles out in the country looking for ornamental furniture and a blue ball on a pedestal.

Feeling certain I was the victim of a practical joke, I turned the car around and started back toward Bloomington. When I came up to the stop sign, I looked up at the sign on the storefront which read "Bentown Store." I wasn't in Holder; I was in Bentown and Holder was a couple of miles south. Again feeling stupid I turned left and headed down to Holder. When I reached the grain elevator, there on the corner sat the white house with the two white iron ornamental chairs and the blue gazing ball in the front yard. I parked the car and went up to the door. I rang the doorbell and she opened the door and asked me to come inside and meet her parents. We then headed back to Bloomington to a movie. After the movie, I drove her home, walked her to the door and told her I needed to ask her a question. You may have told me earlier, but I don't know your name? She laughed and told me her name was Linda Boaz. I then told her if she would like to go out again I'd like that. She said yes and we started dating. For a while I also had a few other dates but, as we continued to go out, I found myself wanting to spend more time with her. She was working at the State Farm Illinois Regional office and rode back and forth in a car pool. When we wanted to go out, it was convenient for me to just drive from work to her house, and we'd go on into Bloomington. Linda came from a very large family and she was the youngest, her oldest sister was twenty years older. She had two brothers, five sisters, more than forty aunts and uncles, and who knows how many cousins. Her brothers and brothers-in-law had all served in the military, and we enjoyed telling stories about all the crazy things guys do while in the service. Linda's mother had always been a homemaker, was a wonderful cook and enjoyed having her family gather at their house on weekends. I really felt comfortable around her family and decided to take her home to meet my family. Little did I know my dad knew two of her sisters, Laverne and Phyllis, who operated a downtown restaurant called "The Little Chef" in Bloomington.

Me and Linda at Miller Park

Before long I realized that time does have a way of building a sound relationship. It's based on common interest, compatibility, trust, mutual respect, sharing feelings and most important, enjoying being together. I suddenly realized there was no one else I would rather spend my time with. We enjoyed dating, dancing, double-dating and going to parties with friends. We spent a lot of time with her brother Jim and his wife Darlene. Jim also worked at State Farm and he and Darlene had recently moved back to Bloomington from Indiana with their two children Kelli and Kirk. They were fun to be with and from that time forward they became not only family, but very close personal friends. During the work week I would occasionally stop in other stores in LeRoy and visit with the owners. Louie Folks and his wife Millie ran the local jewelry store directly across the street from Webb's. During the holiday season I stopped in and Louie started showing me some diamonds he had ordered for a woman in Bloomington. With his magnifying glass piece attached to his head by a thin wire headband, he looked up and mentioned I should consider buying a diamond to give my girlfriend for Christmas. I replied, "Louie, I know you like to sell rings but I'll have to give that some serious thought" and casually went back to the store. I have to admit, Louie definitely sparked my interest and later that afternoon I went back to his store and told him he was right, I wanted to look at engagement rings. I'm sure I'm not the only guy who on the spur of the moment bought an engagement ring and then wondered if the girl I bought it for would accept it. About a week before Christmas the ring came in and I was now ready for Christmas. Having that ring just sitting in that little box was like having a penny burning a hole in my pocket. I finally decided not to wait and give it to her on Christmas. The time was now. That night, we stopped by my folks' house and when we were leaving, I pulled up to the stop sign, opened the glove box and handed her the box with the ring inside. Then I asked her if she would marry me, and she said, "Yes". I know that doesn't sound very romantic, but there are times, and they still occur, where I occasionally enjoy being unconventional and spontaneous. If nothing else, it helps to keep things interesting.

From that corner of Douglas and Clinton Street, our next stop was her parents' house where I asked her father for Linda's hand. Her father just smiled and said, "I've taken care of her this far, so I expect you to take care of her from now on." And since our marriage I've made a sincere effort to try to do just that. Being engaged made the Christmas holidays extra special, and we celebrated New Year's Eve traveling to Ron and Carole's home in DeKalb, Illinois. Soon after returning, like every other girl recently engaged, Linda started making plans for our wedding.

A couple months later a sudden unexpected situation occurred. A very nice lady, Mrs. Myrtle Denny, who did our tailoring work for the stores, suddenly became ill and was admitted to the hospital. After her examination, the doctors determined she had terminal cancer and would not be going home.

Mrs. Denny lived in a small cottage-style home at 901 North Chestnut Street in LeRoy that she and her husband built in the late 1940's. Mrs. Denny was Dale's aunt and the mother of A. Lee Pray, a local attorney. When she passed away, Lee came into the store the next morning to tell Dale about her passing. After giving him the news, he began telling Dale and I about an awkward situation that occurred at the hospital shortly after his mother passed. Lee had called the funeral home and told them to come pick up his mother and take her to the funeral home. The driver, a LeRoy resident placed her on the gurney, turned around and said to Lee, "When you sell her house, I want first shot at it". It was unlike Lee to be lost for words, but the blunt request caught him completely off-guard. After leaving the hospital, the more Lee thought about the gentleman's bluntness the more upset he became. Lee made up his mind in no way would he sell his mother's house to that man. As he was finishing his story, he turned to me and said, "Aren't you getting married this summer"?

I said, "Yes I am."

Lee then said, "You'll need a place to live so you should buy my mother's house."

Now I was the one caught off-guard. I told Lee I certainly would like to, but Linda would have to look at the house and we'd have to see if we could afford it.

"Have you decided what you will be asking for it"?

Lee, still upset, replied, "Don't worry, the price will be right. Come over to the office and pick up the keys and take your girlfriend up and look at it and I'll stop back tomorrow." As he turned to leave the store, he added, "If you're interested, call Frank Trantina from the Savings and Loan and tell him to come over here and figure out what needs to be done." This entire conversation took place in less than ten minutes.

I knew we would need to start looking for a place to live but the wedding was still four months away. I knew very little about buying a home but I called Linda at work and told her the news. I also called Frank Trantina and asked him to come over to the store and explain to me the lending requirements. Frank wasted no time and a few minutes later he came in and told me the home loans required 20 percent down and 7 percent interest for a 20 year fixed loan. I told him I did not know the purchase amount, and I would need to know that to determine the amount of money we needed to secure the loan. Frank told me to get the figures and then we'll figure things out.

That evening we looked at the house and we both loved the place. The house was a small two bedroom home with tremendous possibilities. We were really excited about the possibility of buying it. The next day Lee came back and told me he called the fellow and gave him a price he knew he wouldn't pay and he had only twelve hours to give him his answer. I told Lee we really liked the house and Frank had been over to discuss the financing but we needed to know the price. He said, "I'll sell it to you for $10,000 and that's a great price for that house."

I knew the price was a bargain but I told him I needed Frank's approval for the loan to buy it. Again, talking as he was walking towards the door, he said, "Call Frank, keep the keys and we'll talk later." Frank came back and we discussed the loan. When he figured the down payment and all additional expenses, there was a problem. I had used most of my savings to buy my car. With our wedding coming up, I was short of what was needed for the down payment.

Frank looked over at Dale and said, "He works for you, loan him what he needs so we can get this deal done."

Dale was known by everyone to be a very smart businessman and somewhat tight with a dollar. I was actually shocked when he said, "OK, here's what I'll do, I agreed to give you an annual bonus every January. I'll loan you what you need, plus interest, and deduct a portion from your bonus each year until our loan is paid in full."

Frank looked at me and said, "You just bought yourself a house. I'll get the paperwork started." This was astonishing, what an odd way to buy a home, let these three guys negotiate the deal and all I had to do was say yes and OK.

Needless to say, we were very excited about buying the house and now things were really getting crazy. I was working long hours at the store, she was working at State Farm and working hard on wedding plans. Now we had a house to get ready and furnish before the wedding. Our wedding would not only be important to us but also an extra special event for her parents. Of all their seven children, Linda was their youngest, the last one to get married, and she would be the only daughter to have a church wedding. With all that was going on, we were able to find time to work on the house, shop for furniture, and finalize the wedding plans. We do have to give credit where credits are due. Without the generous help of our friends and relatives, the house would not have been ready before our wedding day.

Everything came together perfectly and the wedding day was finally near. Our rehearsal reception dinner was at the Log Cabin, and afterwards the girls went their way and my last night of single life was spent with several of my groomsmen visiting bars in Peoria into the wee hours on the morning of the wedding.

The mixture of staying out too late and the anxiety of getting married that day made it nearly impossible to sleep. Finally, I got up and went downstairs and had breakfast with relatives staying with my parents. Later that morning I put on my tux and Jim and Darlene picked me up at the gas station where I left my car, and we continued on to the church.

That afternoon on June 4, 1967, the wedding party gathered at the LeRoy Methodist Church for the ceremony. Linda's attendants included Chloe Mikel (Maid of Honor) the girl in the car when I met Linda, and Shirley Satterfield Anderson and Patsy Ryan bridesmaids. Ron Bane was best man and Lynn Banta and Jim Boaz were groomsmen. Larry Golden and David Litherland were the ushers with Reverend Jack Christian officiating.

Everyone has heard the old saying, "Opposites attract." Well our marriage was one of those very true examples of just that. Linda was very smart, salutatorian of her class, quiet, calm, very thoughtful, not a risk taker, very conservative and very satisfied simply spending time at home. It was very clear our interest and personalities were different. However, I soon found it was nice to get a different perspective and advice that I otherwise would never thought to seek. In our case, as our married life grew, we seemed to achieve the ideal balance in making decisions about our likes, dislikes, our family and working together toward a common goal for happiness. I have always felt I was a very lucky person having Linda for my wife.

Once everyone took their positions at the altar, Steve Dean, the organist started playing the bride's processional, escorted by her father, down the aisle came my very beautiful wife-to-be. With no noticeable glitches, several minutes later Reverend Christian looked at us and said, "I now pronounce you man and wife." After I kissed my wife, he turned to the audience and said, "It's my pleasure to introduce to you Mr. and Mrs. Davis."

The wedding was short, sweet and beautiful with many of our good friends and family in attendance. After our wedding a cake and punch reception was held in the church reception hall. After the reception, everyone gathered by the steps and threw rice as we exited the church. Because I didn't drive my car, we climbed in the back of Ron and Carol's car, completely covered with shoe polish and they proceeded with the customary ride around town followed by cars and honking horns. Afterwards, Jim and Darlene took us back to Bloomington where I had hidden my car. There was absolutely no way I would have taken my car to our wedding. No one was going to have the opportunity to do to my car what my friends and I had done to their cars.

Wedding Day, Linda and Jerry

With suitcases in the trunk, we were on our way to spend a week at Daytona Beach, Florida. Our first night of marriage was in Eldorado, Illinois. The next day we drove all the way to Daytona Beach and stayed at the Casa Linda Hotel on the beach. We had a great honeymoon, staying on the beach, sunbathing, seeing the sights and spending time walking along the water. Having lived in Florida and familiar with sunburns, I kept telling Linda she needed to be careful of getting sunburned, but guess what, it was me who ended up with the tops of my feet and ankles badly burned.

After several days in Daytona we drove over to Clearwater to visit my relatives. When we arrived at my grandparents' house, my grandmother came to the door and was very excited to see us. Just as we walked into the house the phone rang and it was one of my aunts asking her if we were there and what Linda looked like. Standing right next to us, my Crazy Grandma responded, "She's cute, but a little bit chubby." I'm certainly glad that I had warned Linda about my Crazy Grandma before we got there! God love her!

On the way back home, we stopped to see Linda's aunt and uncle in Vincennes, Indiana. We were shocked to find out that Linda's Grandmother Cope, who lived in Saybrook, had passed away a few days after our wedding. The family decided not to tell us because they did not want to interrupt our honeymoon.

After we arrived at our new home, I carried Linda over the threshold to start our married life together. Another young couple from LeRoy, Larry and Susie Brandt bought the house across the street from ours. Susie and I had gone to school together and she and Larry quickly became our very close friends. Many nights were spent going out or just getting together at each other's homes to visit or play cards. After several years, Susie and Larry divorced and Susie later married Kenny Heavilin. We've enjoyed their friendship and Kenny and Susie have been kind enough to come down to both our home and our cabin for visits.

Chapter 9

Several months after our marriage, there was an interesting article in the Champaign newspaper about two ladies from Nebraska who had traveled to Champaign in search of a "petrified man", supposedly buried somewhere in the Champaign area. Now why would two ladies travel all that distance searching for a petrified man? The answer; the State of Nebraska was about to hold their centennial and it was believed the petrified man was actually a creation of a J.G. Maher, a respected military leader, lawyer, politician and a well-known practical joker. In 1887 a group of archaeologists had traveled to Nebraska in search of dinosaur bones. Colonel Maher decided to have a petrified man made using a mold of a man and filling it with concrete. In the event tests may be taken on his elaborate creation, he went to the trouble to have real human skeleton bones positioned in the arms. Once completed he had it buried in front of the digging site area so they would unearth it the following spring.

As planned, after the ground thawed and the digging started, the workers found and unearthed the petrified man. It was an amazing find but they had serious doubts about it being real, so Colonel Maher suggested they drill a hole into the arm to determine what was inside. To everyone's amazement, the drilling resulted in finding real human bones inside the arm. The story went on to say, after the excitement and numerous local showings of this magnificent find, Colonel Maher became concerned about being found out so he sold the man, and the gentleman who bought it took it on a traveling road show out East. The curiosity in the petrified fellow drew crowds, but the doubt about its legitimacy also grew. The traveling show continued until it reached Champaign, Illinois. There, local authorities demanded proof of its authenticity. Not being convinced with the owner's story, the authorities decided to arrest the showman for cheating the public and ordered the owner to dispose of the hoax and get out of town. It is believed at that time the owner quickly gave the man to some local fellow to avoid having to pay to bury it. That's where the story seemed to end, but the ladies were not ready to give up.

After researching all the records about the story, they decided to travel to Champaign and attempt to find the burial site and hopefully take him back to Nebraska for the centennial celebration. Now for the part that connected the story to LeRoy.

After Dale and I read the stories in the Champaign Gazette and talking about it with a couple local old-timers, one of them said he remembered seeing a cement or petrified man being shown years ago in a local event north of LeRoy. He went on to say when it was being carried from the wagon for display, it was dropped and one of his legs broke off revealing a steel reinforcement rod inside. The break exposing the steel rod proved it was a hoax and it was no longer of any use and the owner now needed to dispose of it. He asked for some help and Alvin Sigler and several other strong young men from LeRoy assisted in giving it a proper burial. A large deep waterway was being cleaned, tiled and filled in on the north part of the LeRoy near the corner of School and Chestnut Street. The workers decided this could solve two problems; his size and weight would make good fill and it would eliminate having to dig a hole large enough to bury him in. At the time, George Rogers was a young boy but also remembered being at the event and told us he remembered the burial and could show us the exact spot where it was buried. We contacted the ladies in Nebraska and after George gave them a description of the cement man, the ladies became excited and were positive their petrified man had been found. They immediately traveled back to LeRoy and Larry Golden borrowed probing rods from the cemetery, and the ladies stood by as we started our search. The property owner had been contacted and agreed to allow us to search for the man and the ladies agreed to pay all costs in removing the object and restoring the yard surface to its previous condition after it was removal.

After a couple days we still had not located the man, and with all the local attention in town, someone jokingly suggested we contact the renowned psychic Jean Dixon, the lady who had warned of President Kennedy's death before his fatal trip to Dallas. Ms. Dixon was often interviewed on WJBC, a local radio show in Bloomington. We contacted the station and they gave us her number to call. We called her office in Chicago and later that day she returned our call. After telling her the story, to our amazement she started giving us directions where to look.

She told us to walk about 40 feet from the north edge of the property line near the alley and directly parallel with a peach, pear or fruit tree. She also suggested the petrified man may possibly actually be petrified. She continued by saying she could see a white street south of the property. We were somewhat confused because we did not see any trees near the site and did not understand the part about the white street. Back at the property we continued our search. To our surprise we found the city had just covered the black top street south of the property with white rock. As we continued our search around the yard, we found a very small branch of a fruit tree growing out of a root almost totally hidden alongside the old foundation of the old garage. We were totally surprised. Her directions appeared to be very close to where George said the man had been buried. Now we had regained our hopes but unfortunately, the property owner refused to let us continue the search. Another neighbor said the property owner was told that the ladies from Nebraska were wives of wealthy doctors, and the petrified man could possibly be worth a lot of money. She ordered us off the property and the ladies who were now running out of time, decided to stop the search and return to Nebraska.

After their return home, they had a "new" fake petrified man made out of plaster of Paris and used it for the centennial event. In parting, the ladies regretted not being able to unearth and take the petrified man home but felt sure J.G. Maher's hoax petrified man was now resting in peace in LeRoy, Illinois.

The so-called Petrified Man

Linda and I adapted very well to married life and we enjoyed living in our house on Chestnut Street. We made lots of new friends in LeRoy and often spent time visiting our family and friends living away. We also enjoyed attending local events and, whenever possible, taking short trips together.

The house was small but a great place to live because we were financially able to enjoy going places and doing things while building up our savings.

In July of 1969, people around the world were excited to finally see the first man land on moon. Hundreds of years from now no one will remember much about what happened in the 20th century - but they will remember when Neil Armstrong placed his foot down on the lunar surface and uttered those famous words; "That's one small step for man, one giant leap for mankind." A short time later the City of Chicago held a ticker- tape parade and Linda, Nancy Barling and a couple other friends from State Farm drove up to watch Neil Armstrong and Buzz Aldrin ride through the streets of Chicago.

After a couple of years being married, we decided it was time to start our family. As excited as we were about telling everyone Linda was pregnant, the news was met with far less enthusiasm at work. When I told Dale, his reaction was simply, "I guess if you never want to have money or do anything, having kids is OK."

On August 1, 1970, Linda woke up early that morning and announced it was time to go to the hospital to have our first child. After she was admitted to the hospital, I was beginning to think this was going to take days rather than hours. Finally, after 14 hours of anxiously pacing around waiting for something to happen, Linda was taken to the delivery room. Shortly afterward, Dr. Calhoun came out and told me I now had a healthy beautiful baby girl. We had predetermined if it was a girl, her name would be Jodi Lee Davis. Her middle name "Lee" came from Ron Bane's middle name and we wanted her godparents to be Ron and Carole.

It's hard to explain what went through my mind when I saw our daughter in her mother's arms for the first time. I marveled at her little fingers, checked her toes, and watched her lips scrunch up as she tried to reach her tiny fingers around anything or anyone near her. It was pretty intense, and it only took a second to fall in love with what Linda and I had created. Jodi was beautiful, even though there was only a faint trace of red hair on top of her head. But we both thought that too was cute. I was really excited about being a dad. I always loved being around kids, making them laugh, listening to the unexpected cute things they say or just the enjoyment of watching them play. I had enjoyed my years of being a kid and being around our little girl brought back some of those wonderful memories of my youth.

There was real excitement in the air when it was time to bring Jodi home. Having a family was a big change to our lives, but we soon found having a baby in our house was a real delight. Like all new parents, she became the center of our world. She was a very active child and would climb out of or onto almost anything. It didn't take long before she started standing, walking and talking. She did have quite a temper (which I think comes with a mix of Irish blood and red hair). Occasionally she would throw a tantrum to the point where we thought she would quit breathing. But after a while, she would turn right around and be happy again like nothing had happened. She was always good about going to bed. As soon as we put her down she would fall asleep within minutes. It was a wonderful sight for me to see her light up with joy when I came home from work. With my work schedule, I had less than three hours to spend with her before bedtime. It was a balancing act playing with Jodi, spending time with Linda, working on the house and spending over 65 hours a week at the store. We felt fortunate that Linda was not working and could stay home to take care of Jodi. She enjoyed being home, playing with her, taking her shopping and visiting our parents and families. Grandma Boaz was amused knowing Jodi, her new grand-daughter, was younger than one of her great- grand-children.

Not long after Jodi was born, I started having health issues. I've always been somewhat hyper, but suddenly I became extremely hyper and rapidly losing weight. I went to a doctor in Bloomington and after my examination and several tests, he said it was colitis and prescribed medicine to correct the problem. The medicine didn't help and I had dropped over thirty five pounds in four months. I had not been overweight and the weight loss became noticeable to everyone. I continued seeing the doctor but he kept insisting it was just nerves. With the excessive weight loss, profuse sweating, upset stomach and starting to not hold down food, I began to think my problem was not nerves or colitis, it may be cancer. Over the holidays we'd planned to go out for New Year's Eve. That morning, I was extremely sick and thought I had now caught the flu. I decided to call our local doctor, Dr. Pliura, and asked him if I could come over to his office and get a shot. He agreed to see me and when I walked into his office, he looked at me and said, "What the hell is wrong with you?"

Doctor Pliura was a regular customer at Webb's but I hadn't seen him in the last several months. He continued on by saying, "Jerry, there's something terribly wrong." He quickly examined me and said, "'Go home and get your wife and some pajamas, you're going to the hospital right away. I'll be there later." Before leaving he gave me three shots, I went home and told Linda what Dr. Pliura said. She put Jodi in the car and we dropped her off at Linda's parents' house on our way to Saint Joseph hospital. By the time I was in my room I had a serious nose bleed and my heart was pounding rapidly. Dr. Pliura, who worked around the clock, stopped by later that evening and was back in my room early the next morning. After two days of tests, the doctors came in and told us they thought I may have histoplasmosis, a sometimes life-threatening fungal disease normally caused by inhaling spores of rat or bird droppings for long periods of time. Having returned from Vietnam three years earlier, I thought the prognosis could very well be possible. Dr. Pliura ordered more tests. When the news got back to LeRoy, Judson Chubbuck, a retired lieutenant colonel in the Army Reserves, called the VA to see how and where returning veterans were being treated for this disease. However, the latest test concluded I did not have histoplasmosis, instead I had a goiter and a severe case of hyperthyroidism. The doctors explained before I could have surgery, I would be taking medicine for several months to control my thyroid and regain my weight and strength.

After five months, I was much better and was ready for the operation. On May 2nd, I was admitted into the hospital for thyroid surgery. After a four-hour operation, I woke up in my room, glad it was finally over, but I was in much more pain than I had anticipated. Later that night, my throat felt like it was ready to burst open and I became very sick. At 3:30 a.m., the doctors called for a surgical room, Linda was called to come back to the hospital, and I was taken back to the operating room. This operation was to stop internal bleeding caused by a hematoma. For eight days I was in the intensive care unit until I was strong enough to be released. The second operation was successful and in a few weeks I was back to work, gaining weight and recovering well.

Linda and I had discussed having another child and decided now would be a good time. This attempt resulted in Linda having a miscarriage. Jodi was growing quickly and we decided to try again.

The following year on July 7, 1973, we welcomed our new son Bradley James Davis to the family. This being our second child, I thought it would be less exciting but that was not the case at all. Again, like all fathers, I started checking him over to make sure there were ten fingers and ten toes. Within minutes, he managed to look up at me giving me a faint smile. When I picked him up, I had forgotten how small a newborn baby was but he seemed quite content to snuggle in his daddy's arms. Having a son is a great gift to a father. Linda and I now had both a daughter and a son and we would soon find out our family was complete. After the delivery, Dr. Calhoun told us he was retiring, closing his practice and moving to Arizona. Based on Linda's previous female problems and difficultly getting pregnant, he strongly suggested we should not have any more children. We respected his honesty and felt fortunate and blessed in having our two healthy children. Brad was not only our last child, but he was also the last grandchild born to both our parents. Brad's middle name came from Linda's father and brother's middle names James.

Another surprise came just before Brad was born. My grandparents had flown up to visit the family and we asked them, along with my parents over for dinner. Grandpa Davis was very excited about the baby and kept saying, "I hope it's a boy." He was concerned that a Davis boy needed to carry on the Davis family name. My father was the only boy and I was the only boy. Two days before they flew back to Florida, Brad was born. This gave my grandparents the opportunity to go to the hospital and meet Brad. Brad's great-grandfather's wish came true; another generation with the name Davis was born and we both hoped other generations of Davis' would follow.

Several months later, my grandpa went to the hospital for a prostate operation and the day after coming out of the surgery he died in his hospital room from a heart attack. He was a wonderful grandfather and I loved him dearly. I was so happy I had the opportunity to know him, and I was thankful both he and my grandmother had the opportunity to visit us and meet our children.

My grandfather enjoyed collecting elephants. After his death, I was given three from his collection. This inspired both Joan and I to start our own elephant collections. It's my hope someone else in my family will enjoy some from my collection and carry on the family tradition. I will admit, they'll be quite a few to pass around.

When we brought Brad home, we both wondered how Jodi would adjust to having a little baby brother. We were pleasantly surprised at how much she enjoyed having Brad around. Brad started crawling and walking and before long there was a lot of activity going on at our house from morning to night. It's amazing how fast children grow. Linda continued staying home with the kids. With my long hours, it was obvious most of the responsibilities in raising our children rested solely on Linda's shoulders. It seemed when I came home, it was time to eat supper, I'd play with the kids and in a couple hours it was time for them to go to bed.

Family in 1978

As our children continued to grow, we enjoyed doing things with them and holidays and birthdays were always special times for everyone. Jodi and Brad were totally different. They had different personalities, different interests, and at times, they each required our undivided attention, and that's OK. I can't say we were strict parents, but I hope they believed we listened to them and tried to be fair. Linda and I have always had a mutual respect for one another. At our 40th anniversary I was asked our secret to a happy marriage, my reply, "Linda and I have never had a major argument. We don't always agree, but we always made a point of not hurting one another with harsh words. After all, once words come out of your month, you can't take them back." We also never argued or fussed in front of the kids. Any differences we had were our problem, not our children's, and when a problem did occur, it was discussed privately between the two of us. The best part of having differences is making up.

Now that our children were quickly growing it was obvious our small two bedroom house no longer was big enough for our family. The time has come to either find something bigger or remodel and add on. We both enjoy antique shopping and liked the idea of finding an old house to put all our "treasures". We started looking but couldn't find a home we really liked. Finally we decided to stop looking and remodel by adding another bedroom, bath, garage and outdoor deck to our house. As happens so many times, as soon as the remodeling was about to be completed, the old large stately home of Dud and Vera Berry came up for auction to settle their estate. We looked at it and it was exactly what we wanted. There was lots of work to be done but we decided we would go ahead and buy it.

At about the same time, Linda's sister, Eileen, who lived in Chicago had just lost her husband, Jerry, and wanted to move back to the area. She decided to buy our house while we were working on the other house. The remodeling project took hours of work, but again, with the help of family and friends, walls were torn out, a new large kitchen was added, rooms were painted, plumbing was updated and rolls and rolls of wallpaper were carefully hung on walls. Finally the work inside was mostly done and we started moving in.

It was a grand old house. The previous owner, Dud Berry, had an insurance agency for many years in LeRoy and he and his wife had lived in the house for over fifty five years. They had no children. She was once a LeRoy socialite who enjoyed entertaining but over the years suffered from severe mental depression and later become a total recluse. In the evenings she would sit in the dark and not allow Dud to turn on the lights or watch TV. To avoid sitting there in darkness, Dud started spending his evenings going across the street to watch ball games in the school gym. After the games ended, he would go home, and because his wife had often threatened him, he locked himself in his bedroom and went to bed.

Several years earlier he had shared that story with me and when we moved into the home, there were several hook locks still on the door of the small upstairs bedroom and scratches on the floor where he had nightly moved the dresser back and forth to block the door. After he died, in honor of his many years of continual attendance, the school gym where he had spent so much of his time was renamed "The Dud Berry Gymnasium."

After Jodi and Brad were both in school, Linda went back to work at State Farm part time. It worked out perfectly; she could drop the two of them off on her way to work and was home when they got out of school.

My mother was again working at Dewey's Cleaners and he decided it was finally time for him to retire. He discussed his retirement with Mom, and before long she was finally the proud owner of her very own business. Dewey was not known for keeping the place clean or organized so the family went to work fixing the place up to make it more presentable. I bought an old wooden store sign from an antique store and repainted the name, LeRoy Cleaners, and we placed it on the front of the building. Mom loved having her own business and with her determination and hard work, the business continued to grow. Dad was still working at Eureka Williams and helped her on Saturday mornings. After a few years, Dad added a section to the front of the cleaners and started selling clocks and candles. Most of the clocks and candles sold, but not to the point where it warranted restocking. The hot item during that time was the CB radio. CB's for years had been the primary communication source for truckers, but suddenly they became the rage for car owners as well. Dad started selling CB's and accessories. He sold quite a few radios, but without offering service repair, that business too, gradually went by the wayside.

After many years of hard work, Dad retired, Mom sold the cleaners, they loaded up their belongings and moved to Clearwater, Florida. There they started working for the owners of a large condo complex. Mom showed potential renters the condos and Dad was doing minor maintenance, changing light bulbs, changing air filters and setting up cleaning and repair appointments for contractors. It wasn't long before they invested in a residential maid service business called "Daily Maid Service".

My uncle Jake, who was semi-retired, had rented some space to start a clock repair shop. Mom and Dad shared the rent and ran their business across the hall. At first they did well, but then things took a turn for the worst. Both my parents and my aunt and uncle became friends with another businessman in the building. He had created a marvelous, completely fail-proof investment plan and needed investors. They suddenly appeared to be almost sworn to secrecy, giving us very little details about this wonderful venture. Joan, Judy and I continually warned them it sounded like a possible scam, but they went ahead and invested their savings. Their newfound friend was in fact a con-man, and before long, their savings was gone. Unhappy about their loss and having to deal with the complicated tax reporting of the cleaning service, they closed their business and decided to move back to LeRoy. That move turned out timely because LeRoy High School had an opening for a school janitor. With Dad's past janitorial experience, he applied and got the job. The move was also perfect in another way; while they were living in Florida, the LeRoy cleaners had burned down. The owner rebuilt the business but wanted to sell it. After knowing my parents were moving back, he sold it back to my parents.

For a year or so things seemed to be going well. However, one night Mom called and said something was wrong with Dad. I rushed to their house and found him sitting in his chair. It was apparent he had just suffered a stroke. After returning home from the hospital, he was no longer able to work, and Mom now was trying to take care of Dad and keep the cleaners running. Unable to do both, she finally sold the business to devote full time caring for my father. After five years at home, it was obvious she could no longer provide the care he needed and he was moved to the LeRoy Manor nursing home. He remained there another five years before passing away in 1991.

Strokes affect everyone differently, and in my father's case, it was sad to see him become this little cranky old man who was far too demanding of my mother. He would tell her to take him places to visit or eat and once there, abruptly demand she take him home. He also became inconsiderate of others and the saddest thing was how his grandchildren still remember him. Most of them were very young during his illness and remember him only as their grouchy old Grandpa. They were not able to remember him as the good natured friendly person he was before his stroke.

I never really fully understood my father, particularly when asking him questions about his early years before he married my mother. He certainly enjoyed talking about many subjects but he seldom brought up his youth or the years he spent in the CCC's. I realize the Depression created many difficult problems for young people, and the memory of those times was something they just did not want to reflect on or share. I would bring up the subject about his childhood but he avoided talking about his early life.

Another puzzle was the time period he spent serving in the CCC's. It appeared he enjoyed it as he kept a large scrapbook of photos taken of the places he traveled and the guys he served with, but he never talked about that either. There was one exception; Hilton Moss, a fellow who lived in LeRoy, was talking to my dad one day and mentioned he had also been in the CCC's. During their discussion they realized they were in the same camp in the Northwest at the same time. After talking to Hilton, Dad looked through his photo albums and found a photo he had taken of Hilton standing on a bridge in either Washington or Oregon. That was the only person I ever heard my dad mention of the many men he had served with for over five years.

Shortly before Dad passed away, I bought the small business building downtown next to the cleaners. It was formerly a beauty shop owned by Dewey Holderly's wife, Dorothy. It was a single-story brick building with a business office in the front area and a small one bedroom apartment in the back. At the rear of the property was a small fenced-in yard and a parking area. It certainly wasn't a palace but once remodeled, Mom moved into the apartment and loved living there. Everything was within walking distance and she enjoyed spending time planting flowers in her small yard. Weather permitting, she took daily walks and stopped in the downtown stores to visit with the shop owners. She and her little dog Mindy became a common sight walking around the city park or back and forth between the stores and her apartment. She enjoyed visiting friends, going on bus tours and going out with her lady friends. They often went to dances in Bloomington or to each other's homes to play cards.

Almost every morning I would stop by for a cup of coffee before going on to work. Over our coffee we discussed everything from what was on the TV the night before, politics or what was going on around town. Those morning visits are what I miss the most. She continued living there until she could no longer drive because of poor eyesight. She started falling and had difficulties going up and down the basement stairs. After several mini strokes, she finally agreed to move into the Hillcrest Assisted Living facility. We had already sold our home and moved to Alabama before Mom's health took a turn for the worst. Joan and Judy watched over her until she was later placed into LeRoy Manor where she passed away in 2006. She was a wonderful mother, a good friend and I miss her very much. She, unlike my father, enjoyed telling me about her early years and all the good times she had with her family and friends while growing up in Cadillac, Michigan. I now often think of questions I wished I had asked and now realize the answers to those questions will never be known. When I think of my mother I reflect on a wonderful quote from Abraham Lincoln; "All I am, or ever hope to be, I owe to my angel Mother."

I have many fond memories of my childhood, growing up, getting married and living near my parents. Even in their absence I continue to think of my parents often. My sisters and I loved our parents even though at times we became frustrated with all their moving, job changes and unfortunately, a general lack of concern for what tomorrow would bring. However, with that said, I'm sure over the years we too caused them frustration and other personal challenges as well. I must admit, from an early age while bouncing around somewhat aimlessly, it did indeed teach us to be flexible, take things in stride, learn from our experiences and have fun along the way. Our parents were good parents. They were kind, generous, and as a family, we sure-as-shootin had a hell of lot of fun during all our many travels and adventures. Our less than perfect, and somewhat wacky past, is evidence the only thing you need to create an adventure is to be spontaneous, think of an idea, and be willing to give it a try. And try we did. All those vivid memories of our childhood is something I would never want to change. All in all, we were blessed and life was good!

Linda and I enjoyed living in our "big white house on Center Street" and watching the kids grow up, active in sports, hobbies and school events. We also enjoyed having their friends over to our house for visits or stay-overs. Because our home was large, it became the center for family gatherings. Linda is a wonderful cook and especially enjoyed decorating the house and planning for holidays. The Boaz family Thanksgiving and Christmas gatherings were always held on the weekend after the holidays to allow each family to spend their holidays at home. The weekend holiday dinners at our house would often bring up to forty people for dinner. The Davis family was much smaller and we spent time together on Thanksgiving Day and Christmas was usually held on Christmas Eve. The Davis Christmas gathering was often blessed with Aunt Judy bringing the words to songs printed out and having everyone sign along while Linda played the piano. I enjoyed all these events and while traveling around the country working. I'd search out a cool magic store and bring home a few magic tricks to perform for the nieces and nephews. I wasn't much of a magician but I gave it my best. I soon found those young nieces and nephews were a hard crowd to please. They sat way to close and it was apparent they were being more entertained watching my blunders than watching the trick itself. I refused to give up and was pleasantly surprised when they showed up the next year asking when the magic show would start. It seemed impossible to believe how fast our kids grew and became teenagers. That brought about many new challenges - pets, friends, report cards, bicycles, dating, curfews, problems riding their dad's motor scooter, and one of all parents' worst fears, driving cars. Like most siblings, they constantly tormented each other and that in itself, drove me crazy. To resolve the problem when traveling, Linda would sit in the back with one of the kids and the other would sit up front with me. Worrying about your kids is just part of the process of having children and that never ends regardless of their age. While the children were home our lives continued to be busy and we managed to be a close family. We both enjoyed being parents, but I will always regret not being home more to help Linda out and being with the kids more during their early years.

Our children are now both grown and on their own. Both have jobs and own their own homes. We are very proud of them and love them both, and they will never know the joy they have brought to both our lives. When we're gone, we hope our children and their children can look back on Linda and me with love and fond memories of being with us, listening to us talk about our lives, and hearing about the early lives and events of their parents. We hope for nothing more.

I'm sure the kids may disagree, but they were not always perfect, but who would want them to be? We feel blessed to have had them for children and thank them for having stayed out of trouble and becoming responsible adults. With that said, there are stories that could be told about them growing up, but I feel those stories would best be told by themselves and I'm sure their versions would be somewhat different than our memories of those events. I get a chuckle when I'm reminded not to bring up some of those stories in front of our grandchildren. Being perfect is nearly impossible but in our family's case, my sister's and I were perfect. Our close friends and family members have heard my mother say many times that we were perfect children. It seemed the older she got the more she would tell others she couldn't understand why parents today could not control their kids. She followed that remark up with, "I had perfect children and I would have never allowed my kids to get away with doing something like that." Respectfully, I'll have to somewhat disagree. Speaking for myself, I'm of the opinion she may have either been in total denial or one of those mini strokes could have caused her to have a total loss of memory. It is, however, nice to know that I've been completely exonerated from all my dastardly deeds and the crazy juvenile antics I did while growing up.

Chapter 10

Webb's Men's Wear

Working 16 years at Webb's in LeRoy was a great experience. It required me to spend not only many hours in the store, but after hours as well. It was not uncommon for someone to call me at home and ask me to open the store for an emergency, going over to the funeral homes to measure bodies for clothing before funerals, and traveling to the merchandise mart in Chicago on weekends to buy inventory. It also included being actively involved with other merchants in the business community. In an effort to promote business, merchants worked together on promotions and advertising. Like other rural communities, LeRoy was facing many changes and the buying habits of residents were changing as well. More and more people started driving further away to shop in other towns and at new larger stores like the new shipping store. Local shoppers also started buying groceries in the new chain grocery stores being built in cities across the country. Local families started shopping at the new malls which provided a much larger variety of stores and a broader selection of merchandise. In an effort to counter these new trends, LeRoy merchants and the LeRoy Promotion Committee started holding larger promotions and special events to keep local citizens shopping in town and bring in new customers from surrounding communities. I enjoyed working on planning promotions and joined the Merchant's Association, the Jaycees, American Legion, and served on the board of the LeRoy Fall Festival. While doing all that, our children were now in school, and like all parents, we became both interested and involved in local school issues. In 1976, I decided to run and was elected to the LeRoy Board of Education. When my four year term on the school board ended, I then ran for city council and served 16 years as a City Councilman.

My original intent was always to someday take over Webb's Men's Wear but after 16 years and Dale's unfortunate health situation, I realized that was not going to happen and it was time to find something else to do. The one job I was most interested in was outside sales. I talked to several of our clothing salesmen and inquired about some possible upcoming sales positions that matched up with products we sold. Most companies felt the real problem was most inside retail sales people normally found it difficult to adjust to the challenges of outside sales and got tired of the quotas, the travel and ended up returning to retail. My mind was made up. I knew I needed to leave Webb's and was convinced I would find a job in outside sales. I interviewed with Red Wing Shoe Company but there were no territories in Illinois open at that time. I was approached by a merchant's group in Farmington, Illinois to consider taking over a clothing store there that had closed after the owner's sudden death. It was a generous offer, but after seeing the condition of the store and its outdated inventory, that store, too, in my opinion, was beyond rebuilding.

Dale's health problems continued and he became incapable of running a business. He stayed in his small office in the back of the store most mornings and around 2:00 p.m. he'd go to the tavern and stay there the rest of the afternoon. The store had been Dale's entire life. For the first 30 years the store was spotless, he carried the latest in men's fashions, the inventory was always fresh, there was something for almost everybody, but that had changed. Over the last couple years the business was being neglected. Dale no longer paid attention to the inventory and was no longer concerned about the store's appearance or its profitability. He loved cats and over the last several years, he and Joanne had amassed over 30 cats living in their home. He started buying cat food by the cases to feed not only their cats, but also to feed stray cats in the alleys uptown.

For more than 16 years I was a loyal employee to Dale and both he and his wife, Joanne, had been very good to me. It was difficult to walk away from the business, but the time had come to seriously make a career change. With the business rapidly falling apart, Dale refused to discuss with me or anyone else his business or drinking problems. The breaking point came when he brought a stray cat into the store as a pet. At first he kept it down in the basement, but before long he let it come upstairs and wander around the store. That was the closest I ever came to being fired. Customers started complaining about the hair, claw marks on the clothes and the smell in the store. Finally, one day when I knew Dale would be gone for a while, I grabbed the cat, put a sign on the door saying "Be Right Back" and drove the cat outside of town and dumped it off. When Dale came back, he looked everywhere for that cat. I told him it must have run out the front door when someone either came in or left the store. He was furious, and I could tell he knew I did something with that cat and mentioned he better not find out I did. For years Dale had discussed of one day retiring and selling the business to me, but over the last couple years, with circumstances being what they were, I lost all interest in buying the stores. The business that he had worked so hard to build over 40 years had declined to the point the chances of restoring the business to profitability was insurmountable.

When I started sending out resumes, my cousin Linda Hampton and her husband Bob moved to St. Louis from Florida. Now living so close, they frequently visited us on weekends. Bob had recently accepted a position as National Sales Manager with his company and was well aware of my situation at Webb's. On one of their visits Bob offered me a position with his company. It was for a territorial sales representative for Illinois, Wisconsin, the lower half of Minnesota, half of South Dakota, Iowa, the eastern half of Missouri and the northeastern quarter of Arkansas. This was a massive territory, and he explained with the downturn of the building industry, he made a special effort to make the territory large enough for it to be profitable for both me and his company. A month later I accepted the job and I will always be grateful to Bob for giving me the opportunity to start my career in territorial sales.

The next day I told Dale I was leaving. He was shocked and offered me more money to stay. However, money was not the issue. The problem was the business was in shambles and Dale's original offer to sell me the business was no longer of any value. After my leaving he remained in the store and it continued to decline. The following year the Farmer City store closed and Dale started closing the LeRoy store for hours at a time. In less than two years after I left he died at home.

Working at Webb's Men's Wear over the years had been rewarding for me and my family, and I thoroughly enjoyed it except for the last couple years. Not only did I like the clothing business, but working in downtown LeRoy gave me the opportunity to really know and enjoy people from LeRoy and be of assistance to the many regular customers who came into the store. We sold dress clothing and shoes to professionals and office workers, work clothing and work boots to laborers and farmers, clothes to students, and rented tuxedos for weddings and local school proms.

It was always enjoyable making friends with the many people who came into the store. Some shopped and others just stopped in to visit or kill time while their wives were shopping in other stores.

Over those years it's amazing how well I got to know some of those people. I not only learned about their families, I learned their buying habits, the type of clothing they wore , what they liked and didn't like and even knew many of our customer's shoe sizes. Some had unusual buying habits. For years one wife told us she only bought her husband's suits at what she called "a high end clothing store in Springfield". After purchasing the suit she would bring it in our store and buy shirts and ties to match. A businessman from a nearby town faithfully came in every year to buy his employees their Christmas presents. He would tell us, "I won't give them cash because they'll just spend it on what they don't need. What they need is warm clothing and work boots. This is how much each can spend this year so help them pick out what they want and send me the bill."

As soon as the Johnny Carson clothing line came out we started stocking his suits and ties. They became so popular, ladies would come into the store to see if we carried the same one they'd seen him wearing on his TV show the night before. Dorothy Wilson was another lady we enjoyed seeing come in at Christmas time. Dorothy's husband was blind and her son, who I had known in my earlier years, lived out west. Every December she would walk in and say, "I hope you aren't busy because I have Christmas presents I need wrapped." I would go out to her car and carry the box full of gifts inside and start wrapping. Then we'd put them in a shipping box and help her take them to the post office. For many years Dorothy was a cook at the elementary school and was well known for her exceptional homemade pies and cakes. Our reward for helping her each year was receiving two fresh homemade pies. To us, it was a great exchange.

I have fond memories of the many people who stopped in Webb's and shopped in LeRoy. They were farmers, businessmen, city residents and people from several neighboring towns. Over time, the store became a regular meeting place and several of the guys stopped by almost daily. They came mostly to visit, find out what was going on around town or give us an update on news they just heard at the park or in the local restaurants. I found it interesting hearing those stories dating back 30 or 40 years about forgotten events; stories of fires, accidents, crimes and interesting historical narratives about families who once lived in LeRoy. One old gentleman told me, "In the old days, everybody was so poor the only thing they had to talk about was how poor they were, and the only exciting things they heard about was 'tall-tales from people who had enough money to go somewhere other than LeRoy." Most of these patrons were descendants from several generations of old LeRoy families. I always laughed when someone I didn't know would come in, talk to the guys and then leave, I would ask who they were and like an FBI computer, they'd spit out the person's name, how long they had lived in town, their family ties and occasionally other interesting bits of personal information. Over time, several of these "regulars" also became my good friends. They were very considerate, and if a customer came into the store they'd leave. However, if we weren't busy, they'd stay for a while and visit. When we were extremely busy and needed something taken over to the other store, we'd load the merchandise in Dale's car and they'd make the delivery. I have to say, I enjoyed the fact that they came in and I enjoyed their friendship and all our conversations. From a political prospective, Webb's was the Republican Headquarters of LeRoy. At one time Dale was the McLean County Republican Chairman, and many county and state candidates stopped in the store when visiting LeRoy. Unlike today and before TV, candidates actually campaigned in large cities and rural communities seeking votes for upcoming elections. Political party caravans would come into town in cars and trucks carrying signs and candidates and supporters with large speakers loudly asking everyone to get out and vote for their candidates.

In rural communities, local voters have a different approach to politics. Like everywhere else, local voters affiliated

275

themselves with one of the two National parties, many times the exact same party their parents supported. However, when it comes to local elections, most local voters have less allegiance to their party when voting for local leaders. As it should be, local elections are usually won by the candidate the voters know and feel would do the best job. National politics was far different and, from my viewpoint, played much like the game of baseball. Sides are picked and no one wants their side to lose. Several of our regular customers were hard-core Democrats and frequently came into the store not only to shop, but to engage in light- hearted political discussions. I quickly found that to be a challenge because, even our Democratic friends had good intentions, it was my opinion they were obviously poor misguided souls. When political discussions came up, eventually someone would throw out a remark to fire up the group. If tempers started to flare, someone would realize the subject needed to be changed and tempers would cool down. I've always been amused how some adults never outgrow their childhood behavior.

A couple of the guys in the "store gang" were also regulars who sat in the city park. There they'd listen to all of the gossip and lies from the other bench sitters. After hearing the latest news, including the "real inside scoop", they'd come into the store like a newspaper delivery boy yelling out "Extra, Extra, Read all about it!" The only problem was the news was normally totally untrue and the guys in the park were delighted in knowing someone would soon be repeating the stories conjured up for their own amusement.

Gene Brown was a Democrat farmer and a good customer who always enjoyed stopping in to discuss upcoming elections. After the election, regardless of who won or lost, he would come in the front door and either smile because his party won or graciously concede his party's loss. I had great admiration for this man. He farmed south of town on 80 acres, raised eight or more children, all great kids, everyone in the family worked hard, the kids never complained about helping with the hogs, and most of his kids attended or graduated from college. The Brown family enjoyed football and I'm sure there are still kids from the Brown clan playing football for LeRoy High. I did have the opportunity to pull off a good joke on Gene. When Jimmy Carter won the election for president, I'd read in *U.S. News and World Report* where President-elect Carter wanted to invite common people to attend his inauguration. In the article it listed the address where to write for a personal invitation. I sent my request and a couple weeks later I received a huge envelope with the official invitations to both the inauguration and a couple of the inaugural balls. The packet included maps and other information needed when visiting Washington, D.C. I anxiously waited for Gene to stop by. When he did, I asked him if he knew of any local Democrats who were invited or planned on attending Carter's upcoming inauguration.

Gene replied with his typical smile. "They don't invite local folks to those things unless you've contributed thousands of dollars to the party." Immediately, I picked up the envelope off the counter and handed it to him. As he was looking through the packet with my name printed on it, he said, "I can't believe Carter would ever invite anyone from around here to go, let alone a darn Republican. Where did you get this?"

I replied, "In the mail. I guess he must like having a few good Republicans around."

His reply,"Ya, like hell!" I never fessed up to Gene how I got the invitation but I certainly got a laugh out of the look on his face, and I still have that packet in one of my boxes of political souvenirs.

During those years, there were a few unusual occurrences that stand out in my mind. The one most unusual involved a motorcycle gang wedding in the LeRoy city park. A local young man, Bobby Head, known by residents as "Cabbage Head," was a member of a notorious central Illinois motorcycle gang from the Peoria area. Bobby was a tall, lean, very polite fellow who at times could be somewhat unpredictable. To the city's surprise, Bobby and his girlfriend decided to get married and have the wedding ceremony in the city park. The town was a-buzz with concerns because Bobby told everyone the entire gang of well over 100 was invited to attend the "biker wedding" in the park. Bobby and his family had been loyal customers of ours for many years. On the day of the wedding, the gang came into town. The riders and their girlfriends were dressed in their riding gear, dew rags tied around their foreheads and gang patches proudly displayed on the back and fronts of their black leather jackets and vests. The local traffic suddenly increased as curious residents started driving around the park staring out their car windows at this most unusual site. Downtown merchants came out of their stores and stood on the sidewalk to watch what was going on. Shortly before the wedding, Bobby realized they forgot to get a photographer. Bobby came running over to the store and said, "Jerry, we need a photographer, someone told me you have a camera and know how to take pictures." I told him I had one, but it was at home and I'm certainly not much of a photographer." Bobby smiled and said, "Can you go get it?"

Dale was standing next to me and said, "Go ahead." So I went home, got my camera and hurried back to the park. When I arrived there were well over 50 motorcycles parked around the bandstand. It took only a few seconds to realize the gang members were big, rough and intimidating. With the exception of the bride and groom's parents, the only two people dressed in a suit and tie were the minister and me. The minister was a small frail gentleman, and totally unaware he was there to perform a "biker" wedding ceremony. He was extremely nervous but suddenly stated his objections to the wedding party standing on the bandstand drinking beer as the ceremony was about to start. I too, was a little uneasy as the gang members seemed curious why I was going around taking pictures. Bobby finally told everyone I was a friend and he'd asked me to be his photographer. From that point on, everyone was friendly and the minister promptly conducted the ceremony and afterward quietly disappeared. After the ceremony, Bobby and his wife walked down the steps where his Harley-Davidson motorcycle proudly stood ready. The bride suddenly unzipped the back of her wedding gown and dropped it to the sidewalk revealing the jeans and top she had carefully hidden under her wedding dress. With loud cheers and everyone clapping, they climbed on his Harley. Within seconds the other gang members mounted their motorcycles and with the thunderous roar from the engines echoing between the downtown buildings, the procession proceeded down Center Street. After riding around town they headed up on the Lexington blacktop to the reception party at Dawson Lake. The last photo I took of the wedding was of Bobby and his bride leading the procession with her holding him tightly with one arm, and her other hand holding the wedding veil on her head as it flowed in the wind. I was invited to attend the reception but respectfully declined. I felt it would be in my best interest to miss the reception and return to work. Thank goodness the pictures turned out OK and Bobby was very happy with them.

Unfortunately the marriage did not last very long. A few years later Bobby was killed along with a girlfriend on his motorcycle. A lady motorist did not see him approaching her car and turned in front of him just as they were riding into LeRoy. His funeral included a long motorcycle procession from the funeral home to the cemetery.

After leaving Webb's Men's Wear, I started my career as a sales representative for Proko Industries in Dallas, Texas. Proko produced exterior coating products and dry wall materials to contractors and commercial accounts. My territory covered a three state area. Proko also sold radiant heat ceiling systems in residential homes and large commercial buildings. One of the largest projects I worked on was a radiant heat ceiling application in a new high rise condominium along Chicago's "Magnificent Mile" on Lake Shore Drive. At the time it was considered to be one of the most fashionable condominiums in Chicago. This is the building where Oprah Winfrey now lives. At least I can say I played a very small part in keeping Oprah happy and warm.

It was nice to no longer have to work on weekends. I now could enjoy spending more time with the family, working on the house and the opportunity to take vacations. Our first vacation was a trip to Florida, Disney Word and Epcot Center. Looking back, it was one of our very favorite vacations. Everyone had fun and enjoyed the rides and spending time together. We were absolutely fascinated with the wonderful Walt Disney theme parks.

After spending a couple years with Proko I was offered a

position as a sales representative with Pitney Bowes, the number one supplier of mailing equipment in the world. My territory was Bloomington, Champaign and Pontiac.

Working for Pitney Bowes presented me with new challenges. It was exciting for me to be working with highly trained professionals and receiving extensive sales and product training courses. I spent many hours doing what I should have done in school, continually learning and setting aside time to study for certification exams.

I enjoyed traveling my territory and visiting the wide variety of businesses and meeting some very interesting people. On one of my trips to Pontiac, I arrived for an appointment at an auto dealership and upon arriving, the parking lot and showroom were completely packed with people.

I went inside and asked to see the business owner. That's when I found out why everyone was there. They were having auditions for "extras" in a movie to be later filmed in Pontiac. After I talked to the receptionist, a lady asked me if I was there for an audition. I responded no, and she asked me if I would consider having my picture taken for a part as an extra. I said sure, and she went on to tell me they needed both local and business type people and very few business people had showed up. After taking my picture, I then met with the dealership's owner and returned to Bloomington. At the time, I was thinking back on all the practices, memorizing lines and hard work I had put into delivering that perfect performance in our high school play. Maybe with all that training and experience I could nab a part in a major Hollywood production. A month later one Saturday morning I received a call telling me to drive up to Pontiac. They were filming and I was needed as an extra. They added I should plan on being there the entire day and bring a suit, sport coat, sweater but no cameras were allowed. When I arrived the large cameras were in place and the shooting had already begun. The movie was "Grandview USA". The stars were Jamie Lee Curtis, Patrick Swayze, C. Thomas Howell, Troy Donahue, Jennifer Jason Leigh, and Joan and John Cusack, now all well- known stars. Before the movie's release, the *Pantagraph* wrote an article about how local people were upset with the cast's conduct during the filming and how most of the local people's parts had been edited out. After reading the article, I never saw the movie at the theater. Finally, a year or so later I rented it. To my surprise, I was in two different scenes, but they were both so small I had to tell people in advance when my part was coming. All in all it lasted less than a couple seconds and then I was gone. I guess I can say I did have a couple seconds of fame, and that may be stretching it, but it was fun. I was paid $55.00, ate supper in the cast members' tent and got to meet most of the stars. I only wish I had taken my camera because several people did and the stars were happy to pose with everyone. To my disappointment, I was not discovered and all chances of my becoming a star were gone. I do want to add Grandview USA was a terrible movie!

One morning in late January, a co-worker, Don Payne and I took a break to have lunch and drove to the Grand Cafe in downtown Bloomington. As we entered the doors of the restaurant, people started getting up from their tables and gathering in the bar in front of the TV. The space shuttle Challenger had just exploded. Everyone watched in silence as the station replayed the launch from its liftoff to the explosion. Tears were in people's eyes and others left the restaurant in silence without finishing their meals. It was certainly a sad day in America to watch those seven brave astronauts die right before your eyes.

From Pitney Bowes I accepted a sales position with MCI Telecommunications. With the rapid growth and advancements in business applications telecommunications was differently the place to be. The position was Bloomington/Normal State Farm Insurance and Country Companies. I found this a great opportunity and it allowed me to concentrate my efforts on only a select few accounts. The vacation package also allowed Linda and I to expand our travels to some faraway places. Our first long distant place was Hawaii for our 25th wedding anniversary. We stayed a week in a condo located near a small fishing village on the southwest coast of Oahu and we drove all around the entire island enjoying the sights. The second week we flew to five other islands renting six cars in seven days. It definitely was a wonderful vacation.

Jerry and Linda's 25th wedding anniversary

The next trip we traveled to London and then on to Ireland to take a bed and breakfast tour starting in Shannon, traveling around Ireland and ending in Dublin. We enjoyed the trip so well we decided to extend our stay a few days and rent a car. Driving in Ireland and driving with the steering wheel on the wrong side, traveling the narrow roads and using the roundabouts can be sometimes extremely challenging. Linda found it to not only to be a challenge, but rather a potential life threatening situation trying to stay calm as I drove. Part of that may have been caused when we were leaving the airport. The traffic was heavy and I suddenly made a wrong turn and realized I was driving around the roundabout the wrong way. Horns were honking and people were waving, and the waves appeared to not be of a friendly type. Finally, I slowly became accustomed to driving and we found there's not a friendlier or fun loving country to visit than Ireland, the country of my ancestors. I love Ireland. It's a beautiful country with hundreds of small villages sprinkled throughout the landscape with hundreds of small pubs, great food and gracious fun-loving people. Once you walk through the door of an Irish pub you're greeted with friendly smiles, everyone is willing to talk to you and share wonderful stories, and the pub grub is fantastic. It's far more than just fun and great food, it's a long lasting wonderful experience. Especially when your meal comes with a Guinness, the cure all for what ills you. I agree with Sigmund Freud's assessment of the Irish; "This is one race of people for whom psychoanalysis is of no use whatsoever."

Our visit to Ireland

After three years working for MCI, I expected a position with AT&T on the State Farm National account team, one of AT&T's largest customers in the country. I also supported the Archer Daniel Midland account in Decatur with their domestic and international data applications. Linda and I continued taking vacations and the following year traveled with Linda's brother and sister in- law, Jim and Darlene, to England and France. We very much enjoyed traveling through cities, villages and country sides and riding the Chunnel high speed train between London and Paris.

I stayed with AT&T for over nine years before leaving and accepting a position with WorldCom Telecommunications as the National Sales Manager for the State Farm account.

In August of 2001 I was scheduled to attend an award ceremony to be held in Las Vegas on September 20th. Weeks before the event everyone was excited, but nine days before leaving everything changed suddenly. On the morning of September 11th, the two towers of the World Trade Center in New York fell to the ground from a terrorist attack. The nation and the world was in complete shock. WorldCom officials considered canceling, but the reservations and flights were already booked. A decision was made to go ahead with the event. It's hard to explain what we found when we arrived in Las Vegas. There were no crowds, hotels had massive cancellations, major acts and big name entertainers canceled their shows. We did however, get to see a few smaller shows and take tours. It was a very nice event but everyone's mind was still on that horrible attack and the thousands of people who lost their lives that morning on September 11th.

Before retiring from WorldCom I was very fortunate to take a most unusual trip spending 10 days visiting Cuba. This trip was not business related.

In Cuba

I was part of a delegation of girl softball players from Illinois invited to play the Cuban Women's Olympic team. Tim Novak, a friend of mine from AT&T, had a daughter who was one of the players. He mentioned if I would be interested in going, there may be extra seats available. The trip provided all members of the group to be issued U.S. authorized visas with no travel restrictions except for military installations. I was listed as a manager but was not required to attend the games. There were a few other available seats on the plane so another friend of mine, Bob Hotkevich gladly traveled with me. It was definitely a trip to remember. We traveled freely around Cuba and did end up attending most of the ballgames. I was overjoyed with what I call the highlight of the trip, seeing and riding in the old cars traveling through the streets of Havana, visiting the bars famously known as "Hemingway's haunts" and being able to watch (from a very far distance) Fidel Castro delivering part of one of his many two-hour speeches.

After many years of work, both Linda and I decided it was time to retire and find the perfect place to spend our golden years. We visited several areas in the Southeast and after numerous trips we found a place to build our retirement home near Alabama's Gulf Coast. The word was getting out that WorldCom was being investigated for some very serious financial dealings. Stories and reports were being covered closely by financial publications and the national media. Everyone was concerned about the future of the company and customers were also concerned how it would affect them. There's the old saying "Timing is everything", and believe me, in this case, it was true.

Linda took her retirement and I did as well. That was a good decision. Soon afterwards, WorldCom did go under and unfortunately, many of the people I worked with lost jobs, their retirement and their stock investments.

I feel blessed to have had the opportunity to be able to work for all the people, businesses and companies I was associated with over the years. I was also fortunate to have worked with many co-workers who were so talented and supportive. After all my years of working with so many wonderful people, my biggest reward is still having many of them staying in touch today. I'm also appreciative of my parents who taught me early the value and need for having good work ethics and the desire to succeed. However, I must confess, a lot of it was just plain damn luck. I believe in what Thomas Jefferson once said, "I'm a great believer in luck, and the harder I work, the more I have of it."

I always enjoyed working; and, when asked, I tell people, "I never had a job I didn't like, because I never had a job I didn't need." Regardless of how bad some of them appeared to be at the time, (like cleaning out chicken coops, scooping manure out of barns or killing and cleaning chickens) I tried my best, worked hard and appreciated having the opportunity to make money.

It's nice to be able to say you're retired but you soon find out that your days are still busy and you never seem to have the free time you imagined. It's a very different way of life, our kids live in different states. Jodi works with State Farm in Colorado and Brad works for Lacledes Gas Company in Saint Louis. In 1998 Jodi married Peter Emsley and in 1999, our lives again changed when Jodi and Peter gave us our first grandchild, Jack Davis Emsley. When they called to tell us Jodi was in labor, we immediately jumped in the car and drove to the hospital in Chesterfield, Missouri where our new grandson was born. He was a beautiful big healthy baby weighing over nine pounds. When they brought him into Jodi's room, they passed him around and finally to me. All of a sudden he started straining and making some unusual facial expressions. That was when we realized he was taking his first poop on his grandpa's lap! What a boy and I'm sure glad he was wearing a diaper! As I looked at him I immediately thought of my grandfather. This little boy, in years to come, will hopefully grow up and start another generation for our family. I instantly became a very proud grandfather. For the next couple years Jack enjoyed visiting LeRoy playing and exploring our old house and chasing our dog Taffy from room to room, much to Taffy's displeasure.

Chapter 11

Christmas Parade

During all my years working and living in LeRoy, I remained involved in my community by serving on committees, boards, and as a councilman for the City of LeRoy. In 1991, upon the sudden resignation of Mayor Jack Moss, I was appointed the new Mayor of LeRoy. At that time, LeRoy like many other rural communities, was not meeting the needs to sustain its growth or the ability to increase its revenues. There were several other service and community issues that also needed to be addressed. After attending several meetings on city planning and attending classes on revitalization of rural communities, I formed a committee of interested citizens to create a strategy plan for LeRoy's growth and development. The goal was to involve local citizens, business owners and civic leaders to work together in addressing community needs, attract new businesses, discuss planned development, form beautification projects, support local businesses, and to create special events and promotions to encourage people to visit and consider relocation to LeRoy. The committee looked for new ways to create revenues and development by focusing on tax incentive programs with the prime goal being growth, maintaining a high quality of life and providing the best services possible, but at the same time, maintaining a tax base that was affordable for all citizens, especially seniors living on fixed incomes. The city formed a new police department providing 24-hour protection with a commitment to reduce crime and assist the school in providing training programs to address drug and safety concerns. An intergovernmental agreement was created with the McLean County Sheriff's department, providing space for their deputies within our police facility, and the city's zoning and building codes were updated. We then formed a community action planning committee to address city needs and a long-range plan with the assistance of the McLean County Regional Planning Commission, giving the city a guide toward reaching that growth and a clear direction to address the future needs of the community. Growth and creation of new jobs was a priority. With full support, we removed the paid position of our economic development consultant, and the council and I took over those responsibilities, resulting in several new businesses starting up along the interstate. Two new subdivisions were opened adding over 200 residential building sites to the city. A group of volunteers called Restoration of Our Town Sensibly (ROOTS) was formed and using money set aside from the cable TV channel agreement, we assisted downtown businesses in repairing and upgrading the storefronts of their buildings. The city purchased the former How Implement building and the city converted the building into a community building for LeRoy's citizens. Volunteer labor was offered by members of the county's labor unions to pour floors and others pitched in to remodel the interior. We worked with the State of Illinois to co-pay adding storm sewers, curbs, gutters and sidewalks when the state was widening Route 150 through LeRoy. We developed a working relationship with the school district to be sure we understood their needs and they understood ours. We contacted the University of Illinois, and they provided us with an engineering student to assist in submitting plans which were approved by the State of Illinois to make LeRoy's downtown an official Illinois Historic District. We worked with a group of concerned parents (PARKS) to secure a $75,000 state matching grant for playground equipment for the restoration of city parks. Working with the LeRoy Historical Society, the city promoted the sale of more than 70 decorative street lamps donated by citizens and friends, for the downtown area and City Park. I would not agree to raising salaries for the Mayor or City Council members during my term, and all city expenditures were constantly being reviewed to keep real estate taxes affordable while providing the best public services possible. During my term as Mayor, the City of LeRoy grew over 20 percent and the financial conditions improved and remained strong while I was in office. Being a Mayor in a small town is very much like living in a large family. Sometimes it's fun and sometimes it can be very challenging. But if decisions are based on a well-planned approach that will benefit both the citizens and the community, ask for a vote and move on it. When citizens can see the results of a successful plan, it unites the entire community.

From left: Becky Reed, Karen Bruning, LeRoy Mayor Jerry Davis and Connie Koerner represented LeRoy's Play and Recreation for Our Kids Safety Commitee at the LeRoy Promotion Association and Chamber of Commerce annual auction and appreciation dinner.

The Pantagraph/SUE BRATCHER

Mary Tompkins received the key to the city from Davis. Tompkins has been active in numerous civic activities including the Christmas parade and historical events.

One of the primary challenges for anyone considering entering politics, is proposing new well thought-out ideas to promote and to improve your community, and having the majority of the citizens accept your proposals. Be prepared, because as Tom Clancy wrote, "No matter what you or anyone else does, there will be someone who says there's something bad about it." After six years as Mayor, some may be surprised, but most of our proposals were accepted and I very much enjoyed my time serving as the Mayor of LeRoy. I'm also proud of the progress we made and feel the time I invested was well worth it. I made a sincere attempt to make myself available to everyone by visiting local groups, attending the many city meetings and listening to citizens who felt passionate about issues facing the city. In no way do I feel the successes made during my term were my successes. The real credit goes the council, employees and those who stepped forward giving their time and energies to move the city forward, making LeRoy an even better community. I have loved politics since I was a young boy riding around McLean County nailing those cardboard political signs on fence posts. However, it's not for everyone. I always think back to Frank Jones Sr. from LeRoy who when asked to run for a local political position responded: " I'm not that willing to find out how many friends I really have." But I enjoyed being involved and over the years served as an election judge, a Republican Precinct Committeeman, worked on several local, State, and National Republican election campaigns, and served on numerous coroner's inquests. I also lost an election by only 34 votes when I ran for the McLean County Board. During the campaign I was traveling extensively with AT&T and did not spend the needed time or the effort to win that position. With that said, I cannot complain about losing that race. In 1998, I had the privilege to be considered for an appointment to the Illinois House of Representatives when our state representative John Turner resigned his seat to become a judge. There were five people considered from five different counties within the district. My county, McLean County, had the fewest residents of all the counties because the cities of Bloomington and Normal were not in our district. I was told up front that it would be a long shot and I did not get the appointment. However, I was flattered just to be considered. I'm now living in the South and have become a true Southern conservative, both politically and financially. Politically, I understand the meaning of being a conservative, and agree with Sir Winston Churchill's definition; "If you're not a liberal at twenty you have no heart, if you're not a conservative at forty you have no brains." Financially, I firmly believe taxing bodies should live within their means and taxes should only be used to serve and benefit those you represent, not burden them. It should be the responsibility of every elected representative/ politician to exhibit common sense and not be self-serving. In reading the writings of James Madison, it was his assumption that politics bring out the worst in people - their selfishness. As Madison saw it, people would always try to use politics to further their own particular interest. Madison could not have imagined what has happened in the last two hundred years. The intent of the framers of our Constitution was to create a government run by the people, for the people and the people were entrusted to elect a person best suited to represent "we the people". Unfortunately, today's system of government has become vulnerable to special interest control, lobbyist manipulation and the influence of money and 30 second commercials on TV. It's sad to realize the voting turnout in the United States continues to decline and is one of the lowest in comparison to other comparable countries. Many Americans today point out they don't vote because; 1. they don't have the time, 2. their vote won't make a difference, 3. they don't like the candidates selected by the party in some back room secret meetings. And last; people simply lose interest when campaigns start well over two years before an election.

Over the years I've had the privilege of meeting several of our presidents; Richard Nixon, Gerald Ford, George H. Bush, Ronald Reagan and George W. Bush. I talked in a hallway with Richard Nixon in Chicago at a Lincoln Day reception shortly after returning from Vietnam. Linda and I attended the McLean County Lincoln Day Dinner in Bloomington and sat at the same table with then Congressman Gerald Ford. We attended a rally for George W. Bush in Pensacola, Florida, and Linda, the kids and I had the special honor of meeting Ronald Reagan at a McLean, Illinois campaign stop. We have a wonderful family story about that event. Brad was about six years old at the time, and after he shook hands with President Reagan, Mrs. Reagan, who was standing right next to him, reached over and patted Brad on the head. To both Brad and her surprise, her diamond ring got caught in his hair. Within seconds, all eyes including the Secret Service's were on Brad. Mrs. Reagan quickly got it loose and gave him a big smile as they continued down the line. I would have thought my children being raised in a Republican home would have followed in my Republican footsteps. That doesn't seem to be the case. Oh well, my efforts were not in vain, they were also encouraged to make their own political decisions and most importantly, always vote. I do however, have to smile every time Linda and I cast our votes because there's a strong possibility we are likely canceling out their vote.

Chapter 12

Linda and I have often been asked how we ended up moving down to Alabama. Throughout our marriage, she has always known it was my intention to someday move back to Florida's Gulf Coast. However, after going down looking at property in the late 90s, the west coast area of Florida had not only changed, it had become so crowded we decided not to retire there and started looking elsewhere. Our longtime friends, Harold and Chloe Misch vacationed in Gulf Shores for many years and asked us to go with them to celebrate an upcoming anniversary. We did and we liked what we saw. I was totally unaware Alabama's coast beaches were that nice and they reminded me of the beaches of Florida's past. We made a second trip with them and with no preconceived intentions, we both purchased lots. They started their home first and the next year we retired and started building ours. Once completed, we sold most of our furniture and the things we no longer needed and made the move. It was hard to believe after more than 50 years, I am again living and enjoying life along the Gulf of Mexico coastline. After all our years living in LeRoy it was hard to leave. We very much enjoyed living there in our old white house, but it seemed the work to keep it up was a never ending battle. What at first seemed to be a labor of love, the older I became, the love had diminished and became simply labor. While living in LeRoy our entire married life, we enjoyed the community, our friends, family and watching all the changes that took place in our family and our lives. If it was my preference, I would have just pulled LeRoy down south to the coast to warmer weather. Since that couldn't happen, we made the move and it was a good move for both of us. We love the South, Foley is now our new home, but we continue to enjoy talking and visiting with our old friends and are always happy to have them visit. And yes, we still occasionally get back to LeRoy and LeRoy will always be "my hometown".

Just before we moved, on September 4, 2002, Jodi gave birth to our second grandchild, Madelyn Grace Emsley, in Highlands Ranch, Colorado. Like all grandparents we were again excited about having another grandchild. We arrived at the hospital just before they were taking her home. What a joy it was to have Maddie come into our lives and become part of our family. It was unfortunate that she was never able to spend time visiting in our home in LeRoy. But since our move, both grandchildren have been back to visit LeRoy several times and have seen where we lived and the town where their mother and grandparents lived. Our family remains very close and our kids take time out of their busy schedule to call us regularly. We enjoy visiting their homes and having them visit ours. Linda and I both enjoy living in our home in Graham Creek Estates just five miles from South Alabama's beautiful Gulf beaches.

Our subdivision is a boating community located on the water near Wolf Bay. It has a community boat launch, dock and pier. Several of our neighbors have boats, some for saltwater fishing and others, including myself, have smaller boats or pontoon boats. The neighborhood ladies are very involved in various social clubs and many of the guys enjoy fishing in the Gulf. I have always enjoyed fishing, but saltwater fishing is by far my favorite. Taking a fishing boat 20 to 40 miles out in the Gulf's deep blue water, gives you a great day in the sun with friends, sometimes an exciting ride bouncing over very rough waves. However, as that may sound, a good day fishing can yield a boatload of fish of all kinds and all sizes. As often stated, "One bad day of fishing is still better than a good day at work." Everyone's local favorite fishing along the Alabama Gulf Coast is during the annual Red Snapper season. It starts in late May and fishermen from all over the country come here to enter the Annual Orange Beach, Alabama Red Snapper World Championship. Anyone willing to pay ten dollars a day can compete and the Gulf becomes packed with hundreds of fishing and charter boats. Every fisherman is looking for and hoping to catch the largest snapper during the tournament. The biggest fish gets the winner twenty-five thousand dollars. If a fisherman can catch a snapper breaking the Alabama state record, they'll win two hundred thousand dollars, and that hasn't happened in a long time.

We very much enjoy our neighborhood and new friends. Linda spends time doing oil painting and I have taken up weaving Nantucket baskets. We continued to travel, visit friends, enjoy stopping in antiques shops and spending time at our log cabin in Mentone, Alabama, on Lookout Mountain. Our vacations included Italy and Spain. We can only hope that the years to come will be as enjoyable and memorable as years past.

Trevi Fountain, Rome, Italy Linda and Jerry

I believe life is much like a book. We create our own pages through life and years later you pick them up to enjoy recounting all the special memories of the past. My desire is to continue adding more chapters of memories for many years to come.

Family on Pier

This story brings us to 2010. It was both fun and interesting for me to sit down and reflect on my life, and I feel very fortunate to have done what I've done and seen the places I've seen. I realize my life has not been anything exceptional, I'm not famous or on any "who's who" list, but I'm thankful I've had the opportunities and the good fortune to be productive and spend so much quality time with my family and friends. There were many more things I could have added and other things that are better left untold, but I've enjoyed looking back and dusting off all these wonderful pages of memories. While reading this story, I'm sure you may find a few errors or a story possibly told inaccurately, but I wrote this from my own memories of the accounts, and I apologize if anything is wrongly stated or could possibly offend someone.

With that said, it's time for us to load up the beach chairs and head to the beach, sit back in the sun, bury our toes in the sand, and hope tomorrow will again be another wonderful day for "making memories".

Jerry and Linda, 2010

Sage Advice

"In order to write about life, first you have to live it."

--Ernest Hemingway

"Life is short, break the rules, forgive quickly, kiss slowly, love truly, laugh uncontrollably, and never regret anything that made you smile. Twenty years from now you will be more disappointed by the things you didn't do than the ones you did. So throw off the bowlines. Sail away from the safe harbor. Catch the trade winds in your sales. Explore. Dream. Discover."

--Mark Twain

About the Author

Jerry C. Davis, 2015

Jerry Davis was a longtime resident and former Mayor of LeRoy, IL. In this book his describes growing up in a family who constantly moved until they finally settled in the small, central Illinois town of LeRoy and made it their hometown. Jerry graduated from LeRoy High School, then served a tour of duty in Vietnam before returning to LeRoy. He married Linda Boaz and for the next 35 years remained active in the community and local and county politics. This book gives you his description of a young boy taking the time to listen to stories from the town's older people and his depiction of growing up in the fifties. With no TV's, cell phones or computers, friendships thrived and opportunities were

304

plentiful for those who remained in their hometown and for those who moved far beyond the city limits.

Jerry spent 16 years working in retailing in LeRoy and over 20 years in management positions for national corporations. He is now retired, loves deep sea fishing, collects classic cars and enjoys life on the beaches of Alabama's Gulf Coast.

Made in the USA
Monee, IL
10 November 2024

69743287R00177